CULTURALLY RESPONSIVE LITERACY INSTRUCTION

50 literacy strategies
· apply

To our families and our families' families, who remind us daily of the benefits of valuing diversity and good teaching.

CULTURALLY RESPONSIVE LITERACY INSTRUCTION

Bob Algozzine
Dorothy J. O'Shea
Festus E. Obiakor

EDITORS

→ Best Place to get Strategy Books.

CORWIN PRESS
A SAGE Company

For information:

Corwin Press
A SAGE Company
2455 Teller Road
Thousand Oaks, California 91320
www.corwinpress.com

SAGE Ltd.
1 Oliver's Yard
55 City Road
London EC1Y 1SP
United Kingdom

SAGE India Pvt. Ltd.
B 1/I 1 Mohan Cooperative
    Industrial Area
Mathura Road, New Delhi 110 044
India

SAGE Asia-Pacific Pte. Ltd.
33 Pekin Street #02-01
Far East Square
Singapore 048763

Printed in the United States of America.

Library of Congress Cataloging-in-Publication Data

Culturally responsive literacy instruction/Bob Algozzine, Dorothy J. O'Shea, Festus E. Obiakor, editors.
    p. cm.
Includes bibliographical references.
ISBN 978-1-4129-5773-1 (cloth)
ISBN 978-1-4129-5774-8 (pbk.)
  1. Language arts—Social aspects—United States. 2. Reading—Remedial teaching. 3. English language—Study and teaching—Foreign speakers. I. Algozzine, Robert. II. O'Shea, Dorothy J. III. Obiakor, Festus E. IV. Title.

LB1576.C853 2009
428.4'2—dc22   2008035121

This book is printed on acid-free paper.

08 09 10 11 12 10 9 8 7 6 5 4 3 2 1

Acquisitions Editor:	David Chao
Editorial Assistant:	Mary Dang
Production Editor:	Eric Garner
Copy Editor:	Paula L. Fleming
Typesetter:	C&M Digitals (P) Ltd.
Proofreader:	Susan Schon
Indexer:	Molly Hall
Cover Designer:	Michael Dubowe

Contents

(Handwritten annotations: Laurie, Kat, Sam *— Ch. 1;* Nat + Bron *— Ch. 2;* Taryn, Jane, Abby *— Ch. 3;* Marcella, Cora, Tammy *— Ch. 4;* Kayla, Abby, Janna *— Ch. 5;* Chelsea, angelina *— Ch. 6;* Owen, Val *— Ch. 7)*

Preface

We wrote this book to address a longstanding and growing need. Many students have reading difficulties, and, among these, students with culturally and linguistically diverse (CLD) backgrounds are a disproportionate group. Teaching foundational literacy skills is necessary to impart to these students that which they missed in the early grades that is necessary to lifelong, literary learning and success. By combining best practices supported by research with instruction that is culturally responsive, we believe teachers and other professionals will improve reading outcomes for students.

Recent advances in research and practice pertaining to literacy acquisition skills and the performance of students on national assessments, combined with federal policy mandates (e.g., Individuals with Disabilities Education Improvement Act [IDEIA]; 2004; No Child Left Behind Act [NCLB]; 2001), have stimulated interest in providing intensive intervention services to students at risk of persistent academic failure. In today's technologically driven, knowledge-based culture, young people need to be expert readers, writers, and thinkers to contend, compete, and succeed in the global economy. Moreover, persistent low national and international literacy standings substantiate that an investment in the education of literacy instruction is a national imperative (Biancarosa & Snow, 2004).

A substantial body of evidence has pointed to five critical areas—phonemic awareness, phonics/decoding, fluency, vocabulary, and comprehension—as essential components of reading instruction (National Institute of Child Health and Human Development [NICHD], 2000; Snow, Burns, & Griffin, 1998). For students who struggle with reading, some or even all of these curricular elements are addressed through systematic and explicit instruction. A 7-year-old or a 15-year-old student who cannot decode words rapidly enough to allow for text comprehension requires instruction in decoding and word attack strategies, along with continuous practice reading connected text. Struggling readers need increased instructional time and scientifically validated methods if they are to close the achievement gap and become proficient.

Diverse students from CLD backgrounds who do not possess the foundational reading skills needed to comprehend written language often score poorly on literacy assessments. In addition to students from CLD backgrounds, poorly performing readers include students identified with language-based learning disabilities, English-language learners, as well as other underachieving or "at-risk" students who may simply have never received appropriate reading instruction. All of these students require effective, research-based interventions provided in culturally responsive ways that put them on the trajectory to developing the higher-level literacy skills needed to succeed in an information-based society (McCollin & O'Shea, 2005).

Reading scores from the 2005 National Assessment of Educational Progress (NAEP) verify the prevalence of severe reading problems in older students, especially those from CLD backgrounds. Results indicate that 27 percent of eighth graders read at "below basic" levels. This means that over 1 out of every 4 eighth graders tested could not demonstrate a "literal understanding of what they read." For many students from CLD backgrounds, the situation is even graver. Consider that while 18 percent of white eighth graders scored below basic, an alarming 48 percent of African Americans, 43 percent of Hispanics, and 41 percent of American Indians scored at that level—revealing significant reading achievement deficits among minority students (Perie, Grigg, & Donahue, 2005). These students are reading considerably below grade level and are far from meeting the proficiency requirements mandated by federal legislation like NCLB. In the face of these widespread reading problems, experts in the field continuously have called for a more informed approach to reading instruction.

Culturally responsive instruction connects students' backgrounds, interests, and experiences to the standards-based curriculum. Culturally responsive instruction is responsive to students of CLD backgrounds both in content and in process. Learning materials take advantage of multicultural literature, themes, and topics. This helps to ensure that students see themselves and their families reflected in the classroom environment. Additionally, instructional practices themselves can be culturally responsive and reflect what we know about the learning preferences, familiar speech patterns, and way of life of diverse groups. Culturally responsive professionals create classroom contexts that reflect cultural values, such as interdependence and communalism, through cooperative learning activities and peer-to-peer interaction.

Research has demonstrated that small-group strategies for instruction, along with a schoolwide climate of acceptance and respect for diversity, more closely match the natural learning patterns that tend to occur in culturally diverse communities. Culturally responsive instruction helps students connect their own cultural knowledge and language experiences to the language and literacy tasks required of them in school. Students are asked to bring the strategic thinking and competence they have in areas outside of school, or what has been called their cultural "funds of knowledge," to academic tasks. For example, families of bilingual young people often select them to carry out the hard work of interpreting and translating to mediate communication with the outside world—between minority and majority communities. The experiences of these young interpreters and the skills they develop to fulfill this role can be utilized to support classroom learning.

ABOUT OUR BOOK ■

Culturally Responsive Literacy Instruction is devoted to content and procedures of culturally responsive literacy instruction, relevant culturally responsive research, and key players involved in literacy instruction to students from CLD backgrounds. *Culturally Responsive Literacy Instruction* aims to help professionals support the growing number of students from CLD backgrounds. It gives practical advice to professionals. We provide a detailed, comprehensive, and practical treatment of *culturally responsive literacy instruction.* We discuss and illustrate a range of interventions, which support the five critical areas of reading instruction. In particular, we explore classroom contexts and learning strategies that are likely to be effective for students from CLD backgrounds at all grade levels, from primary grades through high school.

We begin the book with an introductory chapter framing the importance of culturally responsive instruction and setting the stage for the practical chapters that follow; here we describe how to teach critical literacy skills to students with diverse backgrounds. In Chapter 2, we address phonological processing and its relation to learning to read. Chapter 3 is about teaching skills that are fundamental to sounding out and recognizing words (i.e., decoding and structural analysis). We focus on fluency in Chapter 4, vocabulary in Chapter 5, and comprehension in Chapter 6. Each of these content chapters begins by introducing a student at risk of continued school failure and ends with a summary relating key content to the student's classroom experiences. Within each of these chapters, we discuss the importance and empirical base for the key literacy skill and describe ways to integrate culturally responsive activities into elementary, middle, and high school classrooms. We end with a chapter reframing the importance of focused instruction to meet the needs of students with culturally and linguistically diverse backgrounds.

Teaching is a collaborative process, and this book is a collaborative effort, with assistance from content experts including Jeff Bakken, Gwendolyn Cartledge, Renee Hawkins, Jodi Katsafanas, Kelly Lake, Michelle McCollin, Shobana Musti-Rao, Ellissa Brooks Nelson, Darren Smith, and Cheryl Utley. These contributing colleagues all have extensive experience with cultural and linguistic diversity, reading, and special education that has greatly informed the content of our book.

■ MOVING ON

Culturally Responsive Literacy Instruction is a resource for a variety of professionals, including those established in their careers and those preparing for new careers. General educators, special educators, school administrators, related service professionals, and teacher assistants will benefit from the concepts presented. For professionals in preparation, we believe *Culturally Responsive Literacy Instruction* will be an enlightening supplementary text in upper-level undergraduate- and graduate-level methods courses at colleges and universities. The text puts a broad emphasis on the various levels of general education (i.e., elementary, middle grades, and high school). We hope professionals in school administration programs as well as those taking courses in programs for related disciplines that serve diverse students, such as reading, school counseling, school psychology, social work, physical and occupational therapy, speech and hearing, medicine, and physical education, will also benefit from our book. Finally, *Culturally Responsive Literacy Instruction* should be helpful in community college programs where teacher assistants are prepared for careers in education.

Our book highlights effective practices to help professionals plan, implement, manage, and evaluate instruction for students with culturally and linguistically diverse backgrounds. It will be useful for practitioners who directly use scientifically based literacy practices in classrooms with diverse groups of students. The book, too, is an appropriate guide for professional development workshops intended to increase the knowledge, skills, and dispositions of teachers working with problem readers, including students from CLD backgrounds, readers for whom English is not their primary language, readers with learning disabilities, and readers never provided appropriate literacy opportunities. We hope you enjoy our book.

REFERENCES ■

Biancarosa, G., & Snow, C. (2004). *Reading next: A vision for action and research in middle and high school literacy—A report to Carnegie Corporation of New York.* Washington, DC: Alliance for Excellent Education.

Individuals with Disabilities Education Improvement Act of 2004, Pub. L. No. 108-446 (2004).

McCollin, M., & O'Shea, D. J. (2005). Increasing reading achievement of students from culturally and linguistically diverse backgrounds. *Preventing School Failure, 50*(1), 41–44.

National Institute of Child Health and Human Development (NICHD). (2000). *Report of the National Reading Panel. Teaching students to read: An evidence-based assessment of the scientific research literature on reading and its implications for reading instruction* (NIH Publication No. 00–4769). Washington, DC: U.S. Government Printing Office.

No Child Left Behind Act of 2001, Pub. L. No. 107–110 (2002).

Perie, M., Grigg, W., & Donahue, P. (2005). *The nation's report card: Reading 2005* (NCES 2006–451). Washington, DC: U.S. Department of Education, National Center for Education Statistics. Available August 5, 2008, at http://nces.ed.gov/nationsreportcard/pdf/main2005/2006451.pdf

Snow, C. E., Burns, M. S., & Griffin, P. (Eds.). (1998). *Preventing reading difficulties in young children.* Washington, DC: National Academy Press.

Acknowledgments

Collectively we are grateful to our collaborating authors for their contributions included in the chapters of our book. We are also grateful to David Chao and Mary Dang at Corwin Press for their continuing support in the development and production of *Culturally Responsive Literacy Instruction*. We also acknowledge our reviewers, who provided outstanding supportive and corrective feedback that greatly improved our book:

Akina Canty
Special Education Teacher
National Board Certified Teacher
Birmingham, AL

Phyllis N. Levert, EdD
College Teaching; School Administrator
Clark Atlanta University; Georgia School Districts
Atlanta, GA

Ursula Thomas-Fair, EdD
Assistant Professor of Early Childhood Education
University of West Georgia
Carrollton, GA

Gary L. Willhite, PhD
Teacher Educator
Southern Illinois University
Carbondale, IL

■ PERSONAL ACKNOWLEDGMENTS

I am grateful to Doris and Festus for their continuing friendship over many years. It has been my good fortune to know and work with both of them, and I probably have not told them this enough. I also acknowledge the ever-lasting support of Kate Algozzine, who knows best what it takes to do what I do every day and who has always helped me in many ways to do it.

—BA

I thank my coauthors, Bob and Festus, for seeking, supporting, and valuing what really matters in life. I thank the love of my life, Larry, for helping me to understand and do what really matters in life.

—*DJO*

I want to thank my wife, Pauline, and my children, Charles, Gina, Kristen, and Alicia, for their unwavering support and love. I want to thank my coauthors, Bob and Doris, for their dedication to excellence. Through this book, they have proven that a White male, a White female, and an African-American male can collaborate, consult, and cooperate together without stress!

—*FO*

About the Editors

**Bob Algozzine,** PhD, is a professor in the Department of Educational Leadership at the University of North Carolina and project codirector of the U.S. Department of Education-supported Behavior and Reading Improvement Center. With 25 years of research experience and extensive firsthand knowledge of teaching students classified as seriously emotionally disturbed, Algozzine is a uniquely qualified staff developer, conference speaker, and teacher of behavior management and effective teaching courses. He is active in special education practice as a partner and collaborator with professionals in the Charlotte-Mecklenburg schools in North Carolina and as an editor of several journals focused on special education. Algozzine has written more than 250 manuscripts on special education topics, including many books and textbooks on how to manage emotional and social behavior problems.

**Dorothy J. (Doris) O'Shea**, PhD, currently with the Chester County Intermediate Unit, Downingtown, Pennsylvania, taught special education courses at the tertiary level for more than 25 years, after receiving her doctorate in special education from Pennsylvania State University in 1983. Additionally, she worked as a special education classroom teacher and school administrator for more than 11 years. During her 36-year career, Dr. O'Shea developed an independent line of research and scholarship related to literacy, instructional strategies, legal issues, and work with diverse families.

**Festus E. Obiakor,** PhD, is a professor in the Department of Exceptional Education at the University of Wisconsin, Milwaukee. A teacher, scholar, and consultant, he has served as a distinguished visiting professor at a variety of universities and is the author or coauthor of more than 150 publications, including books, articles, and essays.

1

Teaching Children to Read

Bob Algozzine, Festus E. Obiakor,
Ellissa Brooks Nelson, and Jeffrey P. Bakken

CHAPTER OBJECTIVES

In this chapter, we will

- discuss the critical areas of teaching reading as identified by the National Reading Panel;
- describe what research tells us about reading problems and remediations; and
- identify culturally responsive reading approaches.

DO NOT ASSUME A STUDENT HAS A READING PROBLEM UNLESS YOU HAVE TAUGHT READING!

Ms. Jones has been teaching kindergarten students for more than 18 years. She was known as an excellent teacher in the school and had garnered support from parents, teachers, and principals. The interesting thing here was that Ms. Jones, parents, teachers, and principals were all Anglo-Americans. Ms. Jones had two culturally diverse students in

(Continued)

(Continued)

her class, one Latino named Joe and one African American named Chidi. Joe's parents moved to the town to work in the beef factory, and Chidi's parents moved to the town to work at the university. Meanwhile, Chidi was complaining that Ms. Jones never paid attention to him and how he hated going to school. He observed that Joe was also not called upon in class. Chidi's parents tried to complain to the principal, who indicated that they did not have to worry because Ms. Jones was an experienced teacher with more than 18 years of experience.

During the first parent/teacher meeting, Ms. Jones noted that she was beginning to teach reading. As she noted: "Right now, I am teaching alphabets and word association, that is a for apple, b for ball, c for cat, d for dog, and so on." She added that Chidi was quiet and withdrawn and "that was a red flag for students with reading, learning, and behavior problems." Chidi's parents were shocked that their child, who could read at a second- or third-grade level, was viewed as having reading problems. Additionally, this child was quiet in class because he was brought up to focus on tasks such as schooling. They asked Ms. Jones if she had any book for second or third graders, and she gave them the book. Right there, they asked Chidi to read, and he read fluently and superbly. They wanted to know why she had assumed that their son could not read. She never apologized. When the case was brought to the principal, she expressed surprise and continued to indicate that Ms. Jones was an excellent teacher. Chidi's parents had no option but to move Chidi to a new school, where they felt that his needs might be adequately met. The critical question continued to be "How could a teacher make assumptions about reading deficiency when she had never taught reading?"

When questions arise about how best to teach reading and focus on early literacy, the first instinct of many professionals is to make assumptions about reading and reading deficiency. They sometimes do not teach reading before making reading assumptions. But there are proven ways to teach reading or discover any reading deficiency. The National Reading Panel (2000) identified five critical areas on which general and special educators must focus. In its report, the group responded to a Congressional mandate to help parents, teachers, and policy makers address the key skills and areas central to effective reading instruction and achievement: phonemic awareness, phonics, fluency, vocabulary, and comprehension.

- *Phonemic awareness* means understanding that sounds make words. It is a subcategory of phonological development, which includes other skills such as identifying and manipulating phonemes, syllables, onsets, rimes, and words, as well as other aspects of sound such as rhyming, alliteration, and tone. Phonemic awareness is not phonics.
- *Phonics* means understanding the relationships between the letters (graphemes) of written language and the individual sounds (phonemes) of spoken language. It teaches children to decode these relationships to read and write words fluently.
- *Fluency* means reading accurately and quickly with expression. Fluent readers recognize words automatically.
- *Vocabulary* means understanding that words have meanings and that knowing the meaning of new words is important for reading

higher levels of text. Because it is difficult for children to understand what they are reading without knowing what most of the words mean, vocabulary is critical for comprehension.

• *Comprehension* means understanding what one has read.

TEACHING EARLY LITERACY SKILLS ■

Teachers in sound and effective literacy programs teach these skills and regularly assess their children's development of them. In *Putting Reading First,* Armbruster, Lehr, and Osborne (2003) summarized what researchers have discovered about how to teach each of these skills successfully. Using the findings of the National Reading Panel (2000), they defined each area, reviewed research supporting it, summarized classroom implications, described teaching strategies, and addressed frequently asked questions. In this chapter, we summarize their work as a basis for the content we have included in our book. We also provide an overview of effective teaching and introduce the foundations of culturally responsive teaching to support the use of effective early literacy instruction for learners from diverse backgrounds.

Teaching Phonemic Awareness

Phonemic awareness is the skill of using the individual sounds in spoken words. Before learning to read, children must understand how the sounds in words work. Phonemic awareness is essential for them to do this. Phonemes are the smallest part of sound in a spoken word making a difference in the word's meaning (Flint, 2008; Manzo, Manzo, & Thomas, 2005). Children can show that they have phonemic awareness in several ways, including recognizing which words in a set of words begin with the same sound, isolating and saying the first or last sound in a word, combining or blending the separate sounds in a word to say the word, and breaking, or segmenting, a word into its separate sounds.

Often, phonemic awareness is confused with phonics. Phonemic awareness is the understanding that the sounds of spoken language work together to make words, while phonics is the understanding that a predictable relationship exists between phonemes and graphemes, the letters that represent sounds in written language (Hoosain & Salili, 2005; Lee, 2005). Another misconception is that phonemic awareness has the same meaning as phonological awareness. Phonemic awareness is a subset of phonological awareness. The focus of phonological awareness includes identifying and manipulating larger parts of spoken language while also encompassing awareness of other aspects of sound. Children can show that they have phonological awareness by identifying and making oral rhymes, identifying and working with syllables in spoken words, identifying and working with onsets and rimes in spoken syllables or one-syllable words, and identifying and working with individual phonemes in spoken words.

What Does Research Tell Us About Phonemic Awareness Instruction?

Teachers can teach phonemic awareness, and children can learn it using a variety of instructional activities, including, but not limited to, the following:

- *Phoneme isolation:* Having children recognize individual sounds in a word
- *Phoneme identity:* Having children recognize the same sounds in different words
- *Phoneme categorization:* Having children recognize the word in a set of three or four words that has the "odd" sound
- *Phoneme blending:* Having children listen to a sequence of separately spoken phonemes, combining the phonemes to form a word, and then writing the word
- *Phoneme segmentation:* Having children break the word into its separate sounds, saying each sound as they tap out or count it, and then writing the word
- *Phonemic detection:* Having children recognize the word that remains when a phoneme is removed from another word
- *Phoneme addition:* Having children make a new word by adding a phoneme to an existing word
- *Phoneme substitution:* Having children substitute one phoneme for another to make a new word

Phonemic awareness instruction improves children's ability to read words, helps children learn to spell by helping them segment words into phonemes, and improves their reading comprehension. Some common vocabulary used in research addressing phonemic awareness includes the following:

- *Phoneme manipulation:* When children work with phonemes in words
- *Blending:* When children combine individual phonemes to form words
- *Segmenting (or segmentation):* When children break words into their individual phonemes

Phonemic awareness instruction provides a stronger contribution to the effectiveness of reading and spelling when children are taught to manipulate phonemes by using the letters of the alphabet and when it focuses on one or two types of phoneme manipulation rather than several types.

Keys for Teaching Phonemic Awareness

All children can profit from phonemic awareness instruction regardless of their current literacy level. Of course, it is important to provide them with instruction that is appropriate for their level of development. Teaching one or two types of phoneme manipulation is generally more effective than teaching many types of manipulation.

It is not necessary to devote a significant amount of class time to phonemic awareness instruction; however, children will differ in their levels of phonemic awareness, and some will need more instruction than others.

Similarly, small-group instruction may be more effective than individual or whole-group instruction, because children often benefit from listening to their classmates respond and receive feedback from the teacher. Frequent and ongoing assessment is the best way to identify students who will require more instruction and those who should be taught other early literacy skills (Flood & Anders, 2005; Hoosain & Salili, 2005; Lee, 2005).

Teaching Phonics

Learning the relationships between the letters of written language and the individual sounds of spoken language and learning to use these relationships to read and write words are the goals and benefits of teaching phonics. Professionals use different labels to describe these relationships, including the following:

- Graphophonemic relationships
- Letter-sound associations
- Letter-sound correspondences
- Sound-symbol correspondences
- Sound-spellings

Some professionals argue that English spellings are too irregular for phonics instruction to help children learn to read words. A goal of phonics instruction is to teach children a system for sounding out words when regular rules apply to them.

What Does Research Tell Us About Phonics Instruction?

Scientific research on phonics instruction indicates that systematic and explicit teaching produces a stronger contribution to children's growth in reading when compared with teaching that provides nonsystematic or no phonics instruction (Flint, 2008). Programs of systematic phonics instruction involve the direct teaching of a set of letter-sound relationships in a clearly defined sequence. In addition, these programs provide materials that give children significant practice in applying knowledge of these relationships as they read and write. The many approaches to phonics instruction include the following:

- Synthetic phonics
- Analytic phonics
- Analogy-based phonics
- Phonics through spelling
- Embedded phonics
- Onset-rime phonics instruction

Systematic phonics instruction is most beneficial for children's reading achievement when it begins in kindergarten or first grade. Beginning systematic phonics instruction early results in enhanced growth in children's ability to comprehend what they read rather than nonsystematic or no phonics instruction, and it is beneficial to children regardless of their socioeconomic status or cultural and linguistic background. Programs of systematic and explicit phonics instruction provides practice with letter-sound relationships in a predetermined sequence, helping children learn to use these relationships to decode words that contain them. In addition to phonics instruction, young children should be solidifying their knowledge of the alphabet, engaging in phonemic awareness activities, and listening to stories and informational texts read aloud to them (Flint, 2008; Manzo et al., 2005). Further, they should be reading texts and writing letters, words, messages, and stories.

Keys to Teaching Phonics

A program of systematic phonics instruction identifies a purposefully selected set of letter-sound relationships, which then organizes the introduction of these relationships into a consistent instructional sequence. Nonsystematic programs of phonics instruction are not effective because they are not organized, do not teach consonant and vowel letter-sound relationships in a predetermined sequence, and do not provide practice materials focused on helping children apply what they are learning about letter-sound relationships. Effective programs of phonics instruction help teachers explicitly and systematically instruct students in how to relate letters and sounds; help students apply their knowledge of phonics as they read and to their own writing; can be adapted to the needs of individual students; and include alphabetic knowledge, phonemic awareness, vocabulary development, and the reading of text.

Phonics is effective when taught to the whole class, to small groups, or to individual students. The needs of the students determine how effectively to deliver instruction. Nonsystematic approaches to phonics instruction that should be avoided include these:

- *Literature-based programs* that emphasize reading and writing activities
- *Basal reading programs* that focus on whole word or meaning-based activities
- *Sight-word programs* that begin by teaching children a sight word reading vocabulary of 50–100 words

Systematic phonics instruction helps children learn to identify words that increase their reading fluency, vocabulary, and comprehension. It contributes to growth in the reading of most children, and it produces more growth in spelling among kindergarten and first-grade students than nonsystematic or no phonics programs. Systematic phonics instruction alone may not be sufficient to improve the overall reading and spelling performance of readers beyond first grade, and attention to fluency and other areas of reading must be part of a comprehensive approach to teaching early literacy skills.

Teaching Fluency

Fluency is the ability to read a text accurately and quickly with appropriate expression. Fluency provides a link between word recognition and comprehension. Fluent readers are able to recognize words and comprehend at the same time, whereas less fluent readers concentrate on figuring out the words, leaving them little attention for comprehending the text. Apparently, fluency develops gradually and requires substantial practice. As students are first learning to read, their oral reading is slow and labored because they are just learning to attach sounds to letters and to blend sounds into recognizable words. Once students are capable of recognizing many words automatically, their oral reading may still be less than fluent.

Readers must be able to divide the text into phrases and clauses to read with expression. It is essential that readers know how to pause appropriately within and at the ends of sentences and when to change emphasis and tone. Clearly, fluency changes depending on what readers are reading, their familiarity with the words, and the amount of their practice with reading text. Further, although some readers may recognize words automatically, they may not read the words fluently when the words appear in sentences. Therefore, it is essential that students receive instruction and practice in fluency as they read connected text (Flood & Anders, 2005; Hoosain & Salili, 2005).

What Does Research Tell Us About Fluency Instruction?

There are two major instructional approaches related to fluency: (1) repeated and monitored oral reading and (2) independent silent reading. Research indicates that students who practice repeated and monitored oral reading while receiving guidance and/or feedback become better readers. Repeated oral reading improves word recognition, speed, accuracy, and fluency and improves reading comprehension. Several effective techniques related to repeated oral reading have been established and validated through research. Research has not confirmed whether independent silent reading with minimal guidance or feedback improves reading achievement and fluency, nor has it proven that silent reading in the classroom does not work.

Keys to Effective Fluency Instruction

It is essential that you read aloud to your students daily, because listening to good models of fluent reading enables students to learn how a reader's voice can help written text make sense. Once you have modeled how to read the text, it is important that you have the students reread it and engage in repeated readings. As a rule, having students read a text four times is sufficient to improve fluency, but many teachers find that some students require many more trials before reading fluently. In addition, encourage parents and family members to read aloud to their children (Manzo et al., 2005; Utley, Obiakor, & Kozleski, 2005).

Students should practice orally rereading text that is relatively easy for them and at their appropriate level of reading. This is important because if students are reading text that is more difficult, then they will focus more on word recognition and decrease their opportunity to develop fluency. Students can practice orally rereading text in several ways, including the following:

- *Student-adult reading:* The student reads one-on-one with an adult.
- *Choral reading:* Students read along as a group with another fluent adult reader.

- *Tape-assisted reading:* Students read along in their books as they hear a fluent reader read the book on an audiotape.
- *Partner reading:* Paired students take turns reading aloud to each other.
- *Readers' theater:* Students rehearse and perform a play for peers or others.

Independent reading helps increase fluency and reading achievement, but it should not take the place of direct instruction in reading. Growth in reading fluency is greatest when students are working directly with teachers. Direct instruction is essential for readers who have not yet attained fluency. It is always helpful to encourage students to read outside of the classroom as well (Hannaway, 2005; Lee, 2005).

Teachers should regularly assess fluency formally and informally to ensure that students are benefiting from instruction. The most informal assessment involves listening to students read aloud and making a judgment on their progress in fluency. A general rule for formal assessment is that by third grade students should be able to read more than 90 words a minute and read with expression while also being able to comprehend what they are reading. Monitoring student progress in reading fluency is not only useful in evaluating instruction and setting instructional goals but can be motivating for students as their fluency and reading achievement progress.

Teaching Vocabulary

Vocabulary refers to the words we must know to communicate effectively. In general, there are two types of vocabulary: oral and reading. Oral vocabulary refers to words that we use in speaking or recognize in listening. Reading vocabulary refers to words we recognize or use in print. Vocabulary plays an essential part in learning to read and is very important to reading comprehension. Researchers often refer to four types of vocabulary that help children build literacy skills:

- *Listening vocabulary:* Includes the words we need to know to understand what we hear
- *Speaking vocabulary:* Includes the words we use when we speak
- *Reading vocabulary:* Includes the words we need to know to understand what we read
- *Writing vocabulary:* Includes the words we use in writing

What Does Research Tell Us About Vocabulary Instruction?

According to scientific research, vocabulary instruction reveals that the meanings of many words are learned indirectly, while some meanings must be taught directly. Children learn word meanings indirectly in three ways:

- They engage in oral language.
- They listen to adults read to them.
- They read extensively on their own.

Direct instruction helps students learn difficult words that are not part of their everyday experiences. Direct instruction of vocabulary relevant to a given text encourages better reading comprehension. Direct instruction includes providing specific word instructions and teaching word-learning strategies to students. Specific word instruction provides the following important benefits:

- *Teaching specific words before reading* helps both vocabulary learning and reading comprehension.
- *Extended instruction* that promotes active engagement with vocabulary improves word learning.
- *Repeated exposure to vocabulary* in many contexts aids word learning.

Since it is impossible to provide specific instruction for all the words students do not know, it is essential that students be able to determine the meaning of words that are new to them but that have not been directly taught to them. Therefore, it is important that students develop effective word-learning strategies, such as these:

- How to use dictionaries and other resources to find the meaning of unfamiliar or unknown words
- How to use information about word parts to determine the meanings of words in texts and other reading material
- How to use context clues to figure out word meanings

Keys to Effective Vocabulary Instruction

Indirect learning of vocabulary can be encouraged in two ways: reading aloud to students while discussing the selection before, during, and after reading it and encouraging students to read extensively on their own. Since it is not possible to teach students all of the words in a text, it is better to focus on three types of words:

- *Important words,* or words that are essential for understanding a concept or the text
- *Useful words,* or words that students are likely to see and use consistently over time
- *Difficult words,* or words with multiple meanings and idiomatic expressions.

It is also important to remember that students know words to varying degrees, and they may display three levels of word knowledge:

- *Established:* The word is very familiar, and the student can recognize its meaning and use the word correctly.
- *Acquainted:* The word is somewhat familiar, and the student has some idea of its basic meaning.
- *Unknown:* The word and its meaning are completely unfamiliar.

They also learn vocabulary in different ways: learning a new meaning for a known word, learning the meaning for a new word representing a known concept, learning the meaning of a new word representing an unknown concept, and clarifying and enriching the meaning of a known word.

Effective teachers help students develop vocabulary by fostering *word consciousness,* which is awareness of and interest in words, their meanings, and their power. They do this by calling attention to the way authors choose words to convey particular meanings, by encouraging students to engage in word play, by helping students research a word's origin, and by encouraging students to search for examples of a word's usage in their daily lives. Vocabulary is a building block for comprehension, and developing strong vocabulary skills in these ways supports reading for understanding, which is the ultimate goal of effective literacy instruction for all children (Flint, 2008; Flood & Anders, 2005; Hoosain & Salili, 2005).

Teaching Comprehension

Comprehension is the purpose of reading. Instruction in comprehension helps students understand what they read, remember what they read, and communicate effectively with others about what they read.

What Does Research Tell Us About Comprehension Instruction?

Comprehension strategies are sets of steps that good readers use to make sense of text. Following are six strategies that have a solid scientific basis for improving text comprehension:

- Monitoring comprehension
- Using graphic and semantic organizers
- Answering questions
- Generating questions
- Recognizing story structure
- Summarizing what has been read

Effective comprehension strategy instruction is explicit when teachers tell readers why and when they should use strategies, what strategies to use, and how to apply them. The steps of explicit instruction typically include

- direct explanation,
- modeling,
- guided practice, and
- application.

Effective comprehension strategy instruction can be accomplished through cooperative learning, which involves students working together as partners or in small groups, where they work collectively to understand content-area texts and help each other learn and apply comprehension strategies. Apparently, effective instruction helps readers use comprehension strategies flexibly and in combination. Multiple-strategy instruction teaches students how to use strategies needed to assist their comprehension. In one example of multiple-strategy instruction, called "reciprocal teaching," the teacher and students work together so that the students learn four comprehension strategies: (1) *asking* questions about what they are reading, (2) *summarizing* parts of the text, (3) *clarifying* the words and sentences they do not understand, and (4) *predicting* what might occur next in the text.

Keys to Effective Comprehension Instruction

Text comprehension instruction can begin as early as primary grades to begin building the foundation for successful reading in content areas later in school. Instruction at all grade levels can benefit students by showing them how reading is a process of making sense of text or constructing meaning ultimately leading to understanding and use of information presented in text. Comprehension strategies for the classroom make use of prior knowledge to improve students' understanding and use mental imagery help readers visualize and remember what they read. Comprehension strategies are a means of helping children understand what they are reading, and once they see this helps them to learn, they will be more likely to be motivated and actively involved in learning.

Phonemic awareness, phonics, fluency, vocabulary, and comprehension are key targets for teaching children to read. Implementing components of effective teaching (i.e., planning, managing, delivering, and evaluating) increases the likelihood of achieving success for all students. Culturally responsive teaching builds on these foundations to support teaching reading to children from diverse backgrounds (Obiakor, 2003, 2007; Utley et al., 2005).

EFFECTIVE TEACHING ■

Teaching is the systematic presentation of content assumed necessary for mastery within a general area of knowledge (Algozzine, Ysseldyke, & Elliott, 1997). Effective teachers follow key principles. For example, according to Ornstein and Levine (1993), teachers are most effective when they do the following:

- Make sure that students know how they are expected to perform.
- Let students know how to obtain help.
- Follow through with reminders and rewards to enforce rules.
- Provide smooth transitions between activities.
- Give students assignments of sufficient variety to maintain interest.
- Monitor the class for signs of confusion or inattention.
- Use variations in eye contact, voice, and movement to maintain student attention.
- Use variations in academic activities to maintain student attention.
- Do not respond to discipline problems emotionally.
- Arrange the physical environment to complement instruction.
- Do not embarrass students in front of their classmates.
- Respond flexibly to unexpected developments. (p. 617)

These are just some of the ways in which effective teachers provide knowledge systematically. They are representative of four areas central to effective teaching: planning, managing, delivering, and evaluating (Algozzine & Ysseldyke, 2006; Algozzine et al., 1997).

Planning

If all children in a class were at the same instructional level and if the goals and objectives of schooling were clearly prescribed and the same for all children, then teaching would consist of doing the same things, in the same order, at the same time for everyone. Of course, not all children are alike, and the goals and objectives of teaching are not the same for all of them. This is why planning is such an important part of effective teaching.

Planning involves making decisions about what content to present. It also means deciding how to present the content and how to communicate realistic expectations about it to students (Flint, 2008; Manzo et al., 2005). Planning instruction, then, involves three steps, each contributing to effective teaching of all children and any content: deciding what to teach, deciding how to teach it, and communicating realistic expectations (Obiakor, 2003, 2007).

Managing

Managing involves getting ready for teaching, using time productively, and creating a positive environment. Few of us are comfortable in chaos. We need order around us. Children, too, need an orderly environment in which to learn. They need rules to follow, they need an understanding of those rules and the consequences if they do not follow them, and they need to see that the rules are enforced. In addition to setting rules, getting ready for teaching involves deciding how to deal with disruptions.

Managing also means using time productively. For example, in well-managed classrooms, transitions between activities are brief; few interruptions break the flow of classroom activities; the instructional pace has an active, task-oriented focus; and sufficient time is allocated to academic activities.

Managing also means creating a positive environment because, students are more motivated to learn when teachers accept their individual differences; interact positively with them; and create a supportive, cooperative classroom atmosphere (Obiakor, 2003, 2007; Utley et al., 2005). Students feel better about school and about learning when their teachers manage their classrooms effectively. Delivering content is also easier when teachers effectively manage their classrooms and the activities going on there. Learning is more likely to occur in effectively managed instructional environments.

Delivering

The third component of effective instruction, delivering, involves presenting content, monitoring student learning, and adjusting instruction. A simple but effective model for teaching or delivering content involves four steps: demonstrate, demonstrate, practice, and prove.

Effective teachers present and demonstrate well-crafted lessons with objectives and measurable outcomes. They communicate the goals of their instruction, maintain attention during instruction, and make the content they are teaching relevant for the children they are teaching. They teach thinking skills so their students can apply what they are learning rather than just repeat back memorized facts. Additionally, they monitor children's learning and check for understanding by having children present, identify, say, or write responses before presenting new content. They provide supportive or corrective feedback so that children will know when their responses are correct and so that they will not practice wrong responses when they are incorrect. To motivate their students, effective teachers show enthusiasm, assign work that interests students, use rewards and praise intermittently, and assign work at which students can succeed.

Effective teachers provide opportunities for students to work and practice independently to master content they have been learning. With relevant practice over adequate times, and with high levels of success, students complete tasks and perform skills automatically. Having students engage in extensive relevant practice is important, but if instructional materials are not varied, then practice becomes boring and interferes with instructional goals. Providing supportive or corrective feedback during independent practice is also important so that children will know when their responses are correct and so that they can correct wrong responses before they are asked to show and prove their levels of competence on classroom or standardized assessments.

Adjusting instruction includes varying approaches for presenting content. Not all students learn in the same way or at the same pace. Teachers must adjust their instruction for individual learners. There are no specific rules about how to modify lessons to meet all students' needs. The process usually is one of trial and error. Teachers try alternative approaches until one works.

An example: Mr. Cruise was teaching a lesson on the characteristics of dinosaurs. During the lesson, he noticed that Miguel was not paying attention. Another student, Anna, asked to go to the bathroom, and a third student started drumming on his desk with two pencils. It was clear to Mr. Cruise that the students were not interested in the lesson, so he modified it, assigning to each dinosaur the name of one of the students. He saved the most powerful, *Tyrannosaurus rex,* for the end of the lesson and named him "Mr. Cruise." He believed this slight change was enough to interest the students in the lesson, and he was right.

Teachers also adjust instruction by varying their methods and materials. This increases the chances of meeting individual students' needs. For students who are having difficulty, teachers can provide extra instruction and review, or they can adjust the pace of instruction (Obiakor & Smith, 2005; Utley et al., 2005).

Evaluating

Evaluation is the process by which teachers decide whether the methods and materials they are using are effective—based on students' performance. There are two kinds of evaluation: formative and summative. Both involve using data to make decisions. Formative evaluation occurs during the process of instruction. The teacher collects data during instruction and uses the data to make instructional decisions. Summative evaluation occurs at the end of instruction, when the teacher administers a test or formal assessment to determine whether the students have met instructional objectives. There are six components in the evaluation process:

- Monitoring students' understanding
- Monitoring engaged time
- Maintaining records of students' progress
- Informing students about their progress

- Using data to make decisions
- Making judgments about students' performance

Clearly, culturally responsive teachers use students' interests, experiences, and backgrounds to teach phonemic awareness, phonics, fluency, vocabulary, and comprehension. Culturally responsive teachers consider students' interests, experiences, and backgrounds when planning, managing, delivering, and evaluating their teaching of these skills (Flint, 2008).

■ EFFECTIVE CULTURALLY RESPONSIVE TEACHING

It is not easy to teach reading or literacy the right way and to be also culturally responsive at the same time. There is some multidimensionality involved! Flood and Anders (2005) presented the relationship between literacy and culture. They acknowledged that reading and literacy are connected to myriad issues, such as culture, race, geographical location, socioeconomics, and school policies. As Hannaway (2005) noted, we cannot talk about reading and literacy without talking about parent/family inputs, out-of-school experiences, in-school experiences, economic and social policies, education and social policies, testing and accountability policies, early childhood programs, teacher quality, class size, school resources, and afterschool programs. Why then do some general and special education professionals look at reading unidimensionally? Consider the following unidimensional statements about reading:

- If you cannot read, you will not survive in life.
- Your accent determines your reading ability.
- Good readers speak good English.
- You can predict if a student will have reading deficiency.
- Reading has no connection to socioeconomic and cultural backgrounds.
- Reading can only be evaluated with standardized, conventional methods.

Clearly, reading is connected to multidimensional variables (e.g., cultural, socioeconomic, and environmental backgrounds). The question then is, how can it be taught in a culturally responsive fashion? Culturally responsive instruction involves taking advantage of students' culture, language, values, symbols, and history in designing instruction (Obiakor, 2003, 2007). It is tied to students' interests, experiences, and backgrounds; and by drawing upon students' prior knowledge, learning is made more meaningful and relevant (Guthrie & Wigfield, 2000; Raphael, 1986). Seven characteristics for successful implementation of culturally responsive instruction include (1) teachers setting high expectations for students as they develop the literacy appropriate to their ages and abilities; (2) teachers developing positive relationships with families and the community in terms of curriculum content and relationships; (3) teachers exhibiting cultural sensitivity by modifying the curriculum, connecting the standards-based curriculum with the students' cultural backgrounds;

(4) teachers involving students more by incorporating active teaching methods; (5) teachers acting as facilitators when presenting information; and (6) teachers instructing around groups and pairs, reducing the anxiety of students by having them complete assignments individually but usually working in small groups or pairs with time to share ideas and think critically about the work before it is completed (Schmidt, 2005).

Every elementary classroom is made up of children of varying intellectual abilities, social or cultural backgrounds, language abilities, and physical attributes. Today, more than ever, all teachers must be prepared to meet the varying educational, emotional, and social needs of all children (Nichols, Rupley, Webb-Johnson, & Weaver, 1996; Obiakor, 2003, 2007). When we think about culturally and linguistically diverse (CLD) students specifically, we must remember that they are on the same reading and learning continuum as other children; however, they often have experiences that are different from the mainstream. For example, CLD students often are from lower socioeconomic status homes. As a result, limited emergent literacy experiences and exposure to literature from their own culture or from traditional American literature may inhibit their success in early literacy instruction. Also, CLD students may have literacy experiences that are different from what is expected by the school; thus, traditional early literacy programs may not adequately prepare them for beginning reading instruction (Stahl, 1990). If educators are to strive toward successful academic reading outcomes for "all" children, it is important to develop instructional strategies that empower all children to prosper, and this includes CLD children (Nichols et al., 1996; Utley et al., 2005).

Young children are more willing to learn in school when teachers organize classroom experiences in ways that take into account the language, learning styles, values, and knowledge they encounter at home or in the groups with whom they most identify (Trueba, 1984). Teachers using culturally compatible reading instruction can help the diverse student identify his own cultural individualism while simultaneously learning more literacy instruction (Au, 1993). These students may also not use processing strategies that can help them learn and remember content. While many students think strategically to solve problems outside of school (Holiday, 1985), such reasoning does not always find its way into the classroom of students who experience difficulties with reading. Most children are strategic learners. However, they sometimes are just not able to recognize that the strategies they use in their home cultural context can and should be applied to learning and solving problems at school.

On the whole, culturally responsive teaching involves creative planning and preparation. To teach reading creatively, Manzo and Casale (1985) and Manzo et al. (2005) proposed the L-R-D (Listen-Read-Discuss) method to offer several variations that can be phased into all literacy programs. For instance, Manzo et al. noted that "the L-R-D is a heuristic, or hands-on, activity designed to induce self-discovery about effective teaching by teachers and about effective learning by students" (p. 14). According to Manzo et al., teachers and service providers should do the following:

- Review the reading selection and prepare a brief, organized overview that points out the basic structures of the material, relevant

background information, and important information to look for and that piques interest in the topic.
- Present the summary orally to students.
- Have students read the textbook version of the same material. Students will then be empowered to read material with which they have some familiarity.
- Discuss the material students have heard and read.
- Begin the discussion with the information and ideas students were directed to look for (p. 14).

To motivate weak readers who come from CLD backgrounds, it is important that general and special educators avoid assumptions based on the following:

- *Biological determinism* (i.e., that reading problems/successes are based on genetic attributes)
- *Myth of socioeconomic dissonance* (i.e., that poverty is attributed to reading or learning capability or incapability)
- *Psychopathological problems* (i.e., that reading or learning problems are results of inner mental or delinquency problems)

Rather, general and special educators should create culturally responsive classroom and school environments that can foster collaborative learning. Manzo et al. (2005) concluded that general and special educators should do the following:

- Establish a sustained silent reading (SSR) program.
- Furnish students with interesting reading materials.
- Have students fill out a reading interest inventory, indicating the types of books they enjoy reading.
- Encourage students to join book clubs.
- Become reading motivators.
- Increase collaborative classroom activities.
- Use technology to encourage reading.
- Use bulletin boards.
- Ask students to use media supports (e.g., movies or television programs).
- Involve local writers, parents, and responsible adults.
- Give students incentives for reading.
- Conduct reading conferences with students.

In addition to the aforementioned techniques, Flint (2008) presented guiding principles for effective literacy instruction to help students to lead literate lives in the 21st century. Clearly, the guiding principles are imperatives that center around the fact that literacy practices must (a) be socially and culturally constructed, (b) be purposeful, (c) contain ideologies and values, (d) be learned through inquiry, (e) invite readers and writers to use their background knowledge and cultural understanding to make sense of texts, and (f) expand to include everyday texts and multimodal texts. In the end, it is important to remember that no technique will work unless the teacher or service provider is culturally responsive (Obiakor, 2003). As Obiakor concluded, strategies work when general and special educators (a) know themselves and are confident in what they can do, (b) learn the facts when they are in doubt, (c) change their thinking, (d) use resource persons, (e) build self-concepts, (f) teach with divergent techniques, (g) make the right choices, and (h) continue to learn.

REVISITING CHIDI ■

Remember Chidi? He was labeled as a student with reading problems by his teacher because he was quiet and not rambunctious. He was perceived to have a problem that he never had! The interesting thing here is that perceptions can sometimes be right; however, they have far-reaching, devastating consequences when they are wrong. Apparently, Chidi was misperceived because of his cultural difference as demonstrated by his name. He could have been taught how to expand on his reading skills—his teacher was already introducing the class to alphabets and word association. But his teacher did not know him or his reading capabilities. This lack of awareness prevented her from knowing what strengths he brought to the classroom.

The National Reading Panel (2000) prescribed critical areas of phonemic awareness, phonics, fluency, vocabulary, and comprehension that could help maximize the reading potential of any student with or without a reading problem. All students deserve support in spite of their reading levels. Focusing on the important areas of needs would have helped the teacher to expand on Chidi's reading skills and also on "what is" rather than "what is not." Sadly, teachers spend much time harping on distractions to learning or presumed reading/literacy deficiency instead of what they can do to buttress it. We believe well-prepared, culturally responsive teachers or service providers try to know the present levels of their students as they creatively design, modify, and adapt their instructional techniques. Time spent labeling students and struggling with parents is time spent not teaching and collaborating. Teachers lose teachable moments when they are not paying attention. Clearly, collaboration works in classrooms where consultation and cooperation are in full force!

MOVING ON ■

In this chapter, we have argued that reading is an integral part of learning and teaching. We believe that educators cannot afford to make assumptions about reading unless they are completely sure that reading has been taught. Rather than make assumptions based on biological determinism, the myth of socioeconomic dissonance, or psychopathological disorders, general and special educators should focus on how to address skills and areas central to phonemic awareness, phonics, fluency, vocabulary, and comprehension. It is important that educators understand the different dimensions of literacy and culture. In-school, out-of-school, and past experiences, as well as a host of other variables, affect reading and literacy.

When we fail to understand these critical relationships, we run the risk of either solving a problem that does not exist or using a wrong strategy to solve the right problem. Our hunch is that reading problems cannot be solved by testing alone! We believe that culturally responsive educators and service providers creatively plan and implement culturally sensitive strategies and environments to maximize the potential of all learners.

2

Improving Phonological Processing

Dorothy J. O'Shea and Jodi Katsafanas

CHAPTER OBJECTIVES

In this chapter we will

- establish the importance of phonological processing to developing and becoming a competent reader;
- identify research related to phonological processing and its role in the identification, discrimination, and manipulation of sounds;
- examine how early literacy skills evolve, including development of and difficulties with pronunciation and production of sounds, words, and phonological memory skills; and
- provide examples of culturally and linguistically responsive phonological processing practices important to primary, middle school, and high school readers.

MEET MIGUEL

Miguel Gonzalez began his first year of middle school confident that he could complete his academic requirements and play sports successfully. Throughout his primary school years, Miguel had played basketball daily near his community school. He saw no reason why he couldn't continue to play middle school sports while he completed sixth through eighth grades. After all, he had played well during his elementary school years.

The first week of sixth grade went as expected. Ms. Nichol, Miguel's language arts teacher, met with Miguel and his science teacher/basketball coach, Mrs. Green, to review academic and homework requirements that Ms. Nichol had discussed at the middle school orientation with Miguel and his peers. (Ms. Nichol was Miguel's homeroom teacher.) To Miguel, Ms. Nichol seemed businesslike but supportive in her demeanor. He did have doubts regarding Ms. Nichol and Mrs. Green's expectations. He wondered about how realistic both Ms. Nichol and Mrs. Green were regarding the amount of time he would need to complete his homework.

Miguel knew he had trouble reading. In fact, Miguel still was unsure of recognizing alphabet letters or remembering words quickly. He was not skilled at matching sounds to letters and knew he had problems in recognizing letters that went together to form words. Sometimes, Ms. Nichol asked him to remember the sounds in a word that she modeled for him, such as in the word both. *She then asked him to say other words that sounded similar, such as* this *and* thick. *Sometimes, Miguel couldn't tell sounds apart, and he couldn't say how words started or ended. Whenever his elementary teachers asked him to read aloud, they usually directed him to blend sounds into words or to break up words into parts. When he came to easy words, such as the words* in *or* no, *Miguel was able to read. However, when his teachers said to listen for and find word parts, such as the /n/ sound in the words* win, mental, *and* unknown, *he couldn't understand what to say or how to do these tasks. All of his elementary teachers, however, had helped him to complete his schoolwork, so Miguel wasn't worried.*

During the second week, Miguel spent his time observing his peers read in large-group activities and working in small groups as he participated in content area classes. He never volunteered to read out loud because he knew he would stumble on sounding out the difficult words. He also spent time listening to the tape of his middle school's policies and procedures for its schoolwide sports program. To play basketball, Miguel was aware that he needed to complete all of his homework and make satisfactory grades. He also knew that his grandmother, with whom he lived in their inner-city apartment, would not be able to help him complete his difficult science, language arts, history, computer science, and mathematics homework.

In week three, Mrs. Green had Miguel participate in a one-on-one oral activity with her to compare and contrast the use of science words that his sixth-grade peers were completing independently. After the lesson, Mrs. Green complimented Miguel for listening to the discussion on "photosynthesis" and defining it orally. Mrs. Green, however, expressed concern that Miguel could not follow the text when sounding out key words. She reminded him that he seemed lost when she asked him to practice sounding out key words after hearing longer phrases, such as in the sentence, "Thunder may be involved in rain theory." Miguel took the feedback well and promised to be better prepared for his next lesson.

During the next three weeks, Mrs. Green expressed concern that because Miguel could not complete his homework, basketball should not be his priority. Needless to say, the workload increased dramatically just as Miguel continued meeting his afterschool sports schedule. Upon Ms. Nichol's sixth week of large-group language arts instruction, she also assessed that Miguel's word skills were poor and his homework completion was ineffective as a result.

Prior to meeting with Miguel and his grandmother, Ms. Nichol collaborated with Mrs. Green; Mr. Norton, Miguel's history teacher; and Mrs. Wing, his computer science and mathematics teacher. All teachers verified that Miguel had been having problems with in-class activities and homework completion as they assigned more complex responsibilities. Miguel did not participate in reading and writing activities. He rarely spoke in any class. Ms. Nichol presented Miguel with his teachers' observations. Miguel became defensive and dismissed the feedback. He believed that his participation was sufficient and his homework went well enough. He explained that he had seen students down the hall do half as much as he had.

Three quarters through his first nine-week grading period, Miguel had not made suffi-cient adjustments to improve his reading or homework skills. All of his teachers were frus-trated with his recalcitrance, and Mrs. Green said she had no choice but to terminate Miguel's basketball. The teachers planned to call in Miguel and his grandmother for a team conference meeting. Miguel was devastated.

WHAT IS PHONOLOGICAL PROCESSING? ■

Probably the most significant advance in the scientific study of reading and related skills has been the identification of the role of phonologi-cal processing in learning to read. In the case scenario presented above, Miguel lacked key skills related to hearing sounds and using the sound structure of language. Because of the importance of language sounds in learning to read, Miguel had problems in completing class assignments and complying with his homework activities. Miguel demonstrated diffi-culties in phonological processing, beginning with his knowledge of sounds and letters that comprise the English language. As a result, Miguel displayed problems completing his school tasks and homework.

Listening to and understanding speech involves identifying individ-ual sounds that make up words. These sounds are called *phonemes*. The English language has approximately 40 to 44 phonemes. Individually, phonemes combine with others sounds to make up words. The process of identifying those sounds and subsequently identifying the words that the sounds combine to make is called *phonological processing* (Al Otaiba & Fuchs, 2002; Benner, Nelson, & Gonzalez, 2005; Justice & Pullen, 2003).

Phonological processing involves speech sound perception, memory, retrieval, and pronunciation as a reader sequences, combines, and pro-nounces sounds to make words (Catts, 1991; Chall, 1996; Ehri, 1996). Key phonological processing components are in Table 2.1.

Phonemic Development

Phonological processing includes the ability to hear and manipulate the sound structure of language. In fact, two important findings in reading research over the past decade have been the discovery of (a) the importance of understanding that words are made up of sounds and (b) development of efficient ability to convert a string of letters to a match-ing sequence of sounds (Brady, Fowler, Stone, & Winbury, 1994; Christie, Richgels, & Roskos, 2003; Share, 1995). Snow, Burns, and Griffin (1998) defined important components related to phonological development. A major literacy component is *phonemic awareness*, or the insight that every

| TABLE 2.1 | Phonological Processing Components |

- *Phonemic development:* Includes awareness, recognition, and discrimination of phonemes
- *Alphabetic awareness:* Includes awareness, recognition, and discrimination of letters
- *Acoustic-visual skills:* These are needed to link letter sounds with letters; blend letters and letter sounds; segment letters and letter sounds; and exercise awareness, recognition, and discrimination of beginning, medial, and ending sounds to make words.
- *Shifting understanding of word sounds and/or acoustic blends to word typography*
- *Segmenting and blending individual phonemes or words:* This skill is needed to apply syllabication, rhyme, and alliteration.

spoken word can be conceived as a sequence of phonemes. Because phonemes are the speech phonological units, each sound contributes a difference to meaning. (Thus, the word *lane* is comprised of three phonemes: /l/-/a/-/n/. The word *lap* also is comprised of three phonemes: /l/-/a/-/p/.) When readers acquire phonemic awareness, they can shift focus from the meaning of spoken words to their sounds.

The development of phonemic awareness, the explicit understanding of a word's sound structure, is critical for the efficient decoding of reading print and the ability to form connections between sounds and letters when writing and spelling. Readers need solid phonemic awareness for reading instruction to be effective. Readers must become aware of a relationship between letters and sounds, which letters represent; that words have boundaries and can be broken up into syllables and patterns; and that beginning, medial, and/or ending sounds can be put together, or taken apart, to make up words. Readers able to connect and manipulate the sound structure successfully will be unable, most likely, to express how they obtain meaning through a set of written symbols. They demonstrate, however, that symbols represent the sounds they hear, as they begin to decipher, store, and retrieve from memory letter symbols to match the sounds. To enhance phonological processing, readers must demonstrate a basic understanding of the alphabet.

Alphabet Awareness

Phonological processing relies heavily on alphabet knowledge; however, alphabet and letter sound knowledge is complex. Letters in the English language have names, sounds, and shapes, and the three are not logically connected. For example, the letter name for *c* is pronounced "see," its pure phoneme should be correctly pronounced /k/, and its shape is an almost-closed "o." To complicate matters, only eight letters of the alphabet have names from which the sounds can be derived (*b, d, j, p, t, k, v,* and *z*), and numerous letter names are similar. That is, the letters *b, e, p, d, t, c, g, v,* and *z* all have the *e* as the final sound in their name (Bear, Invernizzi, Templeton, & Johnston, 1994).

Several letter names begin with a short /e/ sound (*f, m, n*). Many letters make more than one sound, depending on surrounding letters. When learning a letter's shape, there are vertical, horizontal, and diagonal intersections and up-down and circular movements to coordinate (Bear et al., 2003). To learn to read, readers require "awareness that all words can be decomposed into phonological segments" (Shankweiler, 1999, p. 114).

Alphabetic Principle

The alphabetic principle is "the idea that spelling systematically represents spoken words" (Snow et al., 1998, p. 4). In Snow and peers' view, as phonemes are the units of sound that are represented by letters of an alphabet, awareness of phonemes is key to understanding the logic of the alphabet by applying an alphabetic principle and in acquiring skills in phonics, writing, and spelling.

Share (1995) described the role of phonological recoding in phonological processing and applying the alphabetic principle. It "functions as a self-teaching mechanism enabling the learner to acquire the detailed orthographic representations necessary for rapid, autonomous, visual word recognition" (p. 152). Orthography involves an understanding that a written system of letters represents the sounds heard in language. Failure to attain this self-teaching process and early prerequisite skills may lead to the acquisition of more compensatory strategies as reading advances, such as the use of visual memory or an overreliance on content (Stanovich, 1994; Torgesen, Wagner, & Rashotte, 1999).

Acoustic-Visual Skill

In the English language, to a preliterate individual, the individual letters on a page are initially abstract. These abstract shapes must eventually be associated with sounds such that the reader can detect, store, recognize, and recall phonemes. As phonological processing in early literacy skills advances, the reader must use and differentiate syllables and beginning, medial, or ending sounds of words. A reader can learn to differentiate syllables as word components when becoming involved in sound manipulations. In essence, the beginning reader translates the connections between the 26 letters of the alphabet and the approximately 44 English language phonemes. The acoustic-visual understanding that written spellings systematically represent the phonemes of spoken words is tantamount to learning the alphabetic principle while applying blending and segmenting, and it is essential for the development of accurate and rapid decoding and word reading skills (Adams, 1990; Ball & Blachman, 1991; Blachman, 1989; Catts, 1991).

Word Typography

It is now widely recognized that poor readers, such as Miguel, often struggle to learn to decode and comprehend text if they lack phonological awareness skills, including phonemic awareness and segmenting and blending separate sounds within words acoustically and visually (Goswami, & Bryant, 1990; Grace, 2005; McCollin & O'Shea, 2005). Miguel displayed many common problems in phonemic awareness as he lacked the ability to attend to phonemes, differentiate them, and manipulate them in speech. He was not a phonemically aware reader because he was unable to identify sounds in words consistently. He lacked fundamental knowledge of *word typography* (i.e., the visual appearance of printed characters on a page). Because Miguel lacked in phonemic awareness, he was unable to read accurately and to complete higher order academic tasks requiring listening, speaking, reading, writing, and/or spelling.

Segmenting and Blending Individual Phonemes or Words

To begin to read effectively, in addition to sensitivity to individual phonemes and knowledge of the alphabet, phonological processing also involves an understanding of *syllable, rhyme,* and *alliteration.* Thus, a reader must discover that spoken words can be segmented into smaller units of sound, that alphabet letters on the page represent the sounds, and that written words have the same number and sequence of sounds heard in a spoken word. The reader must be able to differentiate beginning, medial, and ending sounds in words. The reader must be able to translate (or map) speech to print and print to speech.

Syllable knowledge entails an understanding of a unit of spoken language that is comprised of one or more vowel sounds alone, a syllabic consonant alone, or any of these with one or more consonant sounds. Readers with knowledge of *syllabication* realize that letters in a word correspond approximately to a syllable of spoken language. The ability to *rhyme* words entails a reader's understanding of the similarity of word endings, while *alliteration* (i.e., the occurrence in a phrase of two or more words having the same initial sound) entails discerning quickly the same beginning sounds and blends in words. Rhyme and alliteration activities support the development of phonemic awareness in readers, especially when reading activities focus readers' attention on and raise their consciousness of individual phonemes (e.g., blending phonemes to make words or segmenting words by phonemes) (Benner & Nelson, 2005; Benner et al., 2005; Chard, Jackson, Paratore, & Garnick, 2000).

Translating skills necessary for phonological development requires advancement through types of cognitive tasks that have a positive effect on reading acquisition and spelling (Ball & Blachman, 1991; Yopp, 1988). Table 2.2 illustrates examples of some tasks often used to assess the extent to which children are developing phonological skills necessary for reading and spelling success.

TABLE 2.2 Examples of Commonly Used Tasks for Assessing Phonological Development

- Orally discriminating sounds that are different
- Blending spoken sounds into words
- Word-to-word matching
- Isolating sounds in words
- Rhyming
- Counting phonemes
- Segmenting spoken words into sounds
- Deleting sounds from words
- Alliteration

Phonological Memory Skills

Cognitive tasks in phonological processing require one to detect sounds, store sounds in memory, and retrieve phonemes and sound sequences in spoken language (Blachman, 1989, 1991; Snow et al., 1998). Memory skills are essential to phonological processing as one hears, differentiates, and manipulates sounds. The reader must rely on memory in his or her mental processing and mental capacity when recognizing, filing to remember, recalling, retrieving, connecting, using, monitoring, and repairing selections of sounds in words and matching letter sequences in print.

Fundamental memory skills first require a reader to detect sounds such that sounds hold meaning. As sound awareness increases, a reader becomes more proficient at storing or filing in memory what sounds represent and how sounds can be used. Recall and retrieval of sounds require the reader to activate memory when repeating those sounds, followed by blending those sounds into words or phrases. When a reader imitates correct production of phonemes as phonemes are articulated, the reader requires memory to differentiate and match phonemes with written symbols (i.e., letters or graphemes). Memory requirements underscore mental capacity used to retrieve sound-symbol relationships when the reader is required to hold sounds in memory to recall letters so that words can be said orally or written down or to spell words from a list (Catts, 1991; Chall, 1996; Ehri, 1996).

EXPLICIT INSTRUCTION ■

Recent reports by the U.S. National Reading Panel (2000; NICHD, 2000) examined evidence regarding the impact of phonemic awareness instruction on reading development. (See Appendix F for more information concerning the National Reading Panel.) From a meta-analysis of over 10,000 research studies, several conclusions evolved regarding the efficacy of explicitly teaching phonemic awareness skills. Beginning readers who are read to at home—especially material that rhymes—often develop the basis of phonemic awareness. Readers who are not read to will probably need to be taught that words can be broken apart into smaller sounds. This report concluded that training in phonemic awareness, combined with letter to sound instruction, is the most effective method of teaching beginning readers to read and spell. These results were the same for both readers at risk of failure at the beginning of reading stages and for older failing readers.

To address reading difficulties experienced by many beginning readers, especially those from diverse backgrounds, teachers must use effective, research-based programs (Shippen, Houchins, Steventon, & Sartor, 2005). One such research-validated reading program is the use of direct instruction (DI) (Adams & Engelmann, 1996), which promotes mastery of meaningful reading through explicit teaching. Explicitly teaching readers sound-letter correspondence and sounding out is essential for readers at risk for reading failure. Systematic phonological and phonemic awareness instruction contributes strongly to reading success (Swanson, Hoskyn, & Lee, 1999). When teachers stress explicit instruction and offer feedback and encouragement, they help to ensure appropriate reading mastery. DI programs also insist on extensive training to prepare for teacher implementation (Grossen, 2004; Kim & Axelrod, 2005).

A program with a 25-year history of success is the SRA/McGraw Hill Corrective Reading Program. It provides a systematic, explicit approach to teach struggling readers the intricate skills necessary to analyze words proficiently with accurate understanding (Greenberg, Fredrick, Hughes, & Bunting, 2002; Kim & Axelrod, 2005). Corrective Reading stresses an increase in phonological awareness and an emphasis on word decoding and comprehension (Grossen, 2004; Jitendra, Cole, Hoppes, & Wilson, 1998; Kim & Axelrod, 2005; Shippen et al., 2005).

Gaskins (1995) argued that teachers could implement explicit strategies by using direct instruction principles that consider well-sequenced and teacher-directed instruction. Direct instruction principles help to ensure a faultless, efficient, and engaging presentation that is tightly linked to the material presentation with specific instruction, prompts, and frequent and positive feedback. Explicit teaching of strategies is needed, because poor readers often do not exhibit awareness and control of strategies unless directly taught to do so. When poor readers learn that the strategies are valuable and applicable to new situations and are functional to them, they are motivated to use them. However, teaching awareness and control strategies ideally occurs at an early age so that readers have enough practice and time to reach the level of needed *automaticity* (i.e., an unconscious use of the skill quickly and without error). Unfortunately, many at-risk readers do not reach automaticity because they struggle with phonological awareness.

The best evidence for the positive effect of explicit instruction on beginning reading comes from data from Project Follow Through, a federal compensatory education program beginning in 1967 for low-income readers in kindergarten through third grade (Grossen, 2002; Kim & Axelrod, 2005; MacIver & Kemper, 2002a, 2002b). A pattern of effectiveness in explicitly teaching beginning literacy skills remained consistent over the years regardless of setting or grade level, both in general education and in special education (Kim & Axelrod, 2005; Shippen et al., 2005).

Examples of reading programs using direct instruction principles include Corrective Reading and Reading Excellence: Word Attack and Rate Development Strategies (REWARDS). Both proved effective in directing basic literacy skills in young and older readers. Table 2.3 describes Corrective Reading (Engelmann et al., 1999). Table 2.4 describes REWARDS (Archer, Gleason, & Vachon, 2000).

TABLE 2.3   Characteristics of Corrective Reading

- Addresses five key components of reading: phonemic awareness, phonics, fluency, vocabulary, and comprehension.
- Designed for readers in grades 4–12 and targets those reading below grade level.
- Is appropriate for use in special education and general education classrooms.
- Stresses accuracy (decoding), reading fluency, and building comprehension.
- Is tightly sequenced in decoding and comprehension.
  - Decoding focuses on identifying words, understanding how the arrangement of letters in a word relates to its pronunciation, and reading rate.
  - Comprehension incorporates word attack skills practice, group reading, individual reading checkouts, and workbook exercises.

| TABLE 2.4 | Characteristics of Reading Excellence: Word Attack and Rate Development Strategies (REWARDS) Program |

- Addresses five components of reading: phonemic awareness, phonics, fluency, vocabulary, and comprehension.
- Is an intense, short-term intervention reading program specifically designed for 4th- through 12th-grade readers who have mastered skills associated with 1st- and 2nd-grade reading but have difficulty reading long words and/or who read slowly.
- Provides flexible strategies for decoding multisyllabic words to build reading accuracy and fluency.
- Helps readers to segment a word into parts, read the word part by part, and read words independently.
- Stresses phonemic awareness through syllable blending and segmenting activities in each lesson.
- Readers move from overt (circling and underlining word parts and vowel sounds) to covert (recognizing the word parts and vowel sounds) strategies of decoding.
- Readers concentrate on circling decodable word parts (affixes); underlining vowel sounds; articulating the word at a normal pace; and then articulating it faster, making it a real word.
- Readers focus on fluency with a flexible decoding strategy that helps them identify known affixes and their meanings as well as vowel sounds.
- Readers use information to form word parts, thus enabling readers to read longer words within sentences and context passages.

IMPROVING PHONOLOGICAL PROCESSING IN DIVERSE READERS

Whether teachers use commercially produced reading programs, such as Corrective Reading or REWARDS, or they implement effective reading practices without a formal program but use components of effective instruction (Algozzine & Ysseldyke, 2006), literacy skills need to be taught explicitly and directly to beginning or struggling readers, emphasizing phonological development and targeting ways to enhance how readers hear and manipulate the sound structure of language (NICHD, 2000a, 2000b).

Diverse students from CLD backgrounds who enter school and who do not possess the foundational reading skills needed to comprehend written language often lack the literacy experiences provided to their peers from literate backgrounds. In addition to students from CLD backgrounds, poorly performing readers displaying limited phonological awareness include those identified with language-based learning disabilities, English language learners, as well as other underachieving or "at-risk" students who may simply have never received appropriate literacy modeling or reading instruction. As they display phonological awareness difficulties, these readers frequently struggle with more complex tasks, just as Miguel continued to face in his middle school experiences. Such readers often benefit from highly structured phonic/linguistic programs (Chall, 1996) that present regular spelling patterns reinforced by decodable text written in patterns. African-American and many other students of color often have a bilingual or bidialectal background because of their exposure to two language varieties. Often, these diverse readers achieve better academically if phonic/linguistic approaches are used—perhaps because these methods are similar to foreign language teaching methods (Hoover, Dabney, & Lewis, 1990).

Paramount to the job of teaching is using strategies that have been shown to increase readers' motivation, such as making reading relevant to home and community settings. By building on what readers already know and what motivates readers, teachers can support readers to want to read (Flood & Anders, 2005). In addition, teachers can supply reading materials that are age, culturally, and developmentally appropriate to reading abilities (Cartledge & Lo, 2006). Struggling readers who are unmotivated tend to have recognizable characteristics, as presented in Table 2.5.

TABLE 2.5   Characteristics of Struggling Readers Lacking Motivation

- Low confidence in their reading ability (low self-efficacy)
- Low confidence in their ability to improve their reading
- Extrinsically rather than intrinsically motivated (e.g., many respond to rewards and incentives)
- Unlikely to read for their own enjoyment or curiosity
- Often feeling socially marginalized and disrespected and, therefore, uncomfortable in school (e.g., many want to avoid looking bad and find ways to protect their egos)
- Often interested in subjects other than academics that capture their interests

For readers who are not proficient in phonological awareness, teachers should explicitly focus on only one or two phonemic awareness skills at a time, such as on segmenting and blending. Beginning with auditory phonemic activities, teachers can then link sounds to letters and provide opportunities for readers to apply their knowledge of phonological awareness when reading and writing. As with other readers who display phonological awareness difficulties, struggling readers can benefit from systematic instruction in identifying and manipulating the sounds of spoken language (Vaughn, Bos, & Schumm, 2005). For many readers, phonological awareness begins long before school years initiate. In essence, many readers receive early literacy exposure from their familial and community experiences.

■ TEACHING PRIMARY-LEVEL READERS FROM DIVERSE BACKGROUNDS

Based on the work of Hiebert (2005), it has become known that most preschool-age children are unable to read and write in the conventional sense. However, their efforts at reading and writing show steady advancement during their primary years. Reading research examining phonological processing and children's literacy development before the onset of formal instruction is known as *emergent literacy research* (Alvermann & Moore, 1991; Sulzby & Teale, 1991). Such research stresses that literacy learning often occurs during the first years of a child's life.

Van Kleeck, Stahl, & Bauer (2003) found that emergent literacy often begins during the period before children receive formal reading instruction. Sulzby and Teale (1991) contended that emergent literacy encompasses learning about reading and print prior to schooling. Emergent literacy can occur through informal home and preschool activities and encompasses a span of settings and language experiences that support literacy learning. For instance, young children's early phonological awareness may develop through exposure to listening to and following directions from parents or siblings, hearing and responding to stories read or songs sung to them by caregivers, using picture cues to discern meaning, and seeing written language throughout their homes or communities. Such exposure may help young children to develop an awareness of phonemic awareness, print, and letter identification, along with language facility, vocabulary, and comprehension.

Early literacy programs emphasizing phonological awareness are typically designed to serve readers at the lowest end of the achievement range and are expected to increase the numbers of average range readers and decrease the numbers of below basic readers requiring additional assistance. Many "early literacy intervention programs" offer explicit instruction in which teachers incorporate reading and writing instruction into familiar activities. For instance, the clapping routines, snapping fingers, playing games, singing, dancing, jumping, coloring, and pasting routines that many young children enjoy can be embedded with sound, letter, and word instruction. In this way, reading and writing can develop concurrently in young readers, fostered by motivating experiences that permit and promote meaningful literacy interaction with oral and written language (Sulzby & Teale, 1991).

Literacy Modeling

According to Van Kleeck et al. (2003), researchers rely on ethnographic studies to gain insight to the literacy artifacts in preschool children's environments and the literacy events to which they are exposed and in which they participate. Adult-child interactions surrounding literacy events discern how others foster literacy development and aid in the study of the relationship between preschool literacy development and later academic achievement (Snow et al., 1998; Teale & Sulzby, 1987).

Certain areas of emergent literacy (e.g., awareness of print, knowledge of the relationship between speech and print, text structure, phonological awareness, and letter naming and writing) underscore modeling and imitation and continue to develop during the preschool and kindergarten periods. Acquisition of these skills is an important part of early phonological processing and substantially affects the ease with which many children learn to listen, speak, read, write, and spell.

Teaching Phonological Awareness and the Alphabetic Principle to Primary Readers

Teachers can directly teach phonological awareness and alphabet awareness by infusing culturally diverse materials with explicit instructional strategies in early reading opportunities. Readers need many opportunities to hear individual sounds and words, count them, determine whether the words are short or long, and think about their order within sentences. Explicit opportunities in phoneme manipulation, in which beginning readers receive meaningful practice to work and play with phonemes in words, can help in the development of phonological development and alphabet awareness.

Phonological awareness activities can be difficult for many readers. Teachers need to allow plenty of time for each skill and pay careful attention to readers' responses and participation. They need to determine who needs more help and where the problems lie and then set aside time to provide additional individualized instruction with selected activities. At the same time, it is important to keep these readers involved in the larger setting so they can listen to and learn from those who are catching on more quickly. Thus, explicit instruction and practice, combined with other ongoing listening, speaking, reading, and print opportunities, helps develop the critical concept of letter, sound, and word. The following tips may help:

- *Use concrete representation (i.e., modeling a neutral object to stand for a sound, such as a blank tile).* For example, *cat* would have three tiles, one standing for the /k/, another for the /a/, and the third for the /t/. This may facilitate primary readers' understanding of letter-sound correspondences to the written symbols. When concrete representation is paired with cultural themes, readers' interests may be piqued. Thus, using Elizabeth Fitzgerald Howard's (1991) *Aunt Flossie's Hats and Crab Cakes Later,* a simple children's story with words familiar to African-American children, teachers help readers to emphasize sound-letter relationships by stressing important letter sounds and letters of key vocabulary from story events.
- *Implement educator scaffolding (i.e., modeling phoneme sound production, explicitly drawing attention to how the sound feels when it is being produced; modeling strategies for detecting, saying, or moving phonemes; and verbally stressing the target phoneme).* Creativity can reinforce young readers' ideas of what a phoneme sounds like, feels like, and looks like. For example, primary readers often enjoy movement and can create animated dance movements to ethnic folk songs, such as modeled by the *Dancing With the Stars* television show. Using hand percussion to imitate targeted phonemes, young readers can listen to ethnic stories and then dance creatively to "how sounds feel."
- *Play Round the Circle Song.* As the readers walk around in a circle, a teacher can increase phonological awareness by randomly calling out names of famous individuals from culturally diverse backgrounds. As the teacher directs readers whose names begin with the same sound as the famous person to sit down, primary readers receive practice opportunities in listening to and following directions that are embedded in fun, early literacy instruction.
- *Play Word Wizard.* A teacher can display a picture card of a famous person from a culturally diverse background whose name is a

one-syllable word. Then the teacher says the word normally, direct-ing readers to break it into a beginning, medial, or ending sound. The teacher may follow up this practice by adding longer names, cueing readers to hear sounds in multiple syllables represented by the first, middle, and last name of the persons' names. These activi-ties can be geared to holiday activities, such as in February to cele-brate Black History month or in November to celebrate Native Americans and their contributions to American society.

- *Play Straw Tap Sounds:* To emphasize sounds, a teacher can stress stretching out the sounds while saying a two-phoneme word, such as *it, go,* or *up.* Then the teacher can direct readers to use a straw to tap the sounds on the table. Readers work up to three- and four-phoneme words. The words can be relevant to cultural holidays, food, dress, activities, or family customs, as teachers explicitly embed culturally sensitive stimuli in phonological awareness games and activities.

- *Sing a version of familiar songs (e.g., "Mary Had a Little Lamb") and substitute culturally associated animals beginning with the same sound for common animals (e.g., replace* lamb *with* llama *or replace* fleece *with* fleur). Young readers receive enriched vocabulary opportunities to understand why and how they are using letters and letter sounds as they receive an introduction to animals, clothing, and vegetation from around the world in a familiar song.

Table 2.6 illustrates other ways to enhance primary readers' phonolog-ical awareness and alphabetic principle skills.

| **TABLE 2.6** | Examples of Enhancing Primary Readers' Skills in Phonological Awareness and Alphabetic Principle |

- *Play What Did I Buy?* Place one-syllable picture cards of ethnic food in a grocery sack. A reader secretly selects a picture and says its name by separating by phonemes. If the rest of the class can guess the picture, it is placed in the pocket chart.

- *Use sound matching.* Place three sound-picture cards in the pocket chart. Readers name each picture and select the ones that begin or end like the focus sound. Use culturally relevant pictures.

- *Use sound sorts.* Readers sort through picture-sound cards to locate all of the pictures that begin or end with the focus sound, again working with culturally relevant pictures.

- *Play Thumbs Up Thumbs Down for Sound.* Call out a word from the home or community and have the readers signal if it matches the focus letter-sound.

- *Use sound boxes.* Give each reader two counters and a paper with two boxes drawn on it. Slowly say a two-phoneme word. Have readers repeat the word and push a counter into a box for each sound. Once they master this, move to three- and four-phoneme words. Use words from cultural events, such as family or community customs.

- *Play Frog Hop.* Say a sentence from a reading story that is culturally and age appropriate. Give each reader some paper cups and counters (or frog

(Continued)

TABLE 2.6 (Continued)

erasers). Let them put a counter (frog) into a cup for each word in the sentence as they say it aloud.

- *Implement block sentences.* Say a sentence from a reading story that is culturally and age appropriate. Give each reader some blocks. Reader places blocks from left to right for each word in the sentence as it is repeated aloud.

- *Implement Be the Words.* Say a sentence from a reading story that is culturally and age appropriate. Give readers word cards from the sentence and have them stand in order from left to right. Another reader may use a long pointer to count the words in the sentence.

- *Implement Walk the Words.* Say a sentence from a reading story that is culturally and age appropriate and then place the word cards on the floor. Have the readers practice saying each word aloud as they repeat the sentence and step from word to word.

- *Play the Categories game.* Call out a category and have readers name two words that fit. They should then determine if one word sounds longer than the other or if the two words sound about the same length. For example: Animal (*duck, elephant—elephant* sounds like a longer word; *camel, monkey—* the words sound like they're about the same length).

- *Ask readers to discern oral messages from wordless picture books* (e.g., based on readers' knowledge of beginning consonant awareness and words from sociomusical interests). For example, discuss readers' interpretations of a picture of "a cute kitty cat counting coupons and corners in Calcutta" and ask readers to clap hands when each /k/ is said and seen (*c*).

Teaching Segmenting and Blending to Primary Readers

To achieve fast and effortless word identification, a reader must understand how letter patterns map onto pronunciation and, for printed words that have not been previously encountered, must be able to produce an approximate pronunciation. If the approximate pronunciation can be mapped onto a known word, lexical and semantic information can then be retrieved. For many readers, the first step of learning associations between letter patterns and pronunciation is difficult, and these readers often do not develop adequate decoding skills. Readers need to refine concepts of phonemes, segmentation, and blending.

Once readers begin working with the concept of the phoneme, they learn to isolate initial and final phonemes, segment a word by onset and rime, and analyze and synthesize by individual phonemes within a word. Following are brief descriptions of each of these processes.

Initial and Final Phonemes

Readers begin attending to individual sounds by focusing on initial phonemes. Once they're comfortable with these, activities are introduced that spotlight ending sounds. Astute teachers refer to letter sounds rather than letter names as readers receive instructions for phoneme activities in fun, culturally and developmentally sensitive foci.

Onset and Rime

Once readers understand rhyme and can isolate initial sounds, they are ready to begin segmenting and blending one-syllable words at the onset and rime level. As expanded in Chapter 3, the *onset* of a word is the first part of a syllable up to the first vowel. The *rime* of a word is the last part of the syllable beginning with the vowel. For example, in the word *dog,* /d/ is the onset, and /og/ is the rime. Readers make this natural division when first learning to segment one-syllable words and eventually learn to make new words by substituting different onsets with the same rime.

Analysis and Synthesis

Next, readers segment and blend complete words by phonemes. Initially, readers tend to work best with two-phoneme words that include easily distinguishable consonants and long vowels. Then they are able to practice with short vowels and other consonants and work up to three-phoneme and four-phoneme words.

The concept of this category of speech sounds can seem complex and meaningless to young readers. Since phonemes in words are affected by the sounds around them, phonemes are often hard to isolate and hear. Many are articulated differently in different words or by different people. Each of these factors adds to the confusion in young or struggling readers.

Teachers can help by thoroughly introducing each activity, allowing plenty of time and repetition, and being more observant of readers who experience difficulty. In addition, support can be offered in varied classroom opportunities for readers to listen to sounds in words throughout the day. Those who haven't mastered rimes, syllables, or onsets will likely struggle with phoneme-level work. Facilitating small-group and one-on-one instruction in areas of need while pairing advanced and struggling readers in the current activities can help.

With opportunities to hear and play with language, segments and blends can come easily to most young readers and are, therefore, the natural skills with which to begin instruction in phonological awareness. Then concentrating on syllabication, rhyme, and alliteration in fun and meaningful activities allows young readers to think about both the meaning and form of language as attention is brought to the similarities and differences in spoken words. Young readers may learn about segmenting and blending by listening to ethnically based songs, nursery rhymes, poems, and finger plays with an auditory focus.

For preschool readers, an overemphasis on word typography can be confusing and divert attention from listening skills. For example, if teachers chart readers' responses as they produce rhymes, readers will encounter words with different spelling patterns, such as *play/they/sleigh* or *show/go/toe*. Directed reader attention should be on sound and not spelling patterns at this early acquisition stage of literacy. Young readers who can identify and hear similarities and differences in syllabication, rhymes, and alliteration need to practice valuable first steps to literacy acquisition, such as in the following activities:

- *Use read-alouds* along with nursery rhymes, songs, finger plays, and carefully selected language games explicitly targeting segmenting and blending skills. Help young readers learn the sounds in words and sentences by isolating and counting syllables within words and counting ending sounds within oral sentences. Use clapping, finger snapping, and jumping routines to stress syllabication, rhymes, and alliteration.

- *Seek out rhymes and cultural themes.* Give readers rhyming words based on cultural themes and ask them to create oral sentences with a given number of words, such as after listening to Joseph Bruchac's *First Strawberries: Cherokee Story* (1998). Follow up with a discussion on syllabication of key vocabulary words. Ask readers to segment and blend the vocabulary.

- *Use whisper rhymes.* Recite a poem in whispers and shout out the rhyming words. Have readers substitute ethnic names for story or poem characters used in the rhymes.

- *Play the game Odd Man Out.* To begin, call out three words from a cultural story, such as Virginia Haviland's *Favorite Fairy Tales Told in England* (1994), and say, "Tell me the two words that rhyme." Follow up with pictures from the story, playing the I Spy Pictures game. Place several pictures in a pocket chart and say, "I spy something that rhymes with __." A few days later, play the game Rhyme Match. Call on readers to choose two pictures out of a bag and place them in the pocket chart if they rhyme. Have readers recall details from the story as they practice syllabication, rhymes, and alliteration.

- *Use echo microphone rhymes.* Have the class listen to a poem from a multicultural collection, such as *All the Colors of the Race: Poems* by Arnold Adoff (1982). Stop after the second rhyming word in the poem and say, "Tell me the two words that rhyme. Now, think of another word that rhymes." (Nonsense words are acceptable.) Allow young readers to use an echo microphone to respond.

Table 2.7 illustrates other ways to enhance primary readers' segmenting and blending skills.

TABLE 2.7   Other Ways to Enhance Primary Readers' Segmenting And Blending Skills

- *Play the Rhyming Beanbag Toss.* This game is based on prominent holidays during a similar period (e.g., Christmas, Chanukuh, or Kwanzaa). Toss a beanbag or ball and name a familiar holiday word. Direct the next reader to say a word that rhymes with the first word. Start over with a new word when ideas have run out.

- *Play the Snatch a Rhyme game.* Grab a holiday object. Say the name of the object and have readers call out real and nonsense words that use syllabication, rhymes, and alliteration representing the objects.

- *Use silly stories based on cultural customs.* Have readers create animal characters whose names rhyme, such as "Babbit the Rabbit and Zunkey the Monkey." Then have the readers dictate a class story using multicultural food, dress, or songs used by the animals. Reread the story on subsequent days, asking readers to act out characters representing animals.

- *Play Turtle Talk.* Have a turtle puppet segment two-, three-, and four-phoneme words and then have the readers blend the sounds together to say the words.
- *Use clues.* Put three picture cards in the pocket chart. Give two clues for a picture—"starts with" and "rhymes with"—and have readers guess the correct word. Use culturally appropriate pictures and clues.

TEACHING MIDDLE SCHOOL-LEVEL READERS FROM DIVERSE BACKGROUNDS

Initial understandings about sounds and print are particularly important, considering that children who are behind in their literacy experiences upon entering school become "at risk" in subsequent years, and primary age children who entered school without understanding the link between their oral language experiences and formal instruction did not advance at the same rate in learning to read and write as children who did make the connection (Snow et al., 1998). There is a strong and essential correspondence between the amount and quality of early language and literacy interactions and experiences and the acquisition of linguistics skills necessary for reading in upper grades (Adams, 1990; Ball & Blachman, 1991; Blachman, 1989; Catts, 1991).

Why Older Readers Have Problems

Over the past ten years, we have learned a considerable amount about what works to improve the reading ability of school-aged children at risk of reading failure. We know that children who are struggling in beginning reading skills come disproportionately from families of poverty, and we know that the gap in performance between middle- and lower-income readers is not closing substantially as these children enter the middle school and high school years (McCollin & O'Shea, 2005; NICHD, 2000a, 2000b).

Additionally, many school and community factors have had a direct impact on readers' achievement gains. These include unconscious racial biases of educators, cultural differences among and across students and educators, lack of highly qualified educators, resource inequalities, and low educator expectations (Harvard Civil Rights Project, 2001; Kozol, 1991; National Research Council, 2002; Obiakor & Wilder, 2003). Further, many older readers' overall academic performance is clearly associated with modeling from significant persons in homes and communities. Many poor readers lack in the ability to listen to and discern sounds that form words, as well as to use letters, words, phrases, and sentences effectively, because others in their everyday lives demonstrate poor modeling.

Teaching Phonological Awareness and the Alphabetic Principle at the Middle School Level

Recent reports found that 38 percent of fourth graders cannot use phonemes, the alphabet, or beginning reading skills at a basic level.

Self-esteem, social development, and opportunities for advanced education (and eventual meaningful employment) are at risk for older students when persistent reading failure occurs. Further, readers from CLD backgrounds living in poverty are disproportionately, and tragically, affected by reading failure. By the time they reach preadolescent years, nearly 70 percent of inner-city and rural students living in poverty cannot read at a proficient level (Boehner, 2002), and national assessments verify the prevalence of severe reading problems in older students, especially those from CLD backgrounds (McCollin & O'Shea, 2006; Perie, Grigg, & Donahue, 2005).

Teachers can explicitly teach phonological awareness and the alphabetic principle to readers in middle school. A key is to engage readers in age appropriate, culturally relevant, and developmentally suitable activities.

- *Teach phonological detections and manipulations explicitly (i.e., modeling, with readers producing specific sounds).* An example for middle school readers might focus on the use of explicit review, guided practice, and scheduled opportunities for readers to apply and develop facility with sounds using culturally specific materials. Developmentally appropriate and culturally relevant literature, such as Tricia Brown's *Konnichiwa! I Am a Japanese-American Girl* (1995) or Sandra S. Yamate's story of a Korean girl, *Ashok by Any Other Name* (1992) may help readers to attend to the modeling of phonological detection, while combining elements of Japanese and American cultures or East Indian and American cultures, respectively. Teachers may follow up with vocabulary identification, asking readers to identify phonemes from the vocabulary.

- *Secure materials and games focusing on explicit phonemic awareness activities.* When words appear in print (such as through books, newspapers, or computers), middle school readers can practice discriminating phonemes found in these media. Readers may be asked to repeat the phonemes before saying the word. Segmenting relevant sociocultural vocabulary words are easy ways to include phonemes practice into reading activities. For example, when readers are directed to count the syllables in words or phrases, or to count the words in spoken sentences or names of culturally relevant role models, they can be generalizing phonemic awareness skills. "Let's count how many syllables are in the name Desi Arnez." "How many syllables are in the name Coretta Scott King?" "What famous person from your community may we include?"

- *Address task adjustment (i.e., purposefully arranging task difficulty).* Alter factors that contribute to difficulty (e.g., alter the number of phonemes in a word, such that *hat* is easier than *hand*); the size of a phonological unit (e.g., a compound word, such as *handsome*, is larger than a phoneme, such as /h/); the phoneme position in words (e.g., initial sounds are easiest, medial sounds the most difficult: *apple* is easier than *tattle*); the phonological properties of words (e.g., consonants like /m/ are easier than stop sounds like /t/); or the phonological awareness dimension (e.g., rhyme is easier than segmentation, *down/town* is easier than *surrounding*). One way to demonstrate task adjustment is when readers participate in cultural games (e.g., circle games, word memory games, or singing in the round to American folk tunes, such as "Kumbaya"), inserting relevant words or phonemes that reinforce the phonological dimensions being introduced or reinforced.

Other examples to teach phonological awareness and the alphabetic principle to readers in middle school are in Table 2.8.

TABLE 2.8	Teaching Phonological Awareness and the Alphabetic Principle to Readers in Middle School

- *Emphasize clapping names.* Call out reader's names. Have readers sort themselves in groups according to number of syllables. Then switch to famous ethnic or culturally diverse individuals' names.
- *Emphasize clapping pictures.* Have readers choose a picture card (or small object) from a box and clap the syllables. Then switch to famous ethnic or culturally diverse individuals.
- *Use picture guess.* Place pictures of famous ethnic or culturally diverse individuals facedown on a table. Have a reader select one and hold it up so only the class can see it. The class says the name of the picture by segmenting the syllables; then the reader guesses what the picture is.
- *Play Which One?* Place three pictures of familiar objects in the pocket chart. Say the name of a picture one syllable at a time and have readers guess which picture was named.
- *Pass out alien gifts based on holiday traditions or customs.* Sitting in a circle, turn to the nearest reader and give him or her a pretend gift, pronouncing the item's name syllable by syllable. The reader guesses the word and then gives a pretend present to the next reader in the same way, continuing around the circle.

Teaching Segmenting and Blending to Middle School Readers

Awareness of segmenting and blending by using syllables, rhymes, and alliteration, as well as sensitivity to the individual sounds of language, is complex yet integral to readers and writers' development of literacy skills throughout their school experiences. Extensive research continues to provide evidence that skills in segmenting and blending remain strong predictors of reading ability. Those who lack these skills remain poor readers in adulthood (Biancarosa & Snow, 2004).

Syllable awareness develops simultaneously with the concept of words for many readers. However, many older, struggling readers are stuck at this step, so teachers must watch closely for readers who have difficulty with this aspect of phonological awareness. Begin by using words that are familiar to readers from their everyday vocabularies or from read-alouds, so they don't have to struggle. Enunciate and articulate words carefully but don't isolate syllables to the point that they sound like individual words. Syllable segmentation and blending develops critical understandings that readers will use repeatedly. Careful observation becomes increasingly important at this level, as does additional support for readers who are progressing more slowly.

Middle school teachers can explicitly address these skills, using age, developmental, and culturally appropriate activities, as stressed in the following activities:

- *Use splitting rhymes.* Direct middle school readers to act out a culturally based poem in two groups. Have the first group say the beginnings of the lines and the second group say the rhyming words. Have the readers concentrate on hearing the ending sounds by chanting the poem up to the second rhyming word. Then stop and say, "Tell me two words that rhyme." For example, use a collection of Native American tales and myths focusing on the relationship between people to integrate the rhyming experiences into cultural feasts, such as in Thanksgiving events.
- *Use alliteration to enhance listening to stories as they are read orally.* Many middle school readers enjoy playing with alliteration in the form of tongue twisters and word challenges. Teachers can challenge readers using a combination of similar beginning sounds in unfamiliar words that are difficult to say quickly. Teachers also want to stress to readers how tongue twisters and word challenges increasingly become easier to pronounce with practice. Challenge readers in alliteration games that ask them to listen for and manipulate letter-sound word problems with multicultural themes, such as in the alliteration: "Say this successfully: Selling saunas and salsa in the sunshine is sometimes a silly scenario." Extend this type of practice by asking readers to create tongue twisters and word challenges with the same initial sound using vocabulary words and alliterations from the traditional foods, games, music, or dance activities of their communities.
- *Create new tongue twisters to stress alliteration using famous community or school models.* Example: The middle school teacher collects all readers' family members' names and says: "Make a tongue twister sentence with all your family names that start with the *R* sound ('Raul and Rodriquez ran right to the rear.'). Share with your peers—as fast as you can!"

As researchers continue to investigate the effects of explicit and direct instruction on diverse readers who did not gain phonological awareness from other experiences, teachers' infusion of relevant, culturally responsive activities can be used to implement, manage, and evaluate effective interventions as the emergent literacy knowledge base continues to grow. A strong emphasis on phonological awareness will help readers to increase attention, differentiation, and manipulation of the individual phonemes that make up spoken language. To help readers increase their skills in shifting focus from the meanings of spoken words to their sounds (i.e., to stress readers' phonemic awareness), teachers can imbed culturally and linguistically appropriate activities that reinforce readers' phonemic differentiation skills as they recognize and create rhymes, manipulate alliteration, differentiate words and recognize word typography. Culturally and linguistically appropriate materials, strategies, and tactics can help readers to differentiate syllables, blend phonemes, segment phonemes (e.g., by directing attention to individual sounds in words), and segment words by phonemes (McCollin & O'Shea, 2005, 2006). Other examples to teach segmenting and blending to readers in middle school are in Table 2.9.

TABLE 2.9   Teaching Segmenting and Blending to Readers in Middle School

- *Use "tongue twisters."* This one may be difficult: "Donna dishes donuts daily during December." The class may be divided into small groups to create their own tongue twisters, which they present to the class. Emphasize ethnic or cultural themes.

- *Use spoonerisms.* Readers correct phrases like "mocolate chilk" (chocolate milk), "chilled grease" (grilled cheese), "card handy" (hard candy). Sentences can be used, too: "You're plaking my tace," (You're taking my place.). Again, readers can be encouraged to use culturally familiar examples.

- *Develop readers' facility with the sounds of language through music.* Hip-hop music, developed from an oral tradition, is, therefore, an ideal medium through which students can exercise auditory discrimination skills. Hip-hop utilizes alliteration, rhyme and near rhyme—all of which can be used in teaching students to discriminate and manipulate phonemes. Hip-hop is a vital part of youth culture, particularly for students of diverse ethnic heritage. While educators sometimes perceive hip-hop music as inappropriate for instruction, it offers unique opportunities.
(One caution is in order: teachers should preview lyrics before playing music in their classes; some hip-hop songs do contain language or messages that may be offensive.) For example, in one activity, the study of rhyme and near rhyme can be examined in popular hip-hop lyrics. Teachers can then have each student write two poems or raps: one that only uses perfect rhyme and one that uses at least four instances of near rhyme. Students can share the poems or raps in class the next day, comparing the effects of perfect and near rhyme (McQuiston, O'Shea, & McCollin, 2007).

- *Compile a class rhyme book.* Have middle school readers illustrate community words that rhyme and compile them into a class book, based on the readers' cultural backgrounds and family histories. Ask family members to contribute data.

TEACHING HIGH SCHOOL READERS FROM DIVERSE BACKGROUNDS

There is considerable research outlining the benefits of preventative strategies for alleviating reading failure in early school years. In spite of the best efforts of the education system and reading specialists to identify young readers at risk of reading failure, some readers still begin their high school years without achieving at least "functional literacy" (Greenman, Schmidt, & Rozendal, 2002; Gregory & Schmitt, 2005).

A history of reading failure without direct intervention is likely to prevent older, low-progress readers from making meaningful gains in reading beyond elementary-level skills. Slow progress in basic skills of reading acquisition, such as phonological awareness, affects academic progress and other areas of learning. Consequently, problem readers experience even greater difficulty throughout high school, and despite the use of compensatory strategies in reading and spelling, young adults continue to experience problems in oral and written expression, which lead to further frustration and low levels of self-esteem (Lenz & Hughes, 1990).

Teaching Phonological Awareness and the Alphabetic Principle at the High School Level

There is evidence that when poor readers receive explicit and effective instruction, they are able to make significant gains in reading outcomes. High school students with reading difficulties benefit most from instruction in the self-teaching mechanism that facilitates generative strategies in word analysis. The importance of ensuring that older beginning readers are not allowed to bypass the initial stages of reading instruction has been viewed as a key in diminishing functional illiteracy (Greenman et al., 2002).

Motivation and engagement are critical factors for providing meaningful learning opportunities to stress phonological awareness and the alphabetic principle to adolescents. Researchers show that if students are not motivated to read, they will benefit very little from reading instruction (Leake & Black, 2005; Moats, 2001; Schmidt, 2005). Moore, Bean, Birdyshaw, and Rycik (1999) contended that adolescents require access to a wide variety of reading material that they can and want to read. These researchers also found that older readers require explicit instruction that builds both skills and the desire to read. Adolescents needing reading support also benefit from increasingly complex material assessment that shows them their strengths as well as their needs, with instruction based on this understanding. As with other areas of academic instruction, readers require expert teachers who model and provide explicit instruction in reading, writing, and study strategies. Culturally responsive reading practices work most effectively when teachers apply principles of direct instruction.

- *Use multicultural affirmations.* Build upon students' cultural funds of knowledge by engaging readers in multicultural affirmations. Multicultural affirmations are brief, energetic, mood-setting ways to develop interest in the written word. For example, have students perform Maya Angelou's poem "I Love the Look of Words." Teachers help readers to emphasize letter-sound relationships by stressing important letter sounds of key vocabulary from the poem.
- *Create a bridge between the spoken and written word.* For example, the high school's reading class begins by a choral chanting of "If it is to be, it is up to me,"—all sight words. A reader stands at the chart pointing to the words while the rest of the class reads loudly, then softly and more softly, until the class is whispering. Repetition is the key. The readers perform increasingly longer passages and eventually commit long passages to memory. The principle is similar to having young beginning readers memorize predictable text during repeated readings. Two critical components have been added for the older readers: the repetitions address important multicultural themes to motivate older readers, and the passages reflect the phonic/linguistic patterns, including phonemic and letter activities, under study.
- *Use connected and culturally relevant, decodable text for readers to practice the sound-spelling relationships they learn.* Readers need extensive practice applying their knowledge of sound-spelling relationships to the task of reading as they are learning. This integration of phonics and reading best occurs with the use of decodable text. Predictable text gives a motivating success, but readers need to

practice the sound-spellings they have learned as well. For instance, when studying holiday words associated with Chanukah, Kwanzaa, or Christmas, readers can reinforce themselves and their reading partners when they hear words in decodable holiday text that start with the hard c, or /k/, such as *candle, candy, cookie, cup,* and *corn.* Ask readers to review other holiday readings, practicing the sound-spelling relationships, such as *Cajun Night Before Christmas by "Trosclair"* (Jacobs, 1973).

Table 2.10 includes other examples of teaching phonological awareness and the alphabetic principle at the high school level.

TABLE 2.10	Teaching Phonological Awareness and the Alphabetic Principle to High School Readers

- *Teach each sound-spelling correspondence explicitly by isolating a phoneme with culturally specific vocabulary.* For example, use the statement "This letter says /mmm/ like in the word *mango.*" Ask readers whether they know community words that begin with the /mmm/ sound. A brief practice of sound-spelling correspondence each day for about five minutes should precede working with phonemes in the context of words and stories.

- *Show readers exactly how to sound out words, using familiar words from multicultural contexts* (e.g., "Let's practice sounding out words we use at home, such as *sombrero, mano, mango, arroz, pollo, dreidle, taper, menorah, latkes, lapiz, kinara,* and *sushi.*"). Activities can be made fun and academically relevant by dividing multicultural words by syllables and then modeling how to clap out the syllables/sounds.

- *Use mail order catalogs.* Readers locate pictures of items beginning with certain consonant blends (for example, *st, tr,* and *spr*) or consonant digraphs (for example, *sh, ch,* and *shr*). Readers glue the pictures onto poster board or construction paper.

- *Use dictionaries.* Readers look up words beginning with a certain phoneme. Readers write down ten words that they know, then read them aloud to the class.

- *Use other resource books.* Readers choose a topic of interest to them and list words in that topic that contain consonant digraphs. For example, the topic could be food and the diagraphs could be *ch* and *sh:* words could be *spinach, squash, cheese,* and *shellfish.* The index of an ethnic cookbook would be helpful for this topic.

- *Use contests.* Select a page from a story being read in class. Readers write each word on the page that contains the selected phoneme. The teacher could turn this into a contest by saying, "Let's see who can be first to find ten words with *sh* on this page." The winner earns a prize.

- *Use newspapers.* Using newspapers, readers choose an article about their community (or heritage) and circle all the words in it that contain silent letters, whether vowels or consonants (rules of silent letters should be discussed prior to this). They may then exchange articles with partners. The partners mark through all the silent letters in the marked words. Readers check their partners' work; then partners switch roles.

(Continued)

| TABLE 2.10 | (Continued) |

> • *Use group work activities.* Cut small squares from oak tag and print a phoneme or a syllable on each. Make several squares for each letter of the alphabet. Sort the cards alphabetically and keep them in separate compartments of an egg carton. Label compartments A-B, C-D, E-F, etc. for alphabetizing. Let readers practice forming words by taking the letters from the carton and laying them out on a desk. Stress making words they know or have heard before. Readers could work in groups and have a contest with this ("Which group can be first to make 20 words containing prefixes we have discussed?"). Use culturally relevant materials.

Teaching Segmenting and Blending to High School Readers

To support the development of high school readers lacking in literacy skills, explicit instruction in segmenting and in blending, using culturally relevant instruction, helps them to discriminate sounds that are different, blend spoken sounds into words, perform word-to-word matching, isolate sounds in words, count phonemes, segment spoken words into sounds, and delete sounds from words.

Poetry seems to bring out the best in readers of all ages and can become a motivating avenue to teach many aspects of language. Poetry seems to breathe life and enthusiasm into reluctant readers, getting them involved and making them feel successful in some part of literacy. Readers with limited English proficiency also seem to pick up and enjoy poetry because of its simplicity and brevity. For syllable recognition, have readers listen to haiku, tanka, cinquain, and diamond poems, clapping the syllables.

Whether the poem is about not wanting to go to school, having too much homework, a father who snores too loudly, or a four-leaf clover that brings good luck, readers tend to become active participants in the reading, listening to, and speaking of poems. For reluctant readers of all ages, the threatening factor of "too many words on a page" is absent.

Poetry offers many opportunities to teach important sounds, rhyme, parts of speech, listening, cooperation, and memory. Poetry also comes in nonfiction form. Reluctant readers can be provided opportunities to experiment with the sounds and rhymes of both fiction and nonfiction poetry. Reviewing word games that stress rhyming and alliteration activities prior to the use of poetry may help some readers.

• *Play word games with culturally specific language.* Readers can create alliteration, rhymes, and other word play with language that is familiar to them. For example, sociorelevant vocabulary can be used: "Maria mixes martinis Monday." These activities can easily be incorporated into daily routines. When readers are ready to be dismissed, for example, the teacher might say that all readers whose names end in /h/ may close their books and prepare to leave. Or start a game by saying, "I'm going on a trip to (have the class decide where they'd like to go), and I'm going to take (an item that begins with the designated sound)." Each reader has to repeat the sentence and the growing list of items that have been named. For example, a reader may recite, "I'm going on a trip to Peru, and I'm going to take a pen, parka, pudding, pot, etc." Readers will naturally think of items that are culturally familiar to them.

- *Choose multicultural modeling for rhyming activities.* Give readers materials and themes relevant to their cultures. Include quotes from great writers, scientists, popular figures, and historical heroes that diverse readers recognize. Ask readers to point out the rhyming pairs of words.

- *Choose multicultural modeling for syllabication activities.* Again using familiar quotes from great writers, scientists, popular figures, and historical heroes, direct readers to talk about the use of language play in the syllables; challenge readers to count syllables of key words and find patterns.

- *Choose multicultural modeling for alliteration.* Use movie clips and music lyrics from holidays or cultural events as examples to motivate readers. Direct the class to write a new ending to the movie clips or music lyrics using alliterative phrases or sentences. For example, listen to the lyrics to the Spanish song "Feliz Navidad." Ask readers to use the melody to the song but sing new lyrics with alliterative phrases starting with the phonemes or syllables discussed that week.

- *Direct rhyming pairs of words foci, as readers recognize rhymes and alliteration, blending phonemes to devise new words, identify sounds in words, and segment words by phonemes.* Direct older readers to create new dance steps using key culturally relevant vocabulary from texts, stressing explicit phonemic awareness. Some examples of how to do this include using instructional materials from readers' cultures or languages in rhyming riddles, set to ethnic songs or dances, as ways to elicit rhymes from readers and encourage reading acquisition ("How many phonemes can we blend using our new vocabulary words as we rhumba to the beat of our words? Now try a salsa dance step.").

Table 2.11 includes examples of other ways to encourage segmenting and blending in high school readers.

TABLE 2.11   Segmenting and Blending in High School Readers

- *Use the power of the arts—music, visual arts, drama, dance, movement.* Segmentation of phonemes can be made more fun to the rhythm of a particular ethnic instrument or beat. For example, an African drum might be used and a student told to tap the drum for each sound in the word *dragon.* Movement activities could also be incorporated, each representing a phoneme whereby readers actually perform the material in some way, reinforcing learning through multisensory approaches.

- *Use multicultural poetry to teach phonological awareness.* Gwendolyn Brooks's poems "The Bean Eaters" and "The Pool Players" appeal to young adults and contain a variety of literary devices that support phonological awareness learning. Playing an audio reading by the author would be a unique way to present this material. Students could also invent their own poems like these. Another example would be to introduce students to counting syllables through the reading and writing of haiku.

- Ask readers to create a rhyme given a first name of a famous person (e.g., Rosa Parks). Share the rhymes in class.

■ REVISITING MIGUEL

Miguel's teachers met during the school year to consider Miguel's phonological development. After the early school year conference, his teachers realized that Miguel did not have sixth-grade reading skills. As a result, they listed and followed through collaboratively on a number of recommendations to support Miguel.

First and foremost, his teachers realized that Miguel needed to be assessed in his cognition, health, language, and reading skills to pinpoint where he functions in reading and why reading tasks are difficult for him. His teachers advised that a school psychologist was necessary to assess Miguel's verbal and performance levels in his intellectual functioning. They acquired the support of a teacher skilled in literacy to ascertain Miguel's early literacy development. They believed it wise, also, to assess both his spoken language and written language, engaging the services of a speech and language clinic to determine whether Miguel displayed more serious difficulties with articulation, voice, fluency, or language than classroom teachers were able to address.

After his psychological and speech-language assessments, and a visual and health screening to rule out more serious concerns, his teachers focused on his reading development. Working with the support of a reading specialist, Miguel, and his grandmother, Miguel's teachers targeted Miguel's skills in phoneme identification, pronunciation, and awareness.

Data analysis revealed that what seemed to work best for Miguel was the use of materials and games focusing on explicit phonemic awareness activities. His teachers purchased and used many readers, newspapers, and computer games, which helped Miguel to practice discriminating phonemes found in these media. His teachers elicited the support of his grandmother to prompt Miguel to repeat phonemes before saying content area vocabulary. The teachers included phonemes practice in class activities by intentionally selecting relevant sociocultural vocabulary words from Miguel's Hispanic background in subject readings and poems, providing many opportunities to have Miguel blend and segment content area vocabulary both orally and through color coding of print.

As Miguel began to correct sound selection in memory tasks, his teachers noted improvements in his skill at detecting, recognizing, and recalling sounds modeled from others. Ms. Nichol and Mrs. Green challenged Miguel by cueing him to use faster recognition of letter patterns, emphasizing written letter symbols and sound patterns for dictated words. Both teachers challenged Miguel to commit multicultural words to sight, and they exposed him to age-appropriate sound games. One such game was a "word chain" using culturally appropriate words, with the adults saying a word and asking Miguel to change it sound by sound to form new words. His teachers focused on helping Miguel to detect and remember important sounds by purposefully directing and cueing Miguel's attention, thinking, and memory skills necessary for his phonological development.

MOVING ON   ■

We have addressed phonological processing as fundamental to academic achievement and reading success. Because reading acquisition requires the refinement of phonological processing skills, a necessary foundational skill that beginning readers must master is that words and syllables heard via oral language are necessary to translate our written language to and from print. Becoming aware of the phonemes within syllables and words represented by sounds and print is essential to communicating orally and in reading and writing. A reader, at any grade level, who cannot hear and decipher words rapidly enough to allow for comprehension requires explicit instruction in hearing and differentiating phonemes and blending, segmenting, matching, and rhyming strategies. Teachers of diverse readers must recognize that in-class activities and homework completion will be deficient when beginning readers, at any age, lack such fundamental strategies.

3

Improving Decoding and Structural Analysis Skills

Dorothy J. O'Shea,
Jodi Katsafanas, and Kelly Lake

CHAPTER OBJECTIVES

In this chapter, we will

- establish the importance of decoding and structural analysis skills to becoming a competent reader;
- identify research related to decoding skills and decoding difficulties, including recognition and use of letters and letter patterns;
- identify research related to structural analysis skills and difficulties, including recognition and use of whole words and spelling skills; and
- provide examples of culturally and linguistically responsive decoding and structural analysis practices important to primary, middle school, and high school readers.

LILLY'S NEEDS

Lilly Wong is in the third grade and spends approximately 15 percent of her daily life in school. Lilly was not born in the United States and is living in a community where a language other than English is dominant. That is, Lilly is an English-language learner (ELL), often speaking her native Mandarin Chinese at home with her family and in her community. Lilly relies on her developing English skills at school.

Lilly spends a great amount of time with her family in their local landscaping business. Lilly is very skilled at working with flowers, plants, bushes, and trees. She already understands the fundamentals of gardening and landscaping, as she is on her way to perfecting a "green thumb."

In her "typical" American family, Lilly has a mother, father, and three brothers with whom she lives. The Wong family members own their modest home near a California coastal community, close to Lilly's maternal grandparents and her uncles, their spouses, and children. Lilly's mother and father both work, as do her older brothers, in the family business. In this supportive living milieu, Lilly loves her family and community, especially when she has opportunities to interact with her cousins and many neighbors. Her family has a limited but steady income in their peaceful community.

In school, Lilly has learned to participate in academics and does well in extracurricular activities. She is learning to expand her socialization skills. She gets along well with her peers and teachers and is always polite. However, Lilly is experiencing academic difficulties. Her teacher, Mrs. Sullivan, attests that Lilly has a high intelligence and seems to grasp academic concepts when Mrs. Sullivan explains them to the class. Nonetheless, Lilly appears to have many individual reading concerns.

Through a translator, Mrs. Sullivan has indicated to Mr. and Mrs. Wong that Lilly demonstrates basic skills in letter sounds, but she often displays much difficulty with sounding out words in meaning-based language activities. Mrs. Sullivan has explained that Lilly doesn't seem to understand phonics, nor does Lilly use her decoding skills when she reads words. She often experiences difficulty with relationships between words and structural elements within words, such as word endings or verb tense.

Lilly has a limited sight word vocabulary, as she encounters new words that contain sound-letter correspondences she barely identifies. For example, Mrs. Sullivan tells Mr. and Mrs. Wong that Lilly cannot tell the differences between words like pen *and* pin *or* beg *and* peg. *Mrs. Sullivan reports that Lilly appears totally confused when she encounters words containing new sound-letter correspondences, even when they are introduced and practiced in class. Lilly gets mixed up reading words such as* louse *and* lease. *Lilly has a great deal of difficulty with affixes and suffixes (e.g., in distinguishing* rearrange *from* arranging) *and doesn't understand how to make or dissect compound words (e.g.,* downtown). *Consequently, because of difficulties in basic word recognition and word skill usages, Mrs. Sullivan believes Lilly will have major problems in understanding increasingly complex content area texts for science, history, mathematics, social studies, and world geography classes.*

WHAT ARE DECODING AND ■ STRUCTURAL ANALYSIS SKILLS?

Decoding and structural analysis skills are fundamental to readers' ability to sound out and recognize words. Readers need to notice, think about, and work with both the sounds in spoken language, as well as use letter and word shapes, and sequences of written language components that represent sounds in the spelling of a word in order to decipher meaning from words quickly and accurately. (National Institute of Child Health and Human Development, 2000; National Reading Panel, 2000)

In Lilly's case scenario, Lilly has trouble with phonics. Her lack of knowledge that letters of the alphabet represent phonemes and that these sounds are blended together to form written words hinders her in sounding out words she hasn't seen before. Because she has not yet mastered phonics, and because of her decoding deficiencies and problematic structural analysis of word skills, Lilly does not apply sound correspondence to letter combinations (e.g., *ea, ate, ou, al,* and *ing*) consistently. She has problems putting letters and letter sounds together to form words (e.g., *seek + ing = seeking*). Because she does not know to add prefixes, suffixes, or other meaningful word units to a base word, Lilly is unable to use word skills consistently to help her obtain meaning from what she hears or reads. She struggles with translating printed words as she misunderstands both silent and oral reading tasks. Lilly needs help with deciphering words so that she understands the English language and what she is reading and communicating. She needs help with decoding and structural analysis skills.

Decoding Initiates Through Sound Awareness

Decoding is the result of sounding out, an initiation of reading that requires a beginning or struggling reader to apply phonics to many skills, occurring before comprehension of words, phrases, sentences, paragraphs, passages, and connected text (Carnine, Silbert, Kame'ennui, & Tarver, 2004). Reading independently involves the orchestration of many different types of knowledge and skills, which begins when a reader uses sounds to make sense of words. Essential to decoding is both *phonics* (i.e., sound structure skills) and *structural analysis skills* (i.e., word recognition and word attack skills), such that a beginning reader can identify words by breaking down words into manageable units while comparing those units with prior knowledge of familiar word parts. Proficient decoding entails translating printed words into a representation of oral language, either silently or aloud. Understanding that representation results in *comprehension.* Effective reading entails fast and accurate knowledge and skills in both decoding and word analysis.

If Lilly encountered an unfamiliar word in context, such as the word *twig,* and if she could identify the word part *ig* as in *wig,* she most likely could decode (that is, decipher by sounding out) the word. Lilly would display structural analysis skills if she were to recognize the word *twig* and then apply her word structure skills to an unknown word *twin* (that is, decipher two words accurately, *twin twigs*). Lilly would display comprehension if she could sound out and discern meaning from unknown or partially unknown words in the context of a sentence, such as in "Twin twigs snapped sharply in the woods." Comprehension could be confirmed if Lilly were to answer correctly that two objects made a certain sound in a particular setting.

Phonics

Decoding starts with a reader's awareness of phonics. Reading research has confirmed that readers who are skilled in phonics can sound out words they haven't seen before without first having to memorize them (NICHD, 2000a, 2000b). The sound-letter associations, sound-letter correspondences, and sound-symbol correspondences embedded within words can be a challenge to many new readers when first learning to decode. To struggling readers, such as Lilly, lack of awareness of the various parts of spoken language (e.g., awareness of sounds, syllables, or words that help to support the sound structure of words) hampers the phonetic acquisition of the skills necessary to read efficiently (Lyon, 1998; Lyon & Moats, 1997). Because she also is a reader from an ELL background, such awareness may be especially hard for Lilly to acquire. Without direct and explicit help in ways that are age-appropriate and culturally sensitive to Lilly's needs, Lilly may continue to display much difficulty in sounding out and gaining meaning from new words.

Teaching Phonics

Many new or struggling readers often benefit from phonics skills instruction taught systematically using methods of intense, direct, and explicit instruction. As awareness of phonics develops, readers can be asked to identify phonemes, categorize phonemes, blend phonemes to form words, segment words into phonemes, delete or add phonemes to form new words, and substitute phonemes to make new words (Armbruster, Lehr, & Osborn, 2003; Goswami & Bryant, 1990; Grace, 2005). To readers from ELL backgrounds or those from other culturally and linguistically diverse (CLD) milieus, phonics instruction can be infused with relevant developmental activities that capitalize on readers' motivation and willingness to decipher new words and apply word component understandings.

Phonics Instruction Can Be Fun and Academically Challenging

The key for teachers working with new or struggling readers is to stress the sounds readers can hear, play with, and rearrange. Examples of tasks important to the development of phonics and useful to decoding success can include practice with culturally and linguistically appropriate themes in mind, such that teachers encourage readers to observe and think about real and imaginary words from the readers' prior knowledge, including family backgrounds, homes, and communities. The following tips for classroom activities that are fun and academically challenging may help:

- *Segmenting and blending skills using phoneme deletion* (e.g., Play directed word games, as in, "What word would be left if the /s/ sound were taken away from *sat*? Now, think of a word from home that your Mom or Dad may have used. What word would be left if the /l/ sound were taken away from *lap*? What word would you say if we took away the /f/ sound in *fog* and replaced it with the /d/ sound . . . the /h/ sound . . . the /r/ sound?)
- *Word-to-word matching* (e.g., "Do *bat* and *bad* begin with the same sound? Do *mano* and *memo* begin with the same sound? Do *matzo* and *mummy* begin the same?")
- *Blending* (e.g., "What word would we have if we put these sounds together: /h/ + /o/ + /p/? What about these sounds: /p/ + /e/ + /s/ + /o/?")
- *Phoneme segmentation* (e.g., "What sounds do you hear in the word *few*? What sounds do you hear in the word *view*?")

- *Phoneme counting* (e.g., "How many sounds do you hear in the word *begin*? How many sounds do you hear in the word *beep*? How many sounds do you hear in *left*? How many sounds do you hear in *lef*?)
- *Rhyming* (e.g., "Tell me all of the words that you know that end the same as the word *can.* Now that you said, '*dan, fan, san,* and *lan*,' how many words can you name quickly that your sister or brother says ending with the same as the word *fin*?")

Readers with difficulties in these tasks requiring phonics often experience difficulty in decoding new words (Mathes, Howard, Allen, & Fuchs, 1998). Readers who are skilled in phonics can sound out words they haven't seen before (even imaginary words) without first having to memorize them (NICHD, 2000a, 2000b).

Graphemes and Sound-Spellings

Decoding skills also rely on a reader's sense of a *grapheme,* the smallest part of written language that represents a phoneme in the spelling of a word. A sense of a *phonological system* can help the individual in applying the 44 speech sounds in English. The phonological system evolves as the individual recognizes that spoken words can be broken into smaller segments of sounds (phonemes), that the letters of the alphabet represent phonemes, and that these sounds are blended together to form written words (Armbruster et al., 2003). That is, as children initially learn to talk, they learn to pronounce the phonemes, and they learn to associate the sounds with letters as they learn to read and write. Phonemes are represented in print with diagonal lines to differentiate them from graphemes (letters or letter combinations). Thus, the first grapheme in *goat* is *g,* and the phoneme is /g/. The phoneme in *toast* that is represented by the grapheme *oa* is called "long o" and is written /ō/. To decode successfully, a reader must use his or her understanding of the relationships between the letters (i.e., graphemes) of written language and the individual sounds (i.e., phonemes) of spoken language. Readers with proficient decoding skills are able to use *graphophonemic* relationships to read and write words. Individual letters (e.g., *b, d, f, p, s*) or letters placed together (e.g., *ch, sh, th, ck, ea, igh*) represent graphemes (Grossen, 1997).

Graphemes and the Alphabetic Principle

When readers begin to recognize that letters of the alphabet are not merely sounds but representations of the phonological segments the sounds of the letters communicate, they are using the *alphabetic principle*—that is, the ability to map speech to print. As addressed in Chapter 2, readers with poor sound skills, who have not attained an understanding of the internal phonemic structure of words, do not automatically understand and apply speech to print.

Oral and written language can be affected by problems in applying the phonological system, especially for children from ELL or CLD backgrounds. Regional and cultural differences exist in the way people pronounce phonemes (Tompkins, 2004). Readers in the southern United

States often pronounce sounds differently from readers in the midwestern United States, just as readers from Great Britain pronounce phonemes differently than readers from the United States. Children from ELL backgrounds who are learning English as a second language in school must learn to pronounce English sounds before learning to read. Children from Hispanic, African-American, or other socioethnic backgrounds, as discussed in Chapter 7, often have learned a culturally derived, rule-governed entity, with a linguistic origin, that differs from (but is not inferior to) English as taught in traditional schools. English sounds that are different from those in their native language or from the language spoken in their homes or communities may be particularly difficult for readers from ELL or CLD backgrounds to acquire as they encounter traditional school tasks. It is especially important for adults working with new or struggling readers to realize the importance these differences play in how individuals are exposed to, hear, and manipulate the sound structure of language as reading acquisition progresses.

Using the Alphabetic Principle

The acquisition of the alphabetic principle is highly dependent on a reader's phonological awareness and the ability to apply the phonological system. A reader requires proficiency in letter recognition, sound-letter relationships, and spelling skills to master the alphabetic principle (Torgesen & Matthes, 1998). Many readers who lack in recognizing graphemes and in applying phonological structures through the alphabetic principle tend to have needs in short-term memory and word comprehension requiring explicit instruction in learning sound-letter correspondences and spelling patterns (Liberman & Shankweiler, 1985; Liberman, Shankweiler, & Liberman, 1989).

Research findings on moving from phonological awareness and use of the alphabetic principle to actual word recognition have found that phonological awareness and sound-spelling correspondence skills are critical to early reading success and play key roles in discriminating between good and poor readers (NICHD, 2000a, 2000b). New and struggling readers often advance in deciphering new words when they receive explicit instruction in letter knowledge, word structure, word recognition, word strategies, and spelling. They benefit from learning to reason strategically and increase their oral and print vocabulary.

Readers advancing in decoding skills usage may be helped by teachers explicitly using concrete representation and oral modeling of individual sounds in English and in the readers' home or native language, reader production and identification of sounds, addition of teaching sound-letter correspondence to phonemic instruction, segmentation of increasingly difficult phonological units, letter shapes, and grapho-phonemic relationships in a predetermined sequence. Readers learn to use these relationships strategically to decode words that contain them. Six principles related to effective decoding instruction have evolved from research on early reading studies ascertaining needs of effective and ineffective use of phonemes and grapheme detection (Armbruster et al., 2003; NICHD, 2000a, 2000b; Torgesen & Mathes, 1998). These are delineated in Table 3.1.

TABLE 3.1   Principles of Decoding Instruction

1. Begin teaching phonemic awareness directly at an early age.

2. Teach each sound-spelling correspondence explicitly.

3. Teach frequent, highly regular sound-spelling relationships systematically.

4. Show readers exactly how to sound out words.

5. Use connected, decodable text to help readers practice the sound-spelling relationships they learn.

6. Use interesting stories to develop language and comprehension.

Predictable Relationships

Readers from CLD backgrounds often benefit from direct instruction and explicit activities, which are meaningful as they use the English language relationships between graphemes of written language and phonemes of spoken language. Being mindful of culturally and developmentally appropriate materials and activities can help young readers to understand that there often are predictable relationships between written letters and spoken sounds. Readers from CLD backgrounds also require an understanding of *units of language* (e.g., applying letters, letter combinations, and syllables to form words). They need *processing skills* (e.g., using auditory listening skills, sounding out, sight-reading, breaking larger words into parts, identifying larger words into parts, identifying letter combinations and structural units), as well as *skills in applying a knowledge base* (e.g., using letter-sound correspondences; familiarity with words, syntax, semantic constraints; and knowledge of letter combinations and structural units). Further, they must use *strategic knowledge* (e.g., skills in monitoring, adjusting, evaluating units; processing; and activating prior knowledge related to deciphering and comprehending text) (Adams & Engelmann, 1996). To apply and benefit from efficient decoding, struggling readers require knowledge of and skills in decoding and applying word structure, activated in a nearly simultaneous process with background knowledge (that is, they need to read words with speed and accuracy in order to gain meaning) (Adams & Engelmann, 1996; Alvermann & Moore, 1991; Bursuck & Damer, 2007; Carnine et al., 2004; Hecht, Burgess, Torgesen, Wagner, & Rashotte, 2000).

■ IMPROVING DECODING SKILLS

Helping beginning readers from CLD backgrounds make the jump between understanding phonics and applying decoding skills quickly to reach automaticity can be supported when teachers follow a sequenced presentation of skills, such as the format suggested by Carnine and colleagues (2004):

- *Introduce letter sounds, followed by letter names.* Because readers need to acquire sounds before they learn the alphabet, it is essential that teachers introduce the sounds of language without naming letters or presenting a visual representation of letters. Gradually, teachers may introduce visual presentations paired with sounds. For readers from CLD backgrounds, it is very important to use culturally and socially appropriate stimuli that pique readers' interests and that are developmentally appropriate.

- *Help readers to sound out new words prior to use of sight-reading.* Teachers can concentrate on helping readers to identify a sound for each letter in a word, blend the sounds, and then concentrate on identifying the word. For readers such as Lilly, the use of culturally appropriate materials is advantageous, because Lilly may attach more meaning to the letters she sees and the sounds she hears as she deciphers new words in English and practices sounding out unfamiliar words. For example, when using the *twin twigs* activity, above, if her teacher knows that Lilly has an understanding of the fundamentals of gardening and landscaping, the teacher can use that background to help Lilly expand her word knowledge and word recognition base, based on Lilly's knowledge and interests.

- *Teach new words in isolation during the beginning reading stage; later, introduce regular words and high-frequency irregular words in context.* Teachers might present word lists in isolation, based on familiar cultural and community people, places, or events, which are familiar to new or struggling readers. A way to do this is by allowing emergent and developing readers ample opportunities to share their cultural knowledge throughout decoding and word activities, helping to make new words in isolation carry more meaning to them.

- *Pay special attention to words in context because of dual pronunciations.* Readers such as Lilly may be perplexed by the many irregularities in the English language. For example, many words sound the same but have different meanings when heard or read in context. Teachers should use scrutiny when presenting words with dual pronunciations, ensuring that context is available to clarify meanings (e.g., *read* as in "I will read the newspaper," and "I have read many new books"; *behind* as in "Patel is standing behind the line leader," and "Mom told me to get my behind on the seat.") By recognizing and addressing differences in dialects and language variations, teachers can be sensitive to the needs of readers from ELL or CLD backgrounds.

- *Teach oral reading* (e.g., readers reading aloud) *then silent reading* (e.g., readers reading to themselves). Because many beginning and struggling readers need to receive prompting and feedback as they tackle new words, when oral reading opportunities occur first, teachers can offer readers from varied backgrounds positive reinforcement to maintain or increase word skills or use corrective feedback when readers mispronounce or misapply syllables, base words, endings, and so forth. A key in direct and explicit implementation of effective instruction is to infuse guided practice with principles of reinforcement schedules that are appropriate to learners (Algozzine & Ysseldyke, 2006).

Even before learning to sound out words by segmenting or blending, readers from ELL or CLD backgrounds initiating the decoding process must be able to identify some sound-letters in isolation automatically. Prior to sounding out unfamiliar words, beginning readers need at least six to eight sound-letter correspondences, including one or two vowels. They require explicit instruction in sound-letter correspondences and provision of extensive reader practice and review. As they read regular words from English and/or from their homes or community backgrounds, readers then have opportunity to gain from practice as they sound out each word orally with explicit help from a literate model, followed by sounding out words silently. Recognition of regular words is achieved when the reader can sound out automatically, without having to think about sounding out (i.e., a reader has reached automaticity, and word recognition is immediate) (Carnine et al., 2004; Goswami & Bryant, 1990; Grace, 2005).

Gaining in Word Skills

Beginning or struggling readers also gain in decoding new words when directed to write or spell the same words that they are learning to sound and read. (Thus, a teacher may present the word list *hat, cat, can, map, top, sat,* directing readers to sound out each separately, followed by meaningful spelling and writing activities using the words in word games and sentences based on prominent, diverse home or community events.) Then when readers approach sight words (i.e., words that do not rely on common sounds or letters and that have yet to be learned and taught in isolation), they are able to read unfamiliar words (NICHD, 2000a, 2000b).

To encourage recognition of familiar words, readers from diverse backgrounds require presentation of words that appear similar during different instructional sequences (i.e., read similar sight words together only after obtaining automaticity when each sight word is presented in isolation). Thus, to encourage readers not to sound out individual words vocally but to say them at a normal rate as they increase in sight words usage, teachers would want to avoid presenting confusing sight words simultaneously, such as in exposing readers to word lists when they have not consistently sounded out a set of consonant, vowel, consonant (CVC) words that begin with continuous sounds without erring (e.g., readers should consistently be able to sound out words in a word list, as in *run, rut, rat, sat*).

Also important to new or struggling readers from diverse backgrounds is structure and guidance. When provided word lists to be sight-read, it is important that readers can apply sound-letter correspondence consistently. Teachers should be careful to use unpredictable presentation of letter position and word order and gradually introduce words of a new type on one third to one half of word list exercises (Carnine et al., 2004). Helping readers from varied backgrounds recognize new and unfamiliar words at the automatic level is enhanced when teachers individualize instruction to meet the range of readers' phonics and decoding awareness. To encourage decoding development, new readers require (1) knowledge about the format of words (e.g., base words, prefixes, suffixes, inflections) and (2) familiarity with sound-by-sound and/or word-by-word analysis of language (Burns, Griffin, & Snow, 1999). Table 3.2 includes key prerequisites that beginning readers, including those from ELL or CLD backgrounds, require to apply the sound-letter correspondences of English as they advance in decoding and word skills.

TABLE 3.2	Key Prerequisites Required to Apply the Sound-Letter Correspondences of English

- all of the single consonant sounds
- all of the consonant blends (e.g., cr, st, tr, pl)
- all of the consonant digraphs (e.g., ch, sh, th)
- short vowels
- long vowels with silent *e* rule
- vowel digraphs (e.g., oa, ea, ai, ay)
- "*r*-controlled" vowels (sounds of ar, er, ir, ur, or)
- syllable patterns and rules
- morpheme patterns (e.g., compound words, prefixes, and suffixes)

Using the Senses

Readers from diverse backgrounds often struggle with decoding, requiring daily or almost daily review of previously learned phonemes. Often, multisensory use of culturally relevant materials and stimuli can help diverse readers reiterate important sound-letter relationships and connect these relationships meaningfully to background experiences. For example, phonemes presented during a first week of instruction can be printed onto visual displays with multicultural themes and purposes to be used for visual, auditory, and kinesthetic drills with readers. *Visual input,* or seeing a letter or letter combination and pronouncing it alongside culture-specific words, may be key to motivation and continued practice. *Auditory input,* hearing letter and letter combination sounds individually, within syllables, or within words based on English pronunciations, can also help diverse readers appreciate the beauty of acoustics as applied to intonations when reading. *Kinesthetic-tactile stimulation,* including hand-arm movements and lip, tongue, and throat movements, can be offered through varied sociocultural music, songs, dance, and performing arts to support beginning readers in sensing and feeling how their voices produce sounds creatively and meaningfully (McQuiston, O'Shea, & McCollin, 2007; Perie, Grigg, & Donahue, 2005; Snow, Burns, & Griffin, 1998).

Using Decodable Texts

The use of decodable texts is an effective way for many readers to understand how phonics affect practice when decoding words they encounter at school. When culturally relevant, decodable texts are not available, it may be necessary to encourage readers to discuss ways in which they can relate the decodable text used in school to their own experiences. For example, when a reader reads, "*A cat sat on the mat,*" he might relate it to the Spanish folk song, "El señor don Gato." Another reader might be able to relate it to the Korean folk tale *The Dog and the Cat.* For some readers, more challenging word study, (including rimes, roots, and affixes, as well as word construction, as addressed below), would be in order (McQuiston et al., 2007). Teachers can engage more capable readers by providing instruction in strategic word attack skills, including *syllabication* (i.e., breaking words into syllables) and *morphemic analysis* (i.e., understanding and generalizing the makeup of words, including word bases and word units). Whenever possible, diverse readers struggling to decode and reach an automaticity level with comprehending what they read require developmental and culturally relevant reading materials to practice word skills.

Once readers demonstrate proficiency in the concept of phonics, they learn to isolate initial and final phonemes, segment a word by onset and rime, and analyze and synthesize by individual phonemes within a word. Following are more detailed descriptions of each of these processes.

Initial and Final Phonemes

As discussed in Chapter 2, readers begin attending to individual sounds by focusing on initial phonemes. As readers become comfortable with individual sounds, teachers can introduce activities that spotlight ending sounds. Whenever possible, teachers can help to reiterate the acoustics of readers' exposure to sound—for example, by stretching targeted sounds, such as by saying "gggame," rather than isolating a sound, such as by saying "g-ame." If sounds are totally isolated, readers often cannot hear and differentiate them within the context of words. In addition, isolating sounds changes them in ways that may cause further confusion to beginning readers. It is important to refer to letter sounds, and not letter names, as teachers explicitly provide instruction for phoneme activities. Table 3.3, below, provides additional examples of correct and incorrect presentations of initial phonemes.

TABLE 3.3   Correct and Incorrect Presentations of Initial Phonemes

• Correct: We're going to listen for the /m/ sound as in *manna*.
• Incorrect: We're going to listen for the "em" sound.
• Incorrect: We're going to listen for the sound of the letter *m*.
• Correct: We're going to listen for the /t/ sound as in *toy*.
• Incorrect: We're going to listen for the "tee" sound.
• Incorrect: We're going to listen for the sound of the letter *t*.
• Correct: We're going to listen for the /b/ sound as in *Bianca*.
• Incorrect: We're going to listen for the "bee" sound.
• Incorrect: We're going to listen for the sound of the letter *b*.

Phonics activities based on initial and final phonemes may be more difficult for some readers. Teachers can set aside time to provide additional individualized instruction with selected activities for readers struggling with sounds. Key instructional considerations are to make the struggling sounds distinguishable so that struggling readers can hear the problematic sounds, play with them, and use them in meaningful ways that link them to readers' prior knowledge and experiences. At the same time, struggling readers need to be involved in the larger setting so that they can listen to and learn from those who are applying the tasks more quickly.

Onset and Rime

Once readers understand rhyme and can isolate initial sounds, they are ready to begin segmenting and blending one-syllable words at the onset and rime level. Again, the *onset* of a word is the first part of a syllable up to the first vowel; the *rime* is the last part of the syllable beginning with the vowel. For example, in the word *rid*, /r/ is the onset, and /id/ is the rime. Readers make this natural division when first learning to segment one-syllable words and eventually learn to make new words by substituting different onsets with the same rime (Bear, Invernizzi, Templeton, & Johnston, 1995). Some relevant activities for readers from CLD backgrounds may be to practice using onset and rime games with words from their homes and communities that are meaningful to them. Teachers help by pairing cueing techniques to listening games based on word endings. Culturally relevant themes using various rhyme schemes that are pleasurable to listen to when read aloud can be very useful to new or struggling readers. For example, a teacher of young readers might say, "All readers wearing red socks today may come to the front of the room to act out the following verse, 'The dog ran in the fog and discovered a hog by the log.'" As readers demonstrate rhyme and isolation of initial sounds, more difficult cueing may be embedded into the practice instructions.

Analysis and Synthesis

When readers start to segment and blend complete words by phonemes, initially it is helpful that they work with two-phoneme words that include easily distinguishable consonants and long vowels. As they show consistency in understanding consonants and long vowels, readers then are able to practice with short vowels and other consonants and work up to three-phoneme and four-phoneme words. Medial sounds can be isolated. The concept of speech sounds in the middle component of words can seem complex, abstract, and meaningless to young and struggling readers. Since phonemes in words are affected by the sounds around them, many phonemes are often hard to isolate and hear. Some are articulated differently in different words or by different people with dialectical differences. Each of these factors adds to the confusion to diverse readers, such as Lilly. (Her teacher informed her parents that Lilly was unable to differentiate words like *pen* and *pin* or *beg* and *peg* and other words, such as *louse* and *lease*.)

Teachers can continue to support readers by thoroughly demonstrating and discussing each activity, allowing plenty of time and practice, and being more cognizant of those readers who do not seem to catch onto the practice. In addition, practice opportunities are vital for readers to listen to sounds in words throughout the day. Those who haven't mastered syllables, onsets, or rimes will likely struggle with fluent reading. Teachers need to be aware of the need to provide small-group and one-on-one instruction in struggling readers' areas of need while including them in the current activities. Table 3.4 shows a summary of a general lesson using a phonetic approach for struggling readers.

TABLE 3.4 A Phonetic Approach for Struggling Readers

I. Opening: Teacher (T) provides the readers (R) with goals for the lesson and states the purpose.

II. Practice Drill

    A. **Visual card drill:** T shows all learned patterns on visual displays in any order; R give sound.

    B. **Auditory card drill:** T says letter/pattern sound; R name letter(s) and write it on paper. T shows card briefly for visual reinforcement, if necessary.

    C. **Blending drill with visual displays:** T places visual displays, such as cards, in three piles: vowels in the middle. T moves one card at a time, and R blend, or read, the word/syllable. Nonsense words or syllables can be used.

III. Review Previously Taught Pattern, Rule, or Concept

    A. T shows prepared short list (10–15 words) representative of previously learned phoneme pattern.

    B. R decode list and read two or three phrases or sentences.

    C. T dictates three to five words from list for R to write on paper.

    D. Go to top of page.

IV. Introduce New Pattern/Concept/Rule

    A. **High-frequency, nonphonetic word:** T makes pattern and tells R the word. T uses word in an oral sentence and has R use it in an oral sentence. R say each letter to selves while tracing the word three times. Go to top of page.

    B. **New pattern:** T shows prepared list of about 10–20 words, depending upon ability, utilizing one new pattern or concept (for example tch, ea, kn, suffix rule, etc.). R decode words (they may underline vowel first and say name and sound if there is hesitation). R read two or three sentences or phrases incorporating words from the list, old and new nonphonetic words, and previously learned patterns and concepts. T dictates some of the words for R to spell on paper.

V. Practice Sentence Dictation

    A. T has R read back all words written on sheet.

    B. T then dictates two or three sentences or phrases incorporating the above.

Some Tasks Are Easier Than Others

Key factors to consider when presenting skills to decipher in words are many; thus, a continuum of practice opportunities is warranted. The level of cognitive-linguistic complexity of sound and letter awareness varies across activities. For example, for beginning readers, recognizing rhymes often is easier than generating rhymes or using rhymes in sentences. Further, reading tasks requiring awareness at the syllable level typically are easier than those requiring awareness at the phoneme level. Teachers, thus, should help new readers play with syllables and word relationships that emphasize ending sounds before addressing tasks requiring word attack skills in differentiation of medial sounds that acoustically are similar. Because isolated sounds are most likely easier for many beginning readers than, for instance, putting sounds together and taking sounds apart, phoneme isolation tasks generally are easier than phoneme segmentation tasks. Additionally, segmentation or blending tasks are easier with continuant phonemes (e.g., *s,sh,l*) than with noncontinuant-stop phonemes (e.g., *p,b,t*).

Teachers also should note that phonological awareness activities help to support early reading success when combined with instruction in sound-letter correspondences, especially when directly teaching each sound-spelling correspondence explicitly. Explicit instruction means that the teacher or other adult shows the new letter and then says it. Each day, readers from diverse backgrounds should practice, especially listening to models and then practicing new phonemes and previously practiced phonemes that have been already introduced in earlier lessons. After practicing phonemes in isolation, diverse readers should have opportunities to practice phonemes in the context of multicultural words and stories that represent the phoneme-letter relationships they know. Frequent, highly regular sound-spelling relationships must be taught systematically. Readers can then begin to read successfully with 50 to 60 sound-spelling relationships. Writing, on the other hand, requires approximately 70 sound-symbol relationships (Catts, 1991; Hecht et al., 2000; Perie et al., 2005).

For readers who are not proficient, teachers can offer explicit and individualized instruction, focusing on only one or two phonemic awareness skills at a time, such as segmenting and blending. Beginning with auditory phonemic activities, teachers can then link sounds to letters and provide opportunities for readers to apply their knowledge of phonological awareness when reading and writing. As with other readers who display phonological awareness difficulties, those from CLD backgrounds can benefit from systematic instruction in identifying and manipulating the sounds of spoken language with materials and activities that are familiar (Vaughn, Bos, & Schumm, 2005). Effective instructional strategies that target decoding can improve literacy learning. By targeting culturally relevant materials and approaches that build upon readers' cultural funds of knowledge, educators can increase reading engagement. The use of explicit instruction, imbedded with multicultural opportunities, can support meaning and reading achievement to readers from CLD backgrounds. Table 3.5 is a summary of key factors to consider when teaching decoding skills to diverse and struggling readers.

TABLE 3.5   Key Factors to Consider When Teaching Decoding Skills

- Level of cognitive-linguistic complexity of phonological awareness varies across activities.
- Reading tasks requiring awareness at syllable level are typically easier than those requiring awareness at phoneme level.
- Phoneme isolation tasks generally are easier than phoneme segmentation tasks.
- Segmentation or blending tasks are easier with continuant phonemes than with noncontinuant-stop phonemes.
- Frequent, highly regular sound-spelling relationships must be taught systematically.
- Initial instruction targets only one or two phonemic awareness skills at a time, such as segmenting and blending.
- Use explicit instruction, imbedded with multicultural opportunities.

Armbruster and colleagues (2003) summarized the rationale that readers require systematic strategies that teach phonics effectively so that they learn how to decode words and apply word meanings. Readers must learn how to relate letters and sounds, break spoken words into sounds, and blend sounds to form words. Adult models must help to ensure that new or struggling readers receive opportunities to understand why they are learning the relationships between sounds and letters as they apply their knowledge of phonics to read words. Such emphases help readers to activate their relevant background knowledge as they decode and comprehend new and unfamiliar words.

■ WHAT ARE STRUCTURAL ANALYSIS SKILLS?

Phonics instruction that emphasizes both phonemic awareness and graphophonemic relationships is important to the development of deciphering words used in *structural analysis skills.* A beginning reader's sense of managing and applying structural analysis skills and the eventual linking of words to form and read phrases or sentences depend on how and whether readers have functional use of sound-letter and sound-spelling relationships (Adams & Engelmann, 1996; Alvermann & Moore, 1991).

Basic skills involved in *structural analysis of words* entail one's ability to add prefixes, suffixes, or other meaningful word units to a base word. Carnine and colleagues (2004) referred to structural analysis as *morphemic analysis,* because morphemes (e.g., prefixes, suffixes, or inflected endings) are the smallest meaningful units of language one speaks or writes. Miscue analysis in oral skills often targets those being unable to read words by adding prefixes, suffixes, or inflected endings quickly and with accuracy.

Word skill instruction focusing on structural analysis relies on the process of using familiar word parts (e.g., base words, prefixes, and suffixes) to determine the meaning of unfamiliar words. In the scenario above, Lilly has demonstrated some skills in sound-letter associations. However, as she deals with harder and unknown words, even as she is able to sound out a word correctly, she often cannot decipher the meaning of the word. Her teacher's directed focus on context strategies and meaningful clues the word itself might contain may help Lilly in her use of structural analysis skills.

Readers need to recognize that many prefixes and suffixes often have more than a single meaning (as in the words *inactive* and *inroad*) and that even when they can identify the correct meaning of an affix, they might still come up with an incorrect definition. Emphasizing the importance of checking a word's context to see whether their guessed meaning makes sense may help struggling readers in applying structural analysis of word skills. Table 3.6 delineates important word structure tasks for emergent and beginning readers demonstrating early skills in word fluency.

Word Structure

Being able to analyze how words form (and how words influence other words) is important to understanding word structure. Language difficulties that many readers from diverse backgrounds possess may interfere with these readers' ability to use structural analysis when applying word

TABLE 3.6   Word Structure Tasks

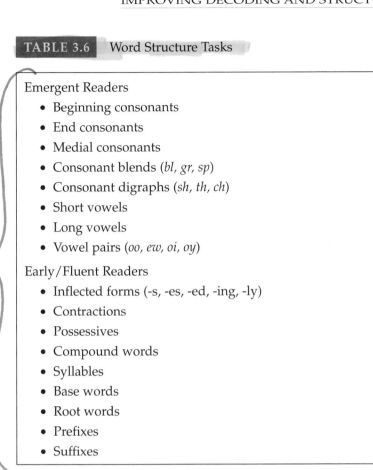

Emergent Readers
- Beginning consonants
- End consonants
- Medial consonants
- Consonant blends (*bl, gr, sp*)
- Consonant digraphs (*sh, th, ch*)
- Short vowels
- Long vowels
- Vowel pairs (*oo, ew, oi, oy*)

Early/Fluent Readers
- Inflected forms (-s, -es, -ed, -ing, -ly)
- Contractions
- Possessives
- Compound words
- Syllables
- Base words
- Root words
- Prefixes
- Suffixes

identification and word attack skills. Often language gets in the way (Carnine et al., 2004; Perie et al., 2005; Snow et al., 1998; Vaughn, Bos, & Schumm, 2007). Many readers from CLD backgrounds or other diverse settings may have language difficulties that affect how they discern sound-letters, sound-letter meaning, words in isolation, sight words, and spelling. Language affects structural analysis and word attack skills, as presented in Table 3.7. The following tips are important in word structure instruction:

- Beginning readers with difficulty adding morphemes to base words may display problems with words ending with a consonant (e.g., *dance + ed = danced*), compound words (e.g., *sun + shine = sunshine*), an ending added to a base word (e.g., *smoke + ing = smoking; tie + ed = tied*), or suffixes or prefixes added to multisyllabic words (e.g., *in + sufficient = insufficient*) (Bursuck & Damer, 2007).
- Although development of structural analysis is necessary to learn to read, these skills alone are not sufficient. Specifically, for new readers to devote the more focused attention and memory capacity to the text such that word comprehension can occur and to read smoothly without errors (that is, to read fluently and with comprehension), structural analysis skills must be acquired and applied accurately and automatically (NICHD, 2000a, 2000b).
- Teachers can support this skill development by providing auditory signals, monitoring responses, and helping readers to pace themselves correctly. Such support by teachers can help beginning readers through visual, auditory, and kinesthetic cueing to become automatic in structural analysis such that word fluency

(i.e., identifying and naming words faster and with fewer errors) can proceed.

- By practicing word knowledge skills in socioculturally relevant games and activities that highlight decoding, word identification, sight words, structural word strategies, and meaningful vocabulary, while they engage in fun and challenging activities, diverse readers can understand better what they are reading as they increase words known automatically and use their knowledge of word structures. Diverse readers increase skills in creating new meaning from words and adding to their prior knowledge.

TABLE 3.7   Language Difficulties Affecting Structural Analysis

- Some readers have difficulties with *morphology* (i.e., understanding the makeup of words, including word base and word units) (Carnine et al., 2004). Readers with morphology problems may not be able to blend word base and suffices and prefixes, such as in *report + ed = reported* or *quick + ly = quickly.*

- A problem in *semantics* refers to readers who have difficulties with the meaning or content of words and word combinations. For example, such readers may be unable to classify letters as consonants or vowels because they do not understand how the terms *consonants* and *vowels* differ or what the terms mean. Teaching reading content helps readers focus on using word skills to increase vocabulary, word categories and relationships, multiple meanings, and figurative language (Vaughn et al., 2007).

- Other readers have difficulties with *syntax* (i.e., order and relationship between words and other structural elements in phrases and sentences). Such readers may be unable to use language rules in letter-sound relationships (e.g., "Use *i* before *e,* except after *c.*").

- Still other readers' difficulties lie in *pragmatics* (i.e., functional language use rather than language structure). For example, a reader with problems in pragmatics may use the wrong verb tense when past tense is written. Instead of reading, "We left early to attend school," the reader might instead say, "We leave early to attend school."

Spelling Skills

Readers advancing in decoding skills are able to apply the alphabetic principle to enhance the oral or written spelling act. Such readers demonstrate a refinement of word details as they connect beginning and ending consonants; recognize medial letters, including vowels and vowel blends; and incorporate letter sequences and patterns in words. Their word knowledge is increasing as they use word bases (e.g., root words) , morphemes (e.g., meaningful word parts), syntax (e.g., rules of grammar and word placement), word parts (e.g., prefixes, suffixes, root words, and endings), familiar sight words (e.g., their names or those of their peers), and high frequency words (e.g., *in, or, and*) to make correct orthographic matches to letters representing sounds in words. Word chunks become meaningful as readers become more proficient in mapping phoneme to grapheme relationships and in discerning predictable letter patterns in words (Catts, 1991; Chall, 1996; Ehri, 1996). Readers' decoding skills advance because they become more familiar with recognition of letter sequences and patterns to form words. Such readers gain in word skills as they recognize and use whole words faster and with more accuracy.

Reaching Automaticity in Structural Analysis Skills

A struggling reader may focus attention on decoding and word recognition (i.e., reducing attention and memory resources) to the point that word fluency becomes impeded. Such readers may not be strategic learners (i.e., they do not plan their reading strategies) and have not learned to activate their background knowledge to derive meaning out of words or text (Adams & Engelmann, 1996; Alvermann & Moore, 1991; Goswami & Bryant, 1990). On the other hand, readers using word recognition skills effortlessly are able to comprehend well and activate their relevant background knowledge when deciphering and applying word strategies. They can relate what has been read to their own experiences. Such readers make meaningful literacy gains as they comprehend oral and written words.

New readers benefit from systematic instruction that clearly helps them to identify a carefully selected and useful set of skills and organize those skills into a logical sequence of instruction (Bursuck & Damer, 2007). In concert with direct and explicit instruction strategies that are developmentally, culturally, and linguistically appropriate, teachers of diverse readers from CLD backgrounds can plan, implement, manage, and monitor research-based literacy strategies related to decoding and structural analysis to support their students.

CULTURALLY AND LINGUISTICALLY RESPONSIVE PRACTICES IMPORTANT TO PRIMARY, MIDDLE SCHOOL, AND HIGH SCHOOL READERS

Because readers may need extensive instruction, especially diverse readers from CLD backgrounds who do not possess the foundational reading skills needed to comprehend oral or written words, teachers need to use engaging beginning reading activities to capture readers' targeted attention. Struggling readers, who may simply have never received appropriate decoding or structural analysis instruction, require research-based interventions that are provided in culturally responsive ways and put them on the trajectory to developing the higher-level literacy skills needed to succeed in an information-based society (Ladson-Billings, 1995). The following tips may help diverse and struggling readers at any grade or developmental level:

- *Allow engaged time for meaningful and fun reading activities.* Teachers purposfully plan and use multicultural materials and opportunities that encourage reading engagement and motivation toward classroom instruction. By so doing, teachers help readers to connect home and school tasks.
- *Assess reading skills frequently, both formally and informally, and identify individual reading area of needs and strengths.* Teachers need to consider each reader's classroom performance in the areas identified as

discrepant from potential. Teachers can monitor progress by examining curriculum-based assessment information of the types, content, and processes of reading materials, linked to individual reading strengths and needs of readers. Formal reading assessment is not required continuously. Rather, teachers observe, generate data, and make instructional decisions daily as they observe readers' progress in literacy activities.

- *Collaborate with other professionals who can assist in providing interventions to address struggling readers' strengths and needs.* For example, classroom teachers may need to team specifically with speech/language therapists and audiologists to address oral language problems exhibited by readers from ELL or CLD backgrounds who had poor modeling prior to school entry.

- *Provide instructional adaptations as necessary to address needs.* For instance, if a reader from an ELL background also has an identified reading disability, then specialized instruction (e.g., related to adaptive equipment, media, or textbook selection) will need to be adapted individually and perhaps even translated into the reader's native language so that the reader can access and comprehend the material more readily.

- *Provide instruction that relates to transition needs of readers.* As readers move into middle school, content area and study skills become critical. Transition planning is imperative to prepare all readers for postsecondary opportunities. In high school, readers struggling with phonics and structural analysis difficulties may make the most gains and benefit greatly from functional literacy activities tailored to their adult goals, life skills instruction, career preparation, further transition planning, and, in some cases, work experiences.

- *Provide support groups for readers making slow progress.* Help middle school and high school struggling readers come to understand what is meant by illiteracy, its characteristics, and the ways reading skills can be manifested and challenged positively as readers mature. As is necessary, teach older challenged readers compensatory strategies in place of limited decoding and structural analysis acquisition (e.g., teach self-advocacy, speaking, and listening skills as priorities).

- *Provide varied instructional arrangements.* For example, using a variety of small groups and pairs helps readers with learning disabilities from ELL or CLD backgrounds to have opportunities to work with typical classmates to complete informal activities and assignments. Teachers need to monitor peer tutoring in dyads, small groups, and classroomwide peer support assignments, making instructional changes based on assignment monitoring.

■ IMPROVING DECODING AND STRUCTURAL ANALYSIS SKILLS IN PRIMARY-LEVEL READERS

To provide an understanding of all the sound units our language encompasses (including phonemes, syllables, and words), primary teachers can carefully select opportunities for read-alouds along with dance, music, art, and carefully selected language games, explicitly targeting decoding and structural analysis skills.

Structure Listening to Literature Activities

By purposively choosing culturally responsive literature that plays with language through rhyming, alliteration, and assonance, primary teachers support emphases on sounds and letter awareness, sound-letter relationships, and decoding.

Use Directed Syllable and Rhyming Activities

Good choices are the use of multicultural songs and poems imbedding various activities, such as the following:

- Identifying and producing oral rhymes in cultural phrases
- Counting words within oral sentences from diverse poems
- Creating oral sentences with a given number of words
- Isolating and counting syllables within oral words
- Isolating and counting phonemes within oral words, followed by dancing, marching, or clapping to the syllabication
- Orally segmenting and blending phonemes
- Orally manipulating initial, medial, or ending phonemes to form nonsense words.

Use Sound Boxes

Teachers can give each reader two counters and a paper with two boxes drawn on it. They slowly say a two-phoneme word, common to readers' homes or communities. Readers repeat the word and push a counter into a box for each sound. Once they master this, readers move to three- and four-phoneme words.

Use Picture Clues

Teachers put three picture cards in a pocket chart. They give two clues for a picture—"starts with and rhymes with"—and have readers guess the correct word. Using relevant pictures familiar to diverse readers, primary teachers may then encourage readers to make up rhyme and rhyming songs or dances using people (or places) words from their families and communities.

Play the Action Game

To introduce the game, the teacher claps her hands and says, "How did I make that sound?" The teacher encourages readers to practice using appropriate vocabulary from the readers' communities. The teacher also reviews common actions, describing what was done to make the sounds, then repeats giving verbal cues only, directing the readers' response. Because readers will learn labels for common objects and the sounds they make, this activity may help readers from ELL backgrounds and those having two or more languages to focus on specific sound-letter relationships. Sample sound cues include the following: Clap your hands. Click tongue. Stamp feet. Pop lips. Tap finger on table. Whistle. Snap fingers. Sing. Cough. Hum. Whisper.

Play the Object Game

The teacher gathers a selection of classroom objects, directing readers to select an object and demonstrate how the object can make a sound. Object examples might focus on book dropping, paper tearing or crumpling, chalk on a board, scissors cutting, pencil writing, and chair scraping. The idea is to start with objects familiar to readers from their homes or communities and gradually introduce unfamiliar ones (e.g., book fanning pages, rubber band squeezing, or flicking retractable pen).

Use Pseudowords Games

If a teacher has not assessed the extent of the reader's decoding problems, "pseudowords" may be used instead of "sight words." These can assist in finding out which sound elements a reader needs to learn. This information helps the teacher to pinpoint problems the reader displays, the sounds associated with written letters, how to put sounds into words, and how to recognize words rapidly. Thus, a teacher may ask readers to substitute words from their primary language with the same beginning or ending sounds as the words under focus when mapping speech to print. The teacher provides a pseudoword from English (e.g., "Start with saying the word *puppy*. Now say the word *tuppy*. Now say the word *huppy*.).

Teach Letter-Sound Correspondence Word Games

Readers need instruction in and practice with understanding that sounds often remain constant, no matter what their position in word typography. For example, the /b/ sound is the /b/ sound no matter where the *b* is in the word (i.e., beginning, middle, or end). Struggling readers often don't decode the last and, especially, the medial graphemes in words, so explicit teaching of these grapheme positions can be important. Using game formats targeting visual letter location, with familiar words from the home and community, can help readers to see constant sounds in word typography and hear phonemes reinforced as games are played.

Use Sounds Directly in Unfamiliar Words

Work toward readers' manipulation of speech segments (e.g., say *spend* without the /p/ or remove the /r/ in the written word *track*) and have readers read the word that's left. Enhancing speech-only phonemic awareness is also helpful (e.g., saying *black* without the /l/). Substitute with words familiar to readers from their homes or communities.

Play "Successive Blending" Games

Successive blending may be useful to readers from CLD backgrounds. The teacher models the blending by linking and blending sounds over multiple trials and systematically "fades out" the direction. Each reader then is responsible for demonstrating blending on his or her own. This activity can be done with small letter cards for the readers to manipulate on their desks and large letter cards for the teacher to manipulate in a pocket chart (so that it is visible for all readers). Blending games can be used to help readers from CLD backgrounds use information in their "tool kits" independently while reading, and teachers can use the blending activities to assess decoding skills. Blending practice can be a very visual, ritualized procedure. Physical actions, focusing on kinesthetic-tactile emphases, such as the readers' opportunities to blend sounds, along with culturally and ethnically favorite songs and dances, can accompany the oral blending.

Use Word-Building Activities

Word building can be done with letter cards (or using small letter tiles). Or a teacher can simply write the words on the board, directing readers to follow along with small dry-erase boards of their own. The teacher focuses readers' attention on a progressive contrast from word to word, but the contrast is minimal (e.g., man-can-cat-hat-hit-hid-had). Readers then receive prompting from the teacher to explain which letter changes each time with verbal emphasis placed on the sounds of the changing letters. Use appropriate words from selected, diverse poems or passages and the readers' homes or communities.

Use Music to Blend Continuous Sounds

A teacher provides readers three sounds and asks them to put the sounds together to their favorite song melody. Example: /th/, /uh/, and /m/ become ththth uhuhuhuhuhuhuhuh mmmmmmm = thumb. Use the continuant sounds (/m/, /n/, /s/, /f/, /sh/, /th/, /r/, /h/, /l/, and /w/) as initial sounds. Examples of melodies might include songs from the latest samba, polka, or country music two-step that readers listen to in their homes.

IMPROVING DECODING AND STRUCTURAL ANALYSIS SKILLS IN MIDDLE SCHOOL-LEVEL READERS

Many middle school readers struggle with and have difficulty decoding words from print. To achieve fast and effortless word identification, readers must understand how letter patterns map onto pronunciation and, for printed words they have not previously encountered, must be able to produce an approximate pronunciation. If the approximate pronunciation can be mapped onto a known word, lexical and semantic information can then be retrieved. For many middle school readers, the first step of learning associations between letter patterns and pronunciation remains difficult (just as content area text and media become increasingly complex for readers in Lilly's position). Activities to support phonics and decoding skills in middle school readers are described below.

Map Phonemes to Graphemes

Mapping phonemes to graphemes on a chart is excellent practice in building decoding skills at the middle school level (Grace, 2005; Moats, 2001). Diagramming the sound-letter relationship is an effective method to help readers use relationships between phonemes and graphemes. Readers who are unable to transfer their phonological awareness to print can learn to map words while diagramming the sound-letter relationship. Teachers can stress the use of words familiar to readers from their homes or communities, such as using the French words *donner, fournir,* and *livrer* to map the phoneme-to-grapheme relationships and then practicing in English words.

Play Onset and Rime Games

The linguistic units of onset and rime may be crucial in explaining the link between rhyming and reading. Readers who recognize onsets and rimes can learn to make analogies between spelling patterns in words to help them read new words. A middle school reader who can read *shape* can more easily learn to read *ship, skip,* and *trip* in an onset and rime game when challenged by the teacher. Adams (1990) concluded that an analogy approach is an effective method for teaching readers to decode. Teachers can cue readers to listen for sound changes and focus on ascertaining word typography changes.

Play With Multisyllabic Words Using Think-Alouds

As they move through the grades, readers are confronted with multisyllabic words (e.g., "*environment, habitat,* and *reusable*"). Older readers often need to develop the ability to read "orthographic chunks" to help them decode these words. Teachers can model and do "think-alouds," to scaffold readers who are practicing blending to improve their ability to read longer words. Lenz and Hughes (1990) offered the mnemonic DISSECT to help secondary-level readers decode unknown words:

Discover the context.

Isolate the prefix.

Separate the suffix.

Say the stem.

Examine the stem.

Check with someone.

Try the dictionary.

Readers can be taught this strategy and then practice using it while reading culturally relevant texts at their instructional level. (Chapter 4 discusses instructional reading levels.)

Play Counting and Syllabication

Teachers can reiterate to middle school readers what a syllable is and how to count the syllables in words. Readers can be taught the six common syllable spelling patterns in order from the simplest (closed and open syllables) through more difficult patterns (like the *r*-controlled and vowel diagraphs). For each syllable type, readers can look for examples in culturally relevant texts, recipe books, or advertisements from community newspapers that are meaningful and functional to them.

Use Relevant Reading Selections

The teacher can divide words selected from upcoming cultural reading selections into syllables, write each syllable on a note card, and display the syllables in jumbled order. Readers then receive teacher cues to unscramble the words. Challenging readers to unscramble the words quickly and accurately can help readers practice and can provide opportunities to chart timed performance changes.

Use Relevant Reading Selections in Dyads

Teachers can assign readers to work in pairs to arrange syllables to form words, given a theme from a selected passage. Another variation would have the teacher write 20 multisyllabic words from an upcoming story. Readers then work with a partner to draw an arc under each syllable as they read aloud. Readers could code each syllable type, or alternatively, readers could code a specific syllable type. For example, the teacher can direct readers to circle all the consonants plus *le* syllables or to underline all closed syllables. Stories with multicultural themes and topics can be used to motivate readers.

Play the Rhyming Game

Teachers can ask readers to create a rhyme given a fictional first name of famous persons from their culture. For example, the teacher models the name *Mame* and demonstrates a creative rhyme: "My name is Mame. I came to Virginia to win some fame. The same day I came to win my fame, I saw a dame who had the same name. I can't blame her for having the same name. Her mom won her name in a game. She became lame trying to tame a lion."

Play the Motown Affixes Scramble

The Motown Affixes Scramble can be a lively game for reinforcing affixes and roots. The teacher divides readers into teams and places a pocket chart or felt board in front of the class. The teacher challenges the readers to divide a word into three parts—prefix, suffix, and base word. Then the teacher challenges the readers to scramble the parts. Each team sends a pair up to the board to attempt to unscramble the word parts and put them into the correct order. For example, a teacher can play a Motown favorite song for one minute. When the music stops, the team cues the readers that they must have the word unscrambled. The team can earn two points: one point for unscrambling the word and a second point for using it in a sentence. Depending on the classroom diversity, teachers may substitute other culturally relevant music. Readers can be cued to write simple poems with movement and rhyme, stressing real or imaginary words.

Play Patterns of Morphologic Elements

Morphology, which includes roots, prefixes, word families, and word origins, can be learned and practiced in both reading and writing. For example, middle school readers can keep a family word notebook with entries such as *suggest, suggestibility, suggested, suggestion, suggestible,* and *suggestive.* Readers from ELL backgrounds can be encouraged to relate English morphological elements to those in their native language through cognates and to list them in notebooks or on index cards for practice and review at school or at home with other family members.

Use Word-Solving Strategies

These strategies may involve shared reading in that the teacher directs the readers to raise their hands during a second reading when they hear a word that contains a certain phoneme. Guided reading is also useful to word solving. For example, after finishing a story based on a multicultural theme, the teacher may direct the readers to review it for compound words. Shared writing can be used in word-solving strategies, as the teacher asks readers to listen to a selection from a multicultural reading and pick out important words that rhyme. The teacher then asks readers to compose a rhyming poem. Further, the teacher may use writing-aloud activities, directing the readers to think aloud as they predict how an unknown word is spelled.

Play Syllable Listening Games

Plan activities involving listening for syllables in relevant home or community words, such as clapping, tapping, or counting the number of syllables. Depending on readers' maturity or motivation, teachers may challenge their syllabic knowledge by timed games stressing physical cue-ing (e.g., "Stand up and clap four times every time you hear words with four syllables from the reading passage.").

Use Cross-Out Techniques

Teachers may select readings from diverse topics representing the readers' heritages and ask the readers to cross out part of a word (to get a better look at the word parts) and then go back and write the whole word. Readers can be encouraged to write creative phrases or simple sentences based on the selected theme for that day's instruction.

Use Word Groupings

The teacher may direct the readers to locate groups of words that begin with the same letter (or words that end with the same letter), using appro-priate vocabulary from diverse newspapers or magazines. The same mate-rials can be used when writing words that sound the same but look different (i.e., homophones).

Use Word Categories

The teacher may have the readers use a selected passage from a diverse reading passage and then classify and write words in categories (e.g., contractions, question words, compound words). The teacher may challenge the readers to write words with different medial sounds (e.g., *ball, bell*), again considering a passage from readers' cultural or language backgrounds.

Play With Word Activities

The teacher may challenge the readers to write plurals (e.g., adding *–s* or *-es*, changing the spellings as in *man* to *men*, changing word endings as in words that end in *y* adding *–ies*, changing word endings as in words that end in *f* changing to *v* and adding *-es*) in stories that hold significance during months of historical holidays or with cultural awareness themes. The teacher may direct the same activity but ask the readers to write words with prefixes and suffixes. Readers might explore base words that are familiar to them in their native languages, then write base words in English, adding endings.

IMPROVING DECODING AND STRUCTURAL ANALYSIS SKILLS IN HIGH SCHOOL READERS ■

It is a challenge to engage the struggling reader, but a number of instructional practices can motivate older struggling readers. Delpit (1995, 2003) found that alphabet knowledge is best learned in a naturalistic, fun, and gamelike manner. Also, an implicit assumption has been that explicit phonological skills training should be an essential component of programs designed to meet the needs of older low-progress readers. The following points are noteworthy:

- *Classroom goals set by the teacher influence the readers' goals.* If learning is a primary aim of the teacher, older readers will internalize that value. If getting a task done quickly is important to the teacher, however, that will become the readers' reason for doing something.
- *Support for learner autonomy and control increases intrinsic motivation.* Teachers can accomplish this by involving high school readers in decisions. For example, by giving them choices and decisions about what they will do for homework, what story to read, or how to compose a response to a story, teachers reinforce high school readers' cooperation.
- *Teacher involvement can show readers that the teacher knows them and knows what they need to learn and want to learn.* Setting short-term goals and tasks increases self-efficacy and is crucial for low-progress learners.
- *High effort fosters a sense of control and accomplishment: "I succeeded because I worked at it—or failed because I didn't put in the effort."* A reader who believes achievement is attributable to luck will not keep at tasks.

Syllable awareness develops simultaneously with the concept of *word* for many readers. Many older, struggling readers are confused, so teachers must watch closely for readers who have difficulty with this aspect of phonological awareness. By using words that are familiar to readers from their everyday vocabularies or from read-alouds so they don't have to struggle constantly, teachers can embed culturally responsive practices into readers' selections. Syllable segmentation and blending develops critical understandings that readers will use again. Careful observation becomes increasingly important at this level, as does additional support for readers who are progressing more slowly. Table 3.8 lists strategies that facilitate motivation for reading in older struggling readers.

TABLE 3.8   Motivating Older Readers

- **Hands-on activities:** Create situational interest by using a hook to get readers' attention.
- **Collaboration:** Involving the reader feeds into adolescent social goals.
- **Personal relevance:** Materials and teachers help to show why the readers should care.
- **Personal involvement:** Materials and teachers help to show how the information will help readers.
- **Meaningful choices:** Allow readers to have some control.

Work With Functional Materials

Teachers can select any real-life materials, such as department store or mail order catalogs. Readers receive cues to locate pictures of items beginning with certain consonant blends (e.g., st, tr, spr) or consonant digraphs (e.g., sh, ch, shr). To focus on hands-on and student-centered activities, readers can be cued to glue the pictures onto poster board or construction paper using creative designs.

Use Resource Materials Linked to Cultural Themes

Using dictionaries, teachers can cue readers to look up meaningful, culturally relevant words beginning with a certain phoneme. For instance, readers receive directions to write down ten words starting with /t/ while compiling a list of clothing from their grandparent's background. The teacher can then direct readers to read aloud to class.

Play a Phoneme Content Game

Teachers can select a page from a culturally specific story being read in class. Readers follow directions to write each word on the page that contains the selected phoneme. The teacher may turn this into a contest by saying, *"Let's see who can be first to find ten words with /bl/ on this page."* The teacher may provide reinforcement to participating readers.

Use English-Language Newspapers or Those in Other Languages

Using newspapers, readers choose an article representing their families' country or countries of origin and circle all the words that contain silent letters—vowels or consonants (rules of silent letters should be discussed prior to this). They then exchange articles with a partner. The partner marks through all the silent letters in the marked words. Readers check their partner's work, then switch roles.

Engage in Word Derivative Games

Since a majority of English words originate from Latin and Greek languages, many lessons at the high school level can use those roots of English words to help diverse readers play with language. For example, the Latin root *scrib* or *script* means "to write." High school readers often enjoy brainstorming and coming up with as many words as they can with that root, such as *transcribe, transcript, inscribe, describe, descriptive, description, manuscript, prescription, scribble,* and so forth. Other derivative words from Romance languages can challenge readers. High school teachers can choose an overhead projector or electronic white board to make a list of readers' ideas for all to see based on new words generated from the list, ensuring that various cultures and heritages are represented in class discussions.

Embed Art Into Literacy

Teachers can guide readers to cut small squares from oak tag and print a phoneme or a syllable on each. Teachers then allow readers to make several squares for each letter of the alphabet and decorate them. Teachers direct the readers to sort the cards alphabetically, keeping them in separate compartments of a decorated egg carton. (Readers label compartments A-B, C-D, E-F, etc. for alphabetizing.) Readers practice forming words by taking the letters from the carton and laying them out on a desk. Teachers stress making words readers know or have heard before. Readers can work in groups and have a contest with this. ("Which group can be first to make 20 words from your community containing prefixes we have discussed?")

Use Syllable Games Infused With Multicultural Readings

For older readers working with multisyllabic words, syllable search games can be used in combination with multicultural readings. Teachers can direct the readers in steps:

1. *Identify words.* Readers become familiar with the words via the teacher reading a set of words aloud from multicultural selections.

2. *Find syllables.* Readers must find the syllables within the unknown words.

3. *Collect the words.* Readers use the syllables that were identified in the previous step to generate different words.

Teachers can select appropriate vocabulary from the readers' homes or community settings for word lists used in syllable search games (e.g., selecting key vocabulary words from new stories to use in syllable search lists, focusing on two- to three-syllable words initially). The activity can be done in whole-group instruction using word cards and syllable cards.

Readers can come up and manipulate the cards either in a pocket chart or on a whiteboard/chalkboard using tape or sticky tac. The teacher can also direct readers in small groups or partnerships to complete syllable search puzzles at their seats or in various classroom locations.

Encourage Strategy Sharing Opportunities

Teachers can explicitly direct readers to think about what they do when they come to words they don't know while reading. Explicitly directing readers to compile a list of reading strategies to share with peers can be embedded in classroom practices. Teachers then allow daily time for sharing prior to the start of each decoding or structural analysis activity.

■ REVISITING LILLY

Because of her teachers' and parents' efforts, Lilly gained in refining her phonemic awareness and structural analysis skills to decode more accurately and faster. Her teachers used explicit teaching activities to plan, implement, manage, and assess as Lilly developed her word recognition skills to be more automatic. Her teachers guided Lilly, coaching her throughout the school year to analyze internal word structures through the use of directed decoding and word recognition skills, infusing activities with culturally responsive practices.

By cueing Lilly's attention to word details and structural analysis activities that were culturally meaningful and age-appropriate, Lilly's teachers sought to build on Lilly's whole word usage and her growing word knowledge skills. Her teachers informed Lilly's parents through the translator that data-supported strategies that cued Lilly to locate letter combinations or sounds (a) individually, (b) within syllables, or (c) paired with known words using kinesthetic-tactile stimulations would increase her decoding skills. All of her teachers encouraged Lilly to use hand-arm movements and voice through Chinese music, songs, dance, and performing arts to support her in sensing how her voice produces sounds creatively and meaningfully. They also integrated her horticultural interests into reading and spelling games whenever activities lent themselves to such accommodations.

Lilly's teachers made a concerted effort to provide corrective feedback to Lilly when she erred in recognizing whole words or in remembering letter sequences. Because of Lilly's strong social interactions, the teachers encouraged Lilly to participate with her peers in word games and activities that stressed rules of capitalization, punctuation, syllabication, and grammar so that Lilly heard and practiced her skills in fun, academic opportunities. Her teachers also encouraged neat handwriting skills when Lilly used her penmanship or participated in spelling activities. They used a buddy system to have her peers give feedback on Lilly's letter spacing, letter and word alignment, as well as margin alignments to help in her manuscript and cursive attempts at writing whole words on pages. Her teachers encouraged use of both uppercase and lowercase letter games in various font sizes and computer formats to reinforce what Lilly knows about letters, sound-letter relationships, word details, and spellings. By reinforcing Lilly to listen to and compare sounds as she pronounced and produced words, her teachers supported Lilly's attempts to make logical associations of letters with speech sounds, word families, blends, and letter sequences or word patterns in culturally appropriate poems, readings, and vocabulary-building activities.

MOVING ON ■

In this chapter, we highlighted culturally responsive practices that professionals employ to improve phonics and structural analysis skills as readers refine the practice of using sounds and of building and analyzing word components. Teachers can capitalize on readers' beginning reading skills using developmentally appropriate and motivational literacy strategies infused with culturally responsive practices. When individualizing instruction for many diverse readers, including those from CLD and ELL backgrounds, or at-risk readers of any age, teachers can support students by stressing the basic phonetic rules of English. Many teaching strategies can be effective with readers who struggle with letters and words, including direct and explicit instruction. Teachers can select instruction that focuses on high-frequency sound-spelling relationships and instruction that offers ample opportunity to practice identification of words. When such strategies are infused with culturally relevant teaching practices, struggling readers make literacy gains.

4

Improving Fluency

Michelle McCollin and Dorothy J. O'Shea

CHAPTER OBJECTIVES

In this chapter, we will

- establish the importance of fluency to developing and becoming a competent reader;
- identify research related to reading fluency strengths and needs, including research on skills needed to read faster, more accurately, and with prosody; and
- provide examples of culturally and linguistically responsive fluency practices important to primary, middle school, and high school readers.

FLUENCY MATTERS!

Latoya Washington, a third-grade African-American student, attends Mary McLeod Bethune Elementary, a large neighborhood, urban elementary school located in the metropolitan Washington, D.C., area. The Title I school's population ranges from families living in public housing communities who receive public assistance (almost 57 percent of the school's student body receives free or reduced lunches) to those living in large and expensive homes. The majority of students, however, are from families of lower socioeconomic status. The school's student demographics are African American 40 percent, American Indian 2 percent, Asian American 35 percent, Caucasian 9 percent, Hispanic

15 percent, and English-language learners (ELL) 47 percent. The school has 49 percent mobility and 79 percent stability ratings of its student population. ELL students and students living in poverty receive supplemental services in reading and mathematics instruction, as well as in speech/language and occupational therapies.

In response to recent standardized test results (in which 85 percent of the students tested at a basic level of proficiency), the school's administration decided to implement a primary curricular and instructional strategy using an integrated language arts/phonics program. This approach was designed to address reading instruction from the perspective of integrated components fundamental to most learning experiences.

The total school enrollment is 869 students from preschool through sixth grade. Only students in early childhood grades 1 through 3 use the Dynamic Indicators of Basic Early Literacy Skills (DIBELS). DIBELS is a set of standardized measures used by schools across the country to gauge early literacy skills development. Measurements of oral reading fluency (ORF) are made by counting the number of words read correctly per minute. For the average performing third grader, DIBELS predicts an increase in ORF from fall to spring of 33 words correct per minute (WCPM) and for fourth graders of 25 WCPM. Likewise, DIBELS predicts ORF from winter to spring to increase by 15 WCPM for third graders and by 13 WCPM for fourth graders (Good & Kaminski, 2002).

Latoya is in an inclusive third-grade class that has a total of 27 students, of whom 7 have Individualized Education Programs (IEPs) for specific learning disabilities (SLD), 2 have therapeutic support personnel for behavioral management, and 1 has a nurse. Latoya receives more than 85 percent of her daily instruction with her nondisabled peers. She receives 45 minutes of "pull-out" reading instruction with other peers three times a week with a reading specialist in the school's resource room, as stipulated by her IEP. She also receives supplemental speech therapy in two half-hour sessions per week. The classroom is assigned a full-time teacher, Mr. Murdock, and a paraprofessional, Ms. Lyde, for three hours daily. Latoya was referred for a multidisciplinary evaluation at the beginning of third grade as a result of a deficient score on her DIBELS in all areas and due to poor performance in first and second grade.

Latoya is a sometimes moody child who is "struggling" with all areas of language arts, including reading, speaking, writing, and penmanship. Aside from speech and language needs, reading difficulties appear to be Latoya's most pressing issue. She can recognize letters and letter sounds in most first-grade vocabulary words presented to her, can read simple sight words and familiar words at the first-grade level, and can articulate and state the meaning of first-grade vocabulary words. Latoya cannot, however, read first-grade textbooks quickly without erring. Second-grade texts are extremely difficult, as Latoya falls more and more behind her peers.

In addition to academic concerns, Mr. Murdock and Ms. Lyde found that Latoya at times displays mild attentional behaviors during reading class, which are described as noncompliance, poor attitude toward reading, and inability to concentrate on reading passages. These behaviors have become more pronounced when Mr. Murdock calls upon Latoya to read orally in front of her peers.

Mr. Murdock met with Latoya's parents, Mr. and Mrs. Washington, to make them aware of Latoya's current academic achievement. The parents mentioned awareness of Latoya's reading difficulties and agreed to have the multidisciplinary team assess their daughter.

Assessment results focused on Latoya's ability, behavioral, health, processing, social-emotional, and achievement measures. Results indicated that Latoya has no known health or serious behavioral concerns, has average intelligence, and displays reading achievement scores that are "significantly below grade level." Latoya does not have emotional or social difficulties but does have receptive language concerns. The team summarized Latoya's learning needs in reading, especially in her reading fluency skills. Mr. Murdock advocated to Latoya's IEP team to consider adding to Latoya's IEP learning support in reading fluency and language arts.

■ WHAT IS FLUENCY?

Fluency is described as the ability to project the natural pitch, stress, and juncture of the spoken word on written text automatically and at a natural rate, coupled with the ability to group words quickly to help gain meaning from what is being read (Carnine, Silbert, Kame'enui, Tarver, & Jungjohann, 2006; Richards, 2000). It is the ability to read a text rapidly and precisely with ease and expression. Accordingly, after it is fully developed, reading fluency is the performance of the reading act, wherein there is great accuracy and rate, unproblematic decoding, and accurately intonated and rhythmic oral reading with attention to comprehension.

When fluent readers read aloud, it sounds as though they are speaking "with expression," "with good phrasing," or "in a meaningful way." In the case scenario above, Mr. Murdock was able to cite how Latoya presented many instances of reading fluency problems, especially when she was asked to read orally in front of her peers, and was unable to decode words quickly and accurately without errors.

Many readers from culturally and linguistically diverse (CLD) backgrounds need to nurture their ongoing fluency to become independent readers. Teachers' use of direct and explicit strategies, focused on culturally and linguistically responsive practices (e.g., use of relevant texts and other instructional materials, teaching strategies targeting fluency building skills, instructional grouping considerations) can facilitate improved reading behaviors. Classroom fluency opportunities encourage and strengthen vocabulary, reading comprehension, and higher-level thinking.

To synthesize how teachers can improve fluency skills of readers from CLD backgrounds, it is necessary to articulate the process involved when readers become fluent. Additionally, deciding what and how to teach requires a most important consideration of valuing and accepting readers' backgrounds and readiness to reach *accuracy* and *fluency,* or the facile and seemingly effortless recognition of words, in connected text (McCollin & O'Shea, 2005).

■ FLUENCY DEVELOPMENT

As part of a continuum of reading progress, fluency is believed to occur in discernable phases. Emergent, developing, and fluent-level behaviors characterize reading fluency (Brady & Moats, 1997; Chall, 1996; Clay, 1993; Cunningham, Hall, & Defee, 1998; Miccinati, 1985; O'Shea & O'Shea, 1994; Stanovich & Stanovich, 1995). Beginning readers at the emergent phase demonstrate fluency by relying mainly on illustrations to attend to print. Often through rote learning, some begin to acquire incidental visual features of a word. They may demonstrate limited attention to features of letters or words, such as through word spacing or letter directionality. Emergent fluency readers begin to identify and name familiar words, such as their names or peers' names. They begin to rely on language patterns found in print as they give auditory and oral responses to text by relating what they know to ideas, events, and information (often using pictures and context).

As developing fluency advances, readers begin to rely less on pictures and more on information from print. They begin to pronounce words on the basis of phoneme-grapheme mapping. These readers display early reading strategy usage, including skills in predicting and retelling. Often, such readers can recognize frequently used words automatically (e.g., *and, book, is, the*). They may read familiar texts with increased word accuracy and speed as they begin to monitor their own reading and self-correction skills.

However, many readers with developing fluency skills still rely on visual and phonetic cues to decode words (e.g., initial-final letters or sounds, simple word patterns known as "chunks") (Brady & Moats, 1997). When readers advance to use of near-fluent or fluent-level skills, many begin to display inferred meaning from print, differentiating available data sources effectively (e.g., diagrams, tables). Such readers have a large body of sight words, often using familiar words in fast and accurate displays. They use multisyllabic words quickly, make analogies easily, and associate word structure with meaning. In addition, as they generalize advanced reading behaviors, fluent readers are able to decode unfamiliar words by relying on chunks, including prefixes and suffixes. They read longer and more complex text, applying correct use of punctuation to adjust phrasing. Fluent readers have available and may display simultaneous reading strategies (e.g., monitoring and self-correcting) to draw meaning from text. Because fluent readers are able to identify text detail to support ideas, most can adjust their reading rates to different types of text (Brady & Moats, 1997; Chall, 1996; O'Shea & O'Shea, 1994; O'Shea, Sindelar, & O'Shea, 1985; Samuels, 1997).

Why Is Fluency a Critical Component of Comprehension?

The National Institute of Child Health and Human Development (NICHD) and the NICHD National Reading Panel (NICHD, 2000; National Reading Panel, 2000) have reported fluency as having critical importance for reading because it bridges word recognition and comprehension. Reading requires one to (a) translate letters into coherent sound representations perceptually and automatically; (b) synthesize the individual sound components into comprehensible wholes and access lexical representations; (c) process meaningful connections within and between sentences, linking text to self and prior experiences and/or information; and (d) make inferences to supply omitted information (Fuchs, Fuchs, Hosp, & Jenkins, 2001). As a result, fluent readers center their thought processes on making text-to-self connections, whereas the dysfluent reader focuses attention on decoding individual words with little to no attention on comprehending the text (NICHD, 2000a, 2000b). Common fluency problems (i.e., dysfluency) stem from the lack of ability to read sight words and an inability to process text meaning, decode unknown words, and read phrases and sentences automatically and rapidly (Chard, Vaughn, & Tyler, 2002).

The reading by dysfluent readers can be characterized as slow, labored, inexpressive, and unenthusiastic (Rasinski, 2000). The reading act to the dysfluent reader becomes a laborious chore that diminishes the reader's ability to understand the text. Such a reader often displays problems with reading *prosody*, in that the rhythm or flow of spoken language, including stress and intonation, does not lend itself to automaticity. The resulting oral reading seems dull and expressionless, almost labored, as if the reader gains no satisfaction or enjoyment from reading. The dysfluent reader does not chunk words into meaningful units and must focus attention on decoding words. Therefore, a dysfluent reader has less attention left to devote to understanding the text

(Carnine et al., 2006; Rasinski et al., 2005). Table 4.1 summarizes differences between fluent and dysfluent readers.

TABLE 4.1 Fluent Readers and Dysfluent Readers

Fluent Readers	Dysfluent Readers
Focus their attention on making text-to-prior knowledge connections.	Focus their attention primarily on decoding individual words.
Focus their attention on making text-to-text connections.	Display an inability to read sight words.
Focus their attention on making text-to-self connections.	Display an inability to process text meaning, decode unknown words, and read phrases and sentences automatically and rapidly.
Focus on comprehension.	Display little attention and skill for multidimensional text comprehension.

Fluency and Automaticity

Fluency encompasses both the process and product of the reading act (Carnine, Silbert, Kame'enui, & Tarver, 2004; Chard et al., 2002; Fuchs et al., 2001; Kame'enui & Simmons, 2001; Stahl & Kuhn, 2002; Vaughn, Bos, & Schumm, 2005; Wolf & Katzir-Cohen, 2001). Fluency is also related to the concept of automaticity. *Automaticity* is defined as fast, accurate, and effortless word identification of words in isolation or in lists. The speed and accuracy at which single words are identified is the best predictor of comprehension (Kuhn & Stahl, 2003).

Automaticity, as well as practicing the mechanics of reading to high fluency levels (e.g., processing letter-sound correspondences rapidly), is believed to allow the reader to allocate more cognitive resources to comprehension (Carnine et al., 2004). Fluency has also been shown to be an important factor in the maintenance, generalization, and application of reading skills and a better predictor of comprehension than direct measures of reading comprehension, such as questioning, retelling, and cloze procedures (Begeny & Martens, 2006; Fuchs et al., 2001; Kuhn & Stahl, 2003).

Fluency is the pathway that the reader must negotiate to get from word recognition to text comprehension. Therefore, automatic word recognition, fluency, and comprehension are inextricably intertwined reading skills (Carnine et al., 2006).

How Can We Help Readers Develop Fluency Skills?

There are two major instructional approaches to fluency:

1. Repeated and monitored oral reading (i.e., repeated reading) approaches in which readers read passages aloud several times and receive guidance and feedback from the teacher as they read aloud (O'Shea et al., 1985)

2. Independent silent reading approaches in which readers are encouraged to read extensively on their own

Significant findings from the scientific research on fluency instruction have found that repeated and monitored oral reading improves reading fluency and overall reading achievement (NICHD, 2000a, 2000b).

Research has not yet confirmed independent silent reading as a means of improving fluency and overall reading achievement. Research has, however, confirmed that repeated oral reading with feedback and guidance improves fluency and has a positive impact on comprehension. In repeated oral reading, readers read and reread a text a specified number of times or until specified levels of speed and accuracy are reached. We now know that readers with fluency problems, such as Latoya, need direct and explicit help.

Addressing Fluency

Researchers and practitioners have defined several techniques for addressing fluency (cf. Chard et al., 2002; Fuchs et al., 2001; Hirsch & Moats, 2001; Kame'enui & Simmons, 2001; Snow, Burns, & Griffin, 1998; Stahl & Kuhn, 2002; Vaughn et al., 2005; Wolf & Katzir-Cohen, 2001). However, addressing the oral language skills and vocabulary of readers of diverse heritages is a special challenge. Many of these readers are English-language learners or spent their preschool years in language-restricted environments. Instruction and practice in recognizing high-frequency words, teaching common word patterns (chunks), and spelling patterns to develop decoding strategies have been shown to be beneficial (Cunningham, 2000; Bear, Invernizzi, Templeton, & Johnston, 1996). High-quality, diverse, and multileveled reading materials should be used. Substantial practice in textual reading is necessary to build fluency (Adams, 1990; Lyon, 1998a, 1998b; Lyon, Alexander, & Yaffe, 1997; Lyon & Moats, 1997; Mathes, Howard, Allen, & Fuchs, 1998). Fluency training with a focus on the component skills of phonological awareness and decoding can be an effective reading intervention for readers with reading disabilities (Mercer, Campbell, Miller, Mercer, & Lane, 2000).

To address the instructional inconsistencies often found among readers from CLD backgrounds, effective fluency instruction, infused with culturally relevant reading, can support increased reading speed with fewer errors. Explicit teaching that targets fluency can improve literacy learning. In addition, by using culturally relevant materials and approaches that build upon readers' cultural funds of knowledge, educators can increase readers' learning and engagement.

Helping Readers to Become More Fluent

Fluency develops as a result of many opportunities to practice reading with a high degree of success (NICHD, 2000a, 2000b). Therefore, poor readers should be provided with good models of fluent reading. By listening to good models, poor readers learn how one's voice can help written text make sense, as well as how to use word identification and comprehension strategies effectively (McCormick, 2003; NICHD, 2000a, 2000b). Thus, it is imperative that adults and peers with good reading skills read aloud daily to problem readers. By reading aloud, effortlessly and with expression, these significant others will model how a fluent reader sounds during oral reading. After an effective reader models how to read the text, it is also important that poor readers reread the same text. By doing this, the readers are engaging in repeated reading. Usually, having readers read a passage three to four times is sufficient to improve fluency (O'Shea et al., 1985).

Opportunities to read passages repeatedly with guidance from the teacher are very important to children such as Latoya. Listening to good models of fluent reading promotes fluency; however, readers must reread the text themselves after listening to the model (Carnine et al., 2004). Teachers can support repeated reading activities in creative ways so that rereading the same passage does not become boring. For example, readers can have the opportunity to repeatedly read passages through other experiences, as described below:

- *Adult-reader reading:* In adult-reader reading, the adult reads the text first, providing the reader with a model of fluent reading. Then the reader rereads the same passage to the adult, with the adult providing assistance and encouragement. To lessen the possibility of boredom, a tape recorder can be used.
- *Choral reading:* In choral, or unison, reading, readers read along as a group with the teacher (or with another fluent adult reader). To further provide support, readers must be able to view the same text that the adult is reading. The readers can follow along as the adult reads from a big book, or they can read their own copy of the book. For choral reading, a teacher should select a book/passage that is not too long and that is at the readers' independent reading level. Patterned or predictable books are particularly useful for choral reading.
- *Prerecorded tape-assisted reading:* Readers read along in their books as they listen to a fluent reader, then read the book aloud on audiotape. The book should be at the readers' independent reading level and should be read at a speed of 80–100 words per minute. Readers should read along with the tape until able to read independently without the support of the tape.
- *Partnered reading:* Paired readers take turns reading aloud to each other. More fluent readers should be paired with less fluent peers to ensure success with this strategy. The stronger reader should read a passage or page first, providing a model of fluent reading. Then the less fluent reader should read the text aloud. The more fluent reader should give assistance with word recognition/word attack skills and provide feedback and encouragement to his or her reading peer until the peer is able to read independently.
- *Readers' theater:* Readers rehearse and perform a play for peers or others. Readers' theater provides readers with genuine reasons to reread text and to practice fluency.

Much of reading fluency determination depends on the accuracy with which one's level of reading is discernable. *Independent* is the level at which readers read successfully without assistance. *Instructional* is the level at which readers read with assistance from a teacher. *Frustration* is the level at which the reader is completely unable to read the material with adequate word identification or comprehension. The frustrated reader may display a word-for-word or hesitant approach. These levels are very important in determining the speed and ease of readers' measurable fluency skills. Table 4.2 describes independent, instructional, and frustration levels of text.

TABLE 4.2   Independent, Instructional, and Frustration Levels of Text

Independent	Instructional	Frustration
Relatively easy for the reader, with no more than approximately 1 in 20 words that may be difficult for the reader (95 percent success)	Challenging but manageable text for the reader, with no more than 1 in 10 words that may be difficult for the reader (90 percent success)	Difficult text for the reader, with more than 1 in 10 words that may be difficult for the reader (less than 90 percent success)

FLUENCY AND READERS FROM CULTURALLY AND LINGUISTICALLY DIVERSE BACKGROUNDS

For diverse readers from CLD backgrounds, dysfluency (i.e., not being able to decode words, unable to process text meaning), which is inextricably linked to academic failure, has been intensified by societal factors and school-based practices that serve to create the large reading discrepancies found between ethnic groups (Hintze, Callahan, Matthews, Williams, & Tobin, 2002; Speece, Mills, Ritchey, & Hillman, 2003; Vaughn et al., 2005).

Many readers from diverse backgrounds have not been motivated to read because of limited reading opportunities and harmful environmental factors (cf. Obiakor & Utley, 2004). Such readers may exhibit achievement difficulties and academic failure because of limited reading resources. Societal factors that present decreased reading opportunities, fewer reading resources or reading models, and less effective educators in schools serving readers from diverse backgrounds may be countered when educators receive training and support in effective school-based, culturally responsive teaching strategies that target reading competency and achievement gains (Artiles, Kozleski, Dorn, & Christensen, 2006; Ladson-Billings, 1994).

CLD readers may require support in the form of reading models, increased afterschool tutoring, reading mentoring programs, and instruction by educational personnel trained in understanding the sociocultural context in which readers live, think, and learn. Limited access to quality literature outside of the classroom may have a significant impact on many readers' motivation and willingness to read. Consequently, providing readers from CLD backgrounds with intense, culturally responsive, and explicit opportunities to experience effective foundational skills may help them to achieve reading comprehension gains and thwart the tremendous long-term negative consequences of limited reading resources and opportunities (McCollin & O'Shea, 2005).

What Is Culturally Responsive Pedagogy?

Culture is fundamental to the teaching-learning process. It dictates how one communicates, receives, interprets, and expresses information. Culture also shapes the very thinking processes of individuals and groups. A pedagogy that recognizes, responds to, and celebrates fundamental similarities among all cultures offers full, equitable access to education for readers from all cultures.

Culturally responsive teaching is a pedagogy that acknowledges the significance of including readers' cultural references in all aspects of learning. This strategy provides a connection between culture and curriculum, home and school, to promote socioemotional wellness and academic achievement (Gay, 2000; Ladson-Billings, 1994; National Research Council, 2002; U.S. Department of Education, 2005; U.S. Department of Health, Education, and Welfare, 2003). Characteristics of culturally responsive teaching must be embedded into educational infrastructures of our diverse schools.

Positive Perspectives on Parents and Families

Parents are the child's first teacher and are critically important partners to readers and teachers. To help parents become aware of how they can be effective partners in the education process, teachers should engage in conversations with parents as early as possible about parents' hopes and aspirations for their child, their sense of what the child needs, and suggestions about ways teachers can help. Allowing parents the opportunities to share their knowledge with the school community helps teachers gain more insight into their readers' background knowledge and abilities and ways in which they learn best (Moll, Amanti, Neff, & Gonzalez, 1992). In so doing, teachers explain their own limitations and invite parents to participate in their child's education in specific ways. Parent involvement need not be just parental participation in school functions; often, religious and cultural differences preclude active participation in school activities. However, parental involvement also includes how parents communicate high expectations, pride, and interest in their child's academic life (Nieto, 1996). The varied strategies for promoting culturally responsive parent interactions are described in Table 4.3.

TABLE 4.3   Strategies for Promoting Culturally Responsive Parent Interactions

- Seek to understand parents' hopes, concerns, and suggestions.
- Conduct needs assessments and surveys (in the parents' first language) of what parents expect of the school community.
- Establish parent-teacher organizations or committees to work collaboratively for the benefit of the readers.
- Provide parents with basic training in methods that can be used to help their children at home.
- Conduct home visits in which parents are able to speak freely about their expectations and concerns for their children.
- Keep parents apprised of services offered by the school.
- Send weekly/monthly newsletters (in the home language) informing parents of school activities.
- Conduct monthly meetings at parents' homes or community centers to inform parents of school activities.
- Host family nights at school to introduce parents to concepts and ideas that children are learning in their classes and to share interactive journals.
- Use cross-cultural skills necessary for successful exchange and collaboration.
- Research the cultural backgrounds of readers' families.
- Visit local community centers to find out about the cultural activities and beliefs of the readers.
- Tour readers' neighborhoods to identify local resources and services.

Communication of High Expectations

All readers should receive the consistent message that they are expected to attain high standards in their schoolwork. All that are involved in readers' academic lives must deliver this message: teachers, guidance counselors, administrators, and other school personnel. They should respect all readers as learners with valuable knowledge and experience. Effective and consistent communication of high expectations helps readers develop a healthy self-concept (Rist, 1971). It also provides the structure for intrinsic motivation and fosters an environment in which the reader can be successful. Table 4.4 provides strategies for promoting culturally responsive expectations.

TABLE 4.4   Strategies for Promoting Culturally Responsive Expectations

- Communicate clear expectations.
- Be specific in what you expect readers to know and be able to do.
- Create environments of genuine respect for readers and belief in their capability.
- Encourage readers to meet expectations for a particular task.
- Offer praise when standards are met.

Learning Within the Context of Culture

Children learn about themselves and the world around them within the context of culture (Meltzer, 2002). Readers from minority cultures may feel pressured to disavow themselves of their cultural beliefs and norms to assimilate into the majority culture. This can interfere with their emotional and cognitive development and result in school failure (Sheets, 1999). Children from homes in which the language and culture do not closely correspond to that of the school may be at a disadvantage in the learning process. These children often become alienated and feel disengaged from learning. People from different cultures learn in different ways. Their expectations for learning may be different. For example, readers from some cultural groups prefer to learn in cooperation with others, while the learning style of others is to work independently. To maximize learning opportunities, teachers should gain knowledge of the cultures represented in their classrooms and adapt lessons so that they reflect ways of communicating and learning that are familiar to the readers. Table 4.5 provides strategies for culturally responsive teaching.

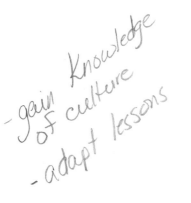

TABLE 4.5   Strategies for Promoting Culturally Responsive Teaching

- Vary teaching strategies.
- Use cooperative learning, especially for material new to the readers.
- Assign independent work after readers are familiar with concept.
- Use role-playing strategies.
- Assign readers research projects targeting issues applying to their own community or cultural group.

(Continued)

TABLE 4.5 (Continued)

- Provide various options for completing an assignment.
- Bridge cultural differences through effective communication.
- Teach and talk to readers about differences between individuals.
- Show how differences among the readers make for better learning.
- Attend community events of the readers and discuss the events with the readers.

Reader-Centered Instruction

Learning happens in culturally appropriate social situations; that is, where relationships among readers and those between teachers and readers are congruent with readers' cultures (Darling-Hammond, 1997). Learning is cooperative, collaborative, and community oriented. Readers are encouraged to direct their own learning and to work with other readers on research projects and assignments that are both culturally and socially relevant to them. Readers become self-confident, self-directed, and proactive. When teachers, such as Mr. Murdock, use reader-centered instruction with students, such as Latoya, it may help decrease the number of incidences of unacceptable behavior from readers who are frustrated with instruction not meeting their needs. Also, readers from cultural groups who are experiencing academic success will be less inclined to form stereotypes about readers from other cultures. Table 4.6, below, describes strategies for culturally responsive, reader-centered learning.

TABLE 4.6 Strategies for Culturally Responsive, Reader-Centered Learning

- Explore readers' experiences with various learning and teaching styles.
  - Ask educators who come from a similar cultural background about effective ways to teach these readers.
  - Visit the communities of the readers to find out how they communicate, interact, and learn in that environment.
  - Survey readers about their learning style preferences.
  - Interview parents about how and what readers learn from them.

- Implement different methods for readers to achieve developmental milestones.
  - Ensure success by setting rigorous and attainable goals for individual readers.
  - Allow readers to set their own goals for a project.
  - Allow the use of the reader's first language to enhance learning.

- Create an environment that encourages, embraces, and respects diverse cultures.
  - Utilize management strategies that are familiar to readers.
  - Allow readers ample opportunities to share their cultural knowledge.
  - Teach readers to reflect on their own beliefs and actions.
  - Promote reader engagement.
  - Have readers generate lists of topics they wish to study and/or research.
  - Allow readers to select their own reading material.
  - Share responsibility for instruction.
  - Initiate cooperative learning groups.
  - Have readers lead discussion groups or reteach concepts.
  - Create inquiry-based/discovery-oriented curriculum.
  - Create classroom projects that involve the community.
  - Encourage a community of learners.
  - Form book clubs and literacy circles for reading discussions.

Culturally responsive pedagogy (CRP) is a multidimensional approach that not only helps bridge the gap between readers, their diverse experiences, and what the school curriculum requires for academic achievement but is also vital in helping CLD readers maintain their cultural identity and community connections, as well as acquire an ethic of success (Banks et al., 2001).

IMPROVING FLUENCY IN ■
PRIMARY-LEVEL READERS

Emergent literacy philosophy emphasizes the connections and interrelationships between reading, writing, and oral language development (Carnine et al., 2006). Creating a "print-rich" environment provides multiple ways for young readers to discover relationships between oral and written language. Labels, signs, charts, calendars, and lists, which children can help create, not only help to organize the environment but also provide opportunities for children to read and write in functional and meaningful ways. Culturally responsive classrooms provide opportunities for children from CLD backgrounds to express themselves using multiple methods, including visual art, music, drama, and dance. Thus, explicit instruction and practice, combined with other ongoing listening, speaking, reading, and print opportunities, help develop the critical concept for reading fluency.

Strategies for Improving Fluency

Effective implementation of a curriculum and environment that addresses the needs of the whole child in relationship to his or her environment is a critical factor in that child's success in academics and in pursuing a livelihood as an adult. This curriculum should be integrated, interdisciplinary, consequential, and student centered. It should include content related to the students' social, cultural, and linguistic background, behavior, and experiences. It should challenge the students to develop critical thinking skills that effectively connect their culturally based knowledge to classroom learning experiences (Villegas, 1991).

Researchers have found viable strategies that, when combined with effective skill-based direct instructional practices, improve fluency of CLD students and those at risk of academic failure. The following suggestions, when integrated into daily instructional practices, could facilitate the improvement of fluency and word recognition for primary-level readers.

Create Literacy-Enriched Activity Centers

Literacy-enriched activity centers expand and enrich students' prior learning and experiences and help them develop divergent thinking and build problem-solving skills. Centers should be organized, have established routines and procedures for using the centers and materials, respond to the students' work, and maintain records of students' progress in center activities. Highly effective centers include the following:

- Appropriate and authentic multicultural materials that increase understanding and appreciation of diversity

Literature Centres

- Manipulatives and other concrete materials at appropriate levels
- Many open-ended and higher-level thinking questions and problem-solving ideas
- Wide range of similar activities at different levels of difficulty
- Room for both enrichment and reinforcement
- Many activities that are structured to develop interpersonal skills, such as sharing, cooperating, giving constructive responses to other students, and exercising responsibility to oneself and the group

Early childhood/primary literacy learning centers may contain tables or desks and materials for writing, telephone books, and picture books to read to dolls. A *housekeeping corner* can contain household items, such as a broom, vacuum cleaners, dishes, a shopping list, and a chores chart. These materials can provide numerous opportunities for children to explore print. A *grocery play center,* complete with newspaper ads, cash register receipts, coupons, food labels, typing paper, inventory sheets, pads of paper, and toy paper money, also provides a natural environment. *An office/career center,* complete with mock cell phones, judge's gavel, doctor's stethoscope, nurse's chart, salesperson's briefcase, and handyperson's tool belt, will provide a natural environment for students to explore and discuss types of workers/careers in the community.

Have Young Readers Participate in Learning Centers

Teachers can purposively create small, culturally relevant centers around the classroom that provide primary readers the opportunity to practice repeatedly the skills involved in reading fluency. This can be accomplished, for instance, through recorded books that help students understand children from other cultures. These books may have microchip processors that offer correct pronunciation for readers. Also on hand can be a language master, tape players, headphones, and microphone. These materials will allow young readers the opportunity not only to listen to a model of fluent reading but also to practice fluency skills in independent read-aloud activities and take a closer look at various cultures. (See Appendix C for an annotated bibliography of multicultural children's literature.)

Model and Have Readers Practice Repeated Readings

Show young readers exactly how to sound out lists of words, using familiar words from multicultural contexts (e.g., "Let's practice sounding out words we use at home, such as *cuffi, sombrero, mano, hermano, mango, pitzells, arroz, pollo, dreidle, souvlakia, feta cheese, taper, baklava, menorah, latkes, lapiz, kinara,* and *sushi.*"). Activities that are fun and academically relevant can involve dividing multicultural words by syllables and modeling how to clap out the syllables/sounds. Clapping or rhythmic beating experiences can precede hopping and rhythmic syllable singing games, as readers acquire new words. Be sure to have readers accurately repeat each word.

Model and Have Readers Practice Accurate and Fluent Reading in Decodable Stories

The words in decodable stories emphasize the sound-letter relationships readers are learning. Use familiar fairy tales, along with cultural themes, such as by changing character backgrounds (e.g., from medieval or ancient characters to modern African-American, Asian, or Hispanic heroes and heroines), while focusing on fluency. Such activities may help readers to acquire accuracy and automaticity in reading unfamiliar words using authentic methods. Using appropriate, culturally relevant and responsive decodable text for readers not only helps them practice sound-spelling/fluency relationships but also builds a sense of self-esteem and cultural respect for diverse cultures. Readers need extensive practice applying their knowledge of sound-spelling/fluency relationships to the task of reading as they are learning. This integration of phonics and reading best occurs with the use of decodable text (Snow et al.,1998; Vaughn et al., 2005). Predictable text gives a motivating success, but readers requiring fluency practice need to repeat the sound spellings they have learned as well.

Use Culturally Relevant Familiar Readings, Such as Nursery Rhymes/Songs

Most readers are familiar with "Are You Sleeping?" Many may enjoy substituting sociocultural vocabulary in opportunities for repetition. For instance, substitute new vocabulary for the passage "Are you sleeping?" After introducing a new word (e.g., *singing*), have the class read in unison at just the right moment to insert the choral reading response "Are you singing, Are you singing, Brother John?" Substitute new vocabulary that is culturally and linguistically sensitive and appropriate for the readers and the curriculum.

Implement Partner Reading

Have readers work in pairs and take turns reading aloud to each other. Plan and implement regular partner reading opportunities, pairing readers from different culturally and linguistically diverse backgrounds and different reading levels. Begin reading a segment of a story or picture book (e.g., the dialogue), using dramatic and dynamic vocal tones, and then ask partners to take turns reading the same segment in a similar manner, providing feedback to each other.

IMPROVING FLUENCY IN ■
MIDDLE-LEVEL READERS

Middle grade classrooms are social settings in which readers read, discuss, and write about literature (Santa, 2006). Effective teachers establish a community of learners in which readers are motivated to learn and are actively involved with reading and writing activities. Characteristics of a culturally responsive middle school classroom that support preadolescent readers' interactions with literature include, but are not limited to, the following:

- *Responsibility:* Readers are responsible for their learning, their behavior, and the contributions they make in the classroom. They see themselves as valued and contributing members of the classroom community.
- *Opportunities:* Readers have opportunities to read and write for genuine and meaningful purposes. They read real books and write for

real audiences—their classmates, their parents, and members of the community.

- *Engagement:* Readers are motivated to learn and are actively involved in reading and writing activities. Readers sometimes choose which books to read, how they will respond to a book, and which reading and writing projects they will pursue.
- *Demonstration:* Teachers provide demonstrations of literacy skills, fluency, and strategies, and readers observe to learn what more capable readers do.
- *Risk taking:* Readers are encouraged to explore topics, make guesses, and take risks.
- *Instruction:* Teachers provide instruction through mini lessons. During mini lessons, teachers provide information and make connections to the reading and writing in which readers are involved.
- *Response:* Teachers provide opportunities for all readers to share and respond to reading and writing activities. Readers are a supportive audience for classmates.
- *Choice:* Teachers encourage readers to choose some of the books they read and projects they develop.
- *Time.* Teachers organize the class schedule with large chunks of time for reading. They plan units and set deadlines with readers.
- *Assessment.* Teachers set grading plans with readers before beginning each unit, meet with readers in assessment conferences, and assist readers in collecting work for portfolios (Santa, 2006).

Direct Fluency Opportunities

Using explicit instruction and practice, combined with directed fluency opportunities, teachers help increase reading fluency. The following strategies, when implemented into an integrated, multidisciplinary, culturally relevant curriculum, may facilitate fluency improvement in middle school-level readers.

Engaging

Readers participate in a variety of supportive reading activities, which middle school teachers can schedule purposively. Activities include the following:

a. *Reading aloud or modeled reading:* For example, the teacher reads aloud, modeling how good readers read fluently and with expression.

b. *Buddy-reading or shared reading:* For example, the teacher reads aloud, and readers follow along individually or in groups.

c. *Choral reading and interactive reading:* For example, the teacher and readers read together and take turns doing the reading. The teacher helps the readers read fluently and with expression.

Demonstrate Multiple Meanings

When words have multiple meanings, their contexts should provide a clue to the meaning to middle school readers. For example, the vocabulary word *character* has 20 meanings in the dictionary. The teacher should go through steps similar to those listed above. For example, The teacher states, "A computer's keys have *characters* on them, such as @, $, 9, ?, and *A*." If the readers mention other meanings of *character*, the teacher can use them as examples of decoding a multiple-meaning word using context clues. Thus, the teacher might challenge middle school readers by writing the following sentences on the board or chart tablet: Whenever my older brother does something silly, my mother says he's a *character* (i.e., a person who is peculiar or eccentric). Among the *characters* in John Steptoe's (1987) *Mufaro's Beautiful Daughters* are Mufaro, Nyasha, Nyoka, and Manyara (i.e., a person portrayed in a story).

The teacher can model fluent expressive reading by reading the sentences aloud to the readers, asking the readers what the word *character* means in each sentence. The teacher then reinforces text clues to the meanings in each sentence by probing readers for how the second example differs from the first sentence where *character* appears. When addressing middle school readers for culturally responsive fluency instruction, it is critical that the teacher

- focus on the vocabulary and related concepts;
- replace abstractions with concrete culturally relevant illustrations; and
- teach by pointing out similarities, using synonyms for the vocabulary word, because ideas and concepts that go together are best learned together.

Use Poetry to Introduce New Words in Context

Middle school students often find studying poetry to be an intimidating and exasperating experience. Teachers can use their knowledge of poetry to help students overcome their fears and to introduce students to a kind of literacy they can get excited about. "Traditional" poets may seem inaccessible to students; therefore, this is an excellent opportunity to focus on poets from multicultural backgrounds that parallel the lives of many students in your class. In the quest to make poetry relevant to middle school students, it is important to take them out of their own lives to help them understand the magnitude of historical events and how those events still affect us today. For example, Nikki Giovanni (1968) wrote a poem in reaction to the funeral of Dr. Martin Luther King, Jr. entitled "The Funeral of Martin Luther King, Jr."

The Funeral of Martin Luther King, Jr.

His headstone read

FREE AT LAST, FREE AT LAST

But death is a slave's freedom

We seek the freedom of free men

And the construction of a world

Where Martin Luther King could have

Lived and preached non-violence

SOURCE: Giovanni, N. (1968). *Black feeling, Black talk, Black judgement.* New York: Morrow.

This poem gives language arts/reading teachers the opportunity to teach using two forms of literary criticism, intertextuality and new historicism, as the framework for a lesson. *Intertextuality* is the practice of studying one piece of literature in relation to another, and *new historicism* allows a reader to study a literary work in a historical context (Wood, 2006). Giovanni's line "FREE AT LAST, FREE AT LAST" links her poem directly to Dr. King's famous "I Have a Dream" speech, which in turn naturally leads to a study of the history behind the speech and King's death. This section allows students to read a poem using its place in history as a tool, rather than just relying on the poem itself to convey meaning. Studying these two texts together, the poem and the speech, is a valuable way to incorporate social studies and literature, specifically the civil rights movement and the life of Martin Luther King, Jr.

Teachers at the middle school level often examine reading materials, identifying new vocabulary words readers will need to comprehend, prior to reading activities. The teacher, or adult model, must decide which words are probably unfamiliar and in what ways they can be unlocked for meaning. The teacher or model then provides sample sentences that incorporate the new vocabulary terms/words and include culturally relevant contextual clues to their meaning. (Teachers or adult models should remember to not present new vocabulary words in isolation). For example, one vocabulary word that could be used is *freedom*. The teacher writes the following sentence on the board or chart tablet and reads it aloud to the class while underlining the focal word: "The wild animal had the <u>freedom</u> to roam in the forest." After reading, the teacher directs the readers to reread the sentence.

When eliciting the meaning of the underlined word, *freedom*, middle school teachers can stimulate readers' thinking processes by asking probing questions, such as these: What do you think *freedom* means as it is used here? Make an educated guess. Look for clues or hints in the sentence. Could *freedom* mean anything else in the sentence and make sense?

The teacher can now use the word in another sentence so the readers can experience it in a different context. Example: "The early American settlers left Europe so that they could experience religious <u>freedom</u>." The teacher can now ask readers to offer original sentences using the word *freedom*. Additional ideas to encourage middle school readers include the following:

- Use pictures and illustrations that are directly related to the material presented to provide added stimuli for readers having difficulty.
- Modify vocabulary to match readers' abilities.
- Spiral in prior learning to correlate present experiences to previously learned concepts and skills.
- Use the power of the arts—music, visual arts, drama, dance, and other movement—as practicing fluency can be made more fun by using the rhythm of a particular ethnic instrument or beat. For

example, a Russian tambourine might be used and a reader told to tap the tambourine for each word on a Dolch word list or content-related vocabulary list. Movement activities could also be incorporated, each movement representing a word, whereby middle school readers actually perform the material in some way, reinforcing learning through a multisensory approach.

- Add a concrete demonstration to accompany instruction by using specific examples.
- Utilize a variety of teaching modalities/multiple intelligence activities to present materials, information, or directions (e.g., visual, auditory, spatial, kinesthetic, mathematical, musical, inter/intrapersonal) suitable for middle school readers' developmental levels.
- Increase repetition to provide opportunities for performing tasks previously presented to ensure retention/fluency.
- Monitor reading and provide immediate feedback and support to inform readers of their rates of success as soon as possible after task completion/achieving standard.
- Adjust the method of evaluation in accordance with reader needs, especially by using fluency probes on selected practices periodically to check for word accuracy and speed.

Implement a Readers' Theater

Readers' theater is a strategy often used to show students how to give voice to a text and to engage reluctant or at-risk readers. It usually involves a group reading from a text without memorizing it or using props. As do young readers, middle school readers often love to perform in skits. Teachers can schedule such that readers rehearse and perform a script before an audience of peers or others, as purposefully created theater opportunities receive attention by inviting other readers, parents, and community members to the classroom.

A simple strategy to support fluency is to choose a familiar speech, skit, or poem and assign readers to roles/passages or lines. Advanced readers may begin the activity, modeling appropriate vocal tone and fluency. Teachers will target relevant dialogue as peers follow along with advanced readers. Then peers collectively respond with missing vocabulary words, using animation and mime. Readers focus their attention to see and hear the speech-to-print correspondence in repeated readers' theater opportunities to present the skit. For example, after repeated readings, readers reenact or retell aspects of various poems or stories with scaffolded materials, using poetry or stories from around the world, such as Dr. Martin Luther King's "I Have a Dream" speech.

After listening to the speech while simultaneously reading it, students can complete a graphic organizer that looks at (a) words that are unfamiliar to them, (b) the definitions of those words, and (c) the meanings of those words in context. This scaffolded activity will continue to build the students' capacity to learn new words, improve their fluency, and essentially improve overall comprehension.

Allow Engaged Time for Practice of Phonics and Other Fluency Prerequisite Skills

Readers learn to use phonics to decode and spell words as they receive time to build up speed and accuracy in their readings. In addition, readers learn other skills, including comprehension, grammar, reference, and study skills, that are useful to reading and writing.

Integrate Content and Interests to Increase Fluency

Teachers help to integrate content-specific themes, oral or written stories, expository or persuasive essays, and research report usage based on readers' backgrounds, interests, and independent reading or writing levels. For example, middle school teachers can use questioning (e.g., factual and analytical questions on Iran) and feedback techniques related to cultural or linguistic experiences (e.g., reinforcement through "Iranian food and dance") after reading about Iranian traditions and customs (O'Shea & O'Shea, 1994).

Direct Readers to Vocabulary-Building Skills

Readers learn meanings of new words though classwide oral readings, as well as by posting key words from books and thematic units on walls (word walls). Teachers can support middle school readers by directing them to participate in word sorts, word maps, and other brainstorming activities from the oral readings.

Direct Readers to Oral Language-Building Skills

Middle school readers can participate in oral language activities as they work in small groups, participate in conversations, and present oral reports. As they participate during read-alouds, mini lessons, and other oral presentations, reading fluency becomes integrated into speaking and listening activities.

Focus Readers on Spelling

Readers apply phonics, syllabication, and morphemic analysis skills to spell and sound out words. They learn to spell high-frequency words first and then other words that they need for reading fluency and writing through a variety of spelling activities, which may include weekly spelling tests. Spelling activities can use the computer to simulate popular video games, such as "Ms. Pac-Man," "Mario Brothers," or "Wheel of Fortune," or traditional games, such as "Bingo" or "Hang-Man." The key is to infuse them with culturally relevant themes to increase vocabulary and word awareness.

Engage Readers in an Oral Class Discussion After Previewing Specific Community or Global Issues From Media

Follow an oral discussion with a tape-recorded rereading of a magazine article, asking readers to focus on an understanding of different perspectives from the article. Have readers repeat in their own words a summary of the article to a nearby peer tutor, who may hold a different perspective on the article's meaning, providing immediate feedback on the summary's accuracy. For example, when readers from culturally and linguistically diverse backgrounds read an article with an important message (e.g., "Let's discuss varied reasons why the United States is involved in the war with Iraq."), teachers might direct the middle school readers to reread, then ask probing questions of a peer holding a different political viewpoint. Teachers could then conduct a whole-class discussion.

IMPROVING FLUENCY WITH ■ HIGH SCHOOL READERS

Students in middle school and high school "read to learn." Reading below grade level in the secondary grades can impair a student's success in other areas of school. The phrase "reading to learn versus learning to read" is typically used to describe the difference between reading in the secondary grades and reading in elementary school. In grades K–3, the focus of reading instruction is on teaching how to decode words. As students are taught skills in phonemic awareness, phonics, fluency, vocabulary, and comprehension, the emphasis is primarily on phonics and phonetic awareness.

As students move through the grade levels, they read to learn, utilizing the skills acquired through early grade instruction. They are required to read a variety of grade-level materials, from stories to textbooks and other items characteristic of various levels of critical thinking and comprehension. It is at the secondary level that the emphasis of instruction shifts to fluency, vocabulary, and comprehension (the skills needed to comprehend the varying materials). For instance, comprehension and critical thinking skills emphasized in the upper grades include paraphrasing authors' ideas, making predictions, making inferences, evaluating the accuracy of the information, identifying and interpreting the author's purpose, using research materials, and identifying bias. When students exhibit difficulties in fluency, for example, secondary reading tasks become insurmountable. And because reading is a requirement of learning in the secondary grades, falling behind in reading can negatively impact a student's success in other subject areas more so than during the elementary grades. Depending on a student's abilities, reading can either be a key or a barrier to math, English, social studies, and science.

Supporting the use of culturally and linguistically relevant text and other teaching materials (e.g., content area kits, reproductions across primary languages, Web sites devoted to cultural themes) helps high school at-risk readers to experience content area fluency through academic exercises. Teachers support understanding of and empathy with characters, settings, and content area themes by directly encouraging high school readers to make connections with other texts they have read and/or with their own experiences.

High school readers who have difficulties in decoding and word recognition skills (who are dysfluent) often are unable to read effortlessly. This lack of fluent reading tends to lower a reader's motivation to continue to read and limits the amount of reading practice. Limited practice results in poor vocabulary knowledge and comprehension. Ultimately, readers with fluency problems face poor academic achievement and underdeveloped literacy skills (Shippen, Simpson, & Crites, 2003). As this achievement gap widens, readers in all areas of academics, especially readers from CLD backgrounds, suffer (Ikpa, 2004).

Reading differences are seen most clearly in secondary classrooms, which tend to be content centered and rarely provide reading-centered instruction (Rinehart & Platt, 2004). With such challenges facing secondary-level readers, the provision of an intense, direct, and explicit intervention program in reading is critical to close the achievement gap (Foorman et al., 1997; Salinger, 2003).

Instructional strategies, such as teachers modeling and guiding readers to use spelling patterns, "chunks," and analogies to decode unfamiliar words, can support a wide range of content-specific exercises tailored for different types of high school readers' literacy enjoyment. Teacher-directed fluency instruction often helps readers to understand more complex text structures and content, increasing readers' understanding of how words operate to derive meaning and building fluency generalization.

High school readers who have failed to succeed in reading are capable of learning to read when they are offered sufficient time and intensity for interventions, as well as the appropriate instructional practices. When secondary-level readers of diverse backgrounds struggle with reading, teachers need to consider instruction in foundational skills with sensitivity to the cultural and linguistic experiences of those readers. Teachers can create classroom structures that provide more socially interactive environments and tap into the cultural and linguistic resources within readers' communities to connect school literacy practices with these readers' own histories and experiences. Using culturally relevant materials and methods is one way of engaging older readers and motivating them to continue the hard work needed to close the gap between them and their normally achieving peers.

Research has demonstrated both cognitive and affective benefits when learning contexts are responsive to readers' familiar home and community experiences (Ladson-Billings, 1995; Rist, 1971; Sheets, 1999). Effective practices include affirmation of ethnic identity, curricular emphasis on readers' cultural heritage, and classroom structures that promote peer-to-peer interaction and sharing of knowledge (Bailey & Boykin, 2001; Foster, Lewis, & Onofowora, 2003; Lee, 2001). The use of culturally relevant materials, including relevant literature and content area texts with multicultural themes and applications, helps to place diverse readers, their histories, and their experiences in the center of the learning process. Opportunities for readers to view themselves as sources of knowledge and valued members of the learning community are yet another. Finally, a climate of respect for cultural and linguistic diversity provides a motivating context for literacy learning (Cummins, 1986).

Culturally responsive pedagogy is not merely a matter of focusing on holidays or ethnic foods; rather, it is instruction integrated into the daily activities of the classroom (McCollin & O'Shea, 2005). The following strategies may help to increase reading fluency in high school readers.

Plan Before Prereading Activities

The teacher may briefly introduce the story, poem, or passage by providing historical references/background knowledge and introducing key vocabulary; some key illustrations, time lines, or characters may be highlighted. Learners are invited to predict the story from the book's cover, illustrations, and other clues. The teacher poses specific listening tasks, such as identifying a particular theme or the use of specific structures. These motivational strategies involve learners in the book/passage and help make text-to-self connections.

Use Reading Aloud Activities

One way to engage secondary students in a book, passage, or poem is to read aloud with expression. The teacher can also move slowly around the room; take time to show the pictures (if applicable); modify the language of the text as needed to facilitate comprehension; and pause occasionally for dramatic effect, to highlight new words or concepts, or to check for comprehension.

Analyze After Discussion and Review Activities

At the completion of the oral reading, the teacher should allow ample time for reflection and discussion. To encourage spontaneous reactions, ask, "What do you think?" or pose more specific questions to focus the discussion. It is also important to discuss the story elements or literary structures identified in the prereading stage. An oral comprehension check can serve as a review of the story and as an informal assessment.

To build the reading-writing connection, students can record their reflections in a journal and use critical thinking skills to respond to issues in the selection. They can copy the title, author, and date at the top of the page and then write briefly about their favorite part; how the story, book, passage, or poem made them feel; something they learned from the selection; or a similar incident that happened to them. They can share these reflections orally, as appropriate.

Use Multicultural Poetry and Folktales to Practice Fluency

A key is to locate poetry and folktales to which adolescents can relate and find meaningful. Teachers might consider using the poetry of Paul Laurence Dunbar (1895/1993), particularly "We Wear the Mask," a poem that looks at the issues of race in America. Such poetry has a universal appeal to young adults and contains a variety of literary devices that support fluency learning. For instance, playing an audio reading by the author would be an intriguing way to present this material. Readers could also invent their own poems using similar strategies and read them aloud to their classmates to practice their fluency. When concrete representation is paired with cultural themes, readers' interests may be piqued.

Teachers can also use literature selections, such as Ralph Ellison's *Invisible Man* (1947/1995; a classic novel of the experience of African Americans who are caught between what white society expects and how black society sees them), Joy Kogawa's *Itsuka* (1992; internment literature, which follows the life of a Japanese-Canadian woman who fights for compensation from the Canadian government for internment of citizens of Japanese descent during WWII), or Gary Soto's *Taking Sides* (1991/2003; Lincoln Mendoza feels his loyalties torn when he leaves the Hispanic inner city for a white suburban neighborhood), to help improve fluency in culturally concrete ways, as well as reinforce the existence of central themes across various cultures.

Play Word Games With Culturally and/or Content-Specific Language

Readers can create alliteration, rhymes, and other wordplay with content-related vocabulary. For example, sociorelevant vocabulary can be used: "Dusk demands daylight." These activities can easily be incorporated into daily high school routines prior to content area class initiation. They can be extended with repeated readings. For example, the teacher might provide a sentence clue to start and direct each reader to repeat the sentence, adding to the growing list of items that have been named. Items may be subject area-related words (e.g., math—square root, pi, circumference; social studies—war, peace, injustice, treaty; sciences—molecule, nucleus, mitochondria) in content area classes. Readers will naturally add items that are culturally familiar to them.

Use Repeated Readings

As with younger readers, in this strategy, high school readers practice repeated oral readings on the same text until a criterion is met, either for speed or accuracy or both (Samuels, 1997).

The use of independent-level text is recommended. With teacher assistance, readers can self-select literature of interest to them that reflects their cultural preferences and are at their independent reading levels. For example, *Children of the River* by Linda Crew (1989) offers students a young Cambodian woman's account of assimilating into a new culture. These pieces lend themselves well to repeated readings and may be at an appropriate reading level for some readers.

Implement a Readers' Theater With Multicultural Literature

Theater experiences are especially engaging for older readers. A story that can be divided into parts (or characters) is selected and read with parts assigned to each reader. Readers read their scripts orally for practice. Groups of readers might work on different sections of a young adult novel with multicultural themes, such as Walter Dean Myers's *Fallen Angels* (1988), a thought-provoking war story of young men who went to Vietnam for different reasons but ended up sharing the same dream. Sections of the story can be rewritten in the form of a screenplay so that it could be easily adapted to the readers' theater format. Additionally, Richard Wright's poem "Between the World and Me," a choreo-poem about a young person facing life-and-death choices, could be utilized to do comparative character studies and enhance fluency through repeated readings/performances for authentic audiences (Chapman, 1968/2001).

Use Partner Reading

Readers of diverse backgrounds often benefit from working together in pairs. Provide engaging materials that incorporate multicultural characters or themes and include role model authors from many cultures, such as Gloria Naylor, Ralph Ellison, Charles Johnson, Theodore Taylor, Tom Feelings, Ernest J. Gaines, Yoshiko Uchida, Joy Kogawa, and Sonia Sanchez. Teachers may ask each reader to read aloud connected text for five minutes. The higher-performing reader reads first, and then the lower-performing reader reads the same material. In this way, the second reader has the opportunity to hear the more capable reader decode unfamiliar words (Fuchs, Fuchs, & Kazdan, 1999).

Utilize Performance Arts in the Oral Tradition

Echo reading, choral reading, and antiphonal reading all have a history in the oral traditions of various cultures. For example, antiphonal reading is an adaptation of choral reading. In antiphonal reading, readers are divided into groups, and each group reads an assigned part, sometimes alternately and sometimes in unison (Miccinati, 1985). The manner of reading is cued by the placement of the text on the page. Rhymes, limericks, and Indian chants lend themselves especially well to this activity. Bombas, Afro-Puerto Rican songs associated with plantation workers in Puerto Rico, have an antiphonal or "call and response" style that can be utilized as well (McQuiston, O'Shea, & McCollin, 2007).

Provide Classroom Multicultural Experiences Using Literacy Themes Across the Curriculum

Readers can participate in small- or large-group literacy activities to enhance reading fluency across content area classrooms. Interdisciplinary teachers collaborate to reinforce concepts and skills, which become the focus of shared literacy activities in their specific content areas. For example, secondary teachers may choose the themes of "predicting outcomes and making inferences" in their large-group lessons during "Black history" or "Puerto Rican heritage" month. Shared reading experiences across content area activities reinforce diverse secondary readers' practice with different types of text and text content, as readers learn from one another to make predictions and inferences in shared curriculum assignments. Practicing a shared passage on joint homework, Web, or Internet assignments may make classroom follow-up to the interdisciplinary lessons nonthreatening, engaging, and enjoyable.

Use Classroom Heritages

By reading and then rereading passages on cultures from readers' heritages, they learn to discern key vocabulary and important concepts while gaining awareness of their own or others' cultural backgrounds. Readers can read faster and with fewer errors by rereading text until story content is familiar and meaningful. They then can create a class quilt, with a background of the books they have read and reread. Teachers can provide the opportunity to create fluency experiences that are integrated with relevant sociocultural themes from readers' heritages. The key is to target reading materials with relevant sociocultural themes and people (e.g., characters from ethnic backgrounds or historical themes relevant to community events and language experiences characteristic of readers' heritages) to support high school readers' fluency efforts.

Create an Oral History

Readers can create an oral history of their cultural and personal experiences using their own writings, including poetry, essays, song lyrics, reflective journals, and stories. They might also include oral readings from collections of diverse adolescent writings, such as *American Dragons: Twenty-Five Asian-American Voices* edited by Laurence Yep (1993), *Rising Voices: Writings of Young Native Americans* selected by Arlene B. Hirschfelder and Beverly R. Singer (1992), or *My Sisters' Voices: Teenage Girls of Color Speak Out* by Iris Jacob (2002). Such audio collages could be performed for parents and community members at a special event or digitally recorded and podcasted from a class weblog, or blog.

Teach High School Readers to Self-Monitor Their Reading Fluency

Many teachers assess for reading fluency by providing readers with opportunities for one-, three-, or five-minute timings of selected reading passages. Teachers then determine both the numbers of words read correctly (or incorrectly) in the timings and chart readers' performance. One variation is to have readers audiotape their independent readings and then listen to the recording while marking their own miscues on a copy of the text by placing a slash through omissions and substitutions. Readers perform three readings of the same selection and can chart their progress as their fluency improves. Another variation is for the teacher to mark phrase boundaries with slash marks to delineate meaningful chunks or phrases (Rasinski & Padak, 2004). Readers practice reading the marked text, then reread the same passage from an unmarked version.

■ REVISITING LATOYA

Latoya's IEP team scheduled an April meeting so that Mr. Murdock would have an opportunity to explain and interpret Latoya's achievement data collected since October. He led a discussion with Latoya's IEP team, suggesting that Latoya's attention and class behaviors were affected greatly by her oral reading. Mr. Murdock provided DIBELS charts that pinpointed Latoya's oral reading data. From these data, Mr. Murdock discussed how he had selected and used explicit practice throughout the year that targeted Latoya's oral reading speed, accuracy, and prosody.

Mr. Murdock's data monitoring supported a number of fluency strategies that helped Latoya's fluency achievement. Data showed that she responded best when the teacher modeled for her exactly how to sound out lists of words, especially familiar words from multicultural contexts. He explained to Mr. and Mrs. Washington that he often reminded Latoya to repeat accurately each word as he introduced and she practiced them. Mr. Murdock explained he would carefully select words and short passages and then ask Latoya to choose from a list of multicultural words with multiple syllables. After modeling how to say and differentiate the syllables/sounds, he would ask Latoya to clap out sounds in syllable singing games.

Mr. Murdock also presented data on Latoya's work with decodable stories in repeated readings. For example, he presented her work samples from a class activity in which students read and reread "The Ugly Duckling," a children's fairy tale, which he had modified with a cultural theme. Data showed that Latoya responded well when he changed the swan character in the fairy tale to a modern child of African-American descent. Mr. Murdock suggested that Latoya's accuracy and automaticity in reading unfamiliar words in the fairy tale helped Latoya's speed and accuracy with sound-spelling relationships, her oral reading prosody, while helping to build her sense of self-esteem.

Mr. Murdock's final data summary related to Latoya's partner reading experiences. Latoya was paired with two peers, Sally and Oscar. All took periodic turns reading aloud to each other. Latoya's data on partner reading supported her increased oral reading gains.

MOVING ON ■

In this chapter, we discussed that fluency building can be integrated into school curricula as teachers work toward increasing the literacy growth of readers from CLD backgrounds. Fluency skills receive attention when teachers consider instructional grouping and specific fluency needs as they provide readers with a variety of opportunities to read relevant texts faster and with fewer errors. Increased individual and small-group opportunities to read orally or silently can lead to large-group classroom discussions on ideas generated from the text.

Extended activities designed to generalize increasing vocabulary and reading comprehension skills can target familiar reading practice in culturally and linguistically responsive texts, oral or written reflections on text meaning and comprehension, and auditory or verbal comprehension reviews. Concurrently, as warranted, secondary teachers can plan, implement, and evaluate the effectiveness of directed discussions on text typography (e.g., punctuation and paragraph structure), integrated with subject area content knowledge. When vocabulary and comprehension skills increase across secondary school content areas, teachers then cue readers to self-monitor and self-correct text with phrasing and speed (Cunningham et al., 1998; Lyon et al., 1997; Moats, 2001). Consistent use of such explicit fluency-building activities encourages readers from CLD backgrounds to become tenacious readers.

5

Improving Vocabulary

Shobana Musti-Rao, Renee O. Hawkins,
Gwendolyn Cartledge, and Cheryl Utley

CHAPTER OBJECTIVES

In this chapter we will

- discuss the importance of developing a strong vocabulary to understanding the meaning of text within a given context;
- identify research related to vocabulary instruction and its role in becoming a competent reader; and
- provide examples of culturally and linguistically responsive practices important to primary, middle, and high school readers.

"LOST IN TRANSLATION"

Jasmine Johnson, a quiet and friendly ninth grader, became anxious at the end of the second week of school when her language arts teacher, Ms. Clark, announced a quiz on the book chapter they had just completed. She did not attend school on the day of the quiz and stayed home with the excuse of having a stomachache. Jasmine had missed school on three different days when quizzes were scheduled. The teacher did not notice this coincidence in absences and quiz days until she was preparing the grade roster for parent-teacher conference night at the end of first term. Ms. Clark had noticed that Jasmine was a bit reserved in her classes and was not one of the students who would volunteer to read or answer questions. Ms. Clark attributed Jasmine's behavior to her quiet personality. On several occasions during in-class activities, Ms. Clark approached Jasmine and asked if she needed any help, and Jasmine always thanked her teacher but refused any help. Jasmine managed to turn in homework on time. Although her writing lacked the diction of a ninth grader performing at grade level, her work contained minimal grammatical and spelling errors.

Some family disorganization had recently forced Jasmine to leave her mother's home and live with her aunt, Elizabeth, who became her legal guardian. Aunt Elizabeth was a college graduate with a professional position. When she tried to help Jasmine with her homework, she discovered that Jasmine was a poor reader and had an extremely limited vocabulary. School evaluations confirmed Aunt Elizabeth's observations and concerns: along with other problems, Jasmine's reading progress was greatly hampered by her poor vocabulary. Aunt Elizabeth and the school personnel noted that Jasmine's speaking vocabulary was equally poor. This was exacerbated by Jasmine's preference to use an urban dialect and speech pattern, especially when conversing with her peers. This meant that Jasmine often purposely left off endings from words (e.g., gettin' instead of getting), deliberately used nonstandard grammar, and chose to use slang instead of standard terms. Although teens often use informal language, especially among peers, Aunt Elizabeth and Jasmine's teachers concluded that Jasmine was not getting enough exposure to more formal language to boost her receptive and expressive vocabulary sufficiently. Her existing classes were inadequate for Jasmine's needs; she needed more explicit vocabulary instruction.

WHAT IS VOCABULARY?   ■

Vocabulary is the ability to understand and use words to acquire and convey meaning. Vocabulary, or word knowledge, plays a key role in the development of reading (National Reading Panel, 2000) to the extent that learning, as a language-based activity, is said to be fundamentally dependent on vocabulary knowledge (Baker, Simmons, & Kame'enui, 1998). As students learn to decode words and read, the intersection of language and literacy allows them to map the words encountered in print to the oral language present in their repertoire. Vocabulary knowledge is one of the most significant predictors of reading comprehension and, in some respects, is a form of comprehension, albeit at the individual word level. Vocabulary knowledge can be thought of as a "bank of words" that individuals possess, and for the bank account to grow exponentially, it depends on the amount of reading that occurs.

Poor vocabulary knowledge is linked to poor reading outcomes for many students. In a review of the related empirical research, Joshi (2005) notes the relationship between meaningful vocabulary development and reading, indicating the importance of vocabulary to reading comprehension. While limited vocabularies impede reading performance, it is also observed that poor readers are less likely to grow their vocabularies due to the fact that they tend to read fewer books with less challenging vocabularies (Joshi, 2005). The phenomenon of the poor getting poorer is particularly relevant for at-risk students who come to school with substantial deficits in word knowledge that are difficult to remediate. Students from low socioeconomic status (SES) backgrounds may be exposed to 50 percent fewer words than students of less educationally disadvantaged backgrounds (Hart & Risley, 1995). From the start of schooling, these students are at a disadvantage. They are limited in the level of difficulty of the material they can read and are, therefore, exposed to less new vocabulary than peers. As a result, the vocabulary knowledge gap between lower and higher income students continues to grow across the grades (White, Graves, & Slater, 1989).

Types of Vocabulary

Vocabulary can be categorized according to the context in which it is used. In general, the two general and widely known forms of vocabulary are receptive vocabulary and expressive vocabulary. *Receptive vocabulary* refers to the vocabulary of words that we can understand when they are presented in text or when we listen to others speak. *Expressive* or *productive vocabulary* refers to the words we use to convey thought in writing or in speaking to others. Table 5.1 lists the different types of vocabulary.

TABLE 5.1	Types of Vocabulary

- *Receptive vocabulary:* Words that the reader can understand when seeing them in print or listening to someone speak
- *Expressive or productive vocabulary:* Words that the reader uses in writing or in speech
- *Oral vocabulary:* Expressive vocabulary containing words that the reader uses in speaking
- *Reading vocabulary:* Words that the reader recognizes or uses in print
- *Sight-word vocabulary:* Words that the reader identifies and reads from previous exposure (or memory) without having to decode them
- *Academic vocabulary:* Words with specific meanings that are central to the understanding of content area
- *Writing vocabulary:* Expressive vocabulary with words that the reader uses in writing composition

■ APPROACHES TO TEACHING VOCABULARY

Despite the unequivocal evidence that suggests a connection between vocabulary knowledge and acquisition of reading comprehension, current reading intervention practices deemphasize vocabulary instruction (Jitendra, Edwards, Sacks, & Jacobson, 2004; Tam, Heward, & Heng, 2006). Blachowicz, Fisher, Ogle, and Watts-Taffe (2006) argue for the need for vocabulary instruction that is a "comprehensive, integrated, schoolwide approach to vocabulary in reading and learning" (p. 526). In such a setting, vocabulary becomes a core consideration in all grades and all content areas across the school day, and teachers share a common philosophy using research-validated practices. Blachowicz et al. also observe that effective vocabulary instruction has certain characteristics that are applicable across teaching contexts:

- Learners are actively involved in the generation of word meanings rather than being passive receptors of information.

- Instruction provides both definitional and contextual information about the words to be learned as well as multiple exposures and opportunities to use them (p. 528).

Due to the wide range of differences in the literature on what entails vocabulary instruction, the National Reading Panel's (NRP) 2000 report included only implicit evidence. Based on a meta-analysis, the NRP provided a taxonomy of methods for vocabulary instruction, which are presented in Table 5.2. The five main approaches to vocabulary instruction identified by the NRP include indirect instruction, explicit instruction, multimedia methods, capacity methods, and association methods. Despite the variety indicated in these methods, most vocabulary instruction can be understood as either indirect or direct/explicit in form.

TABLE 5.2	The National Reading Panel's (2000) Taxonomy of Vocabulary Instruction

---

- *Explicit/direct instruction:* Students are given definitions of words and external cues to connect words with meaning or specific algorithms for determining meaning.
- *Indirect instruction:* Students are exposed to language- and word-rich environments and infer meaning of words from context.
- *Multimedia methods:* Instruction incorporates other media in addition to text, such as semantic maps and graphic organizers.
- *Capacity methods:* Instruction builds automaticity for other reading activities to free cognitive capacity for vocabulary learning.
- *Association methods:* Students are encouraged to make connections between words they know and words that are unfamiliar.

Indirect Instruction

Through the indirect approach, students learn new words and build their repertoire (a) when they hear words in conversation, (b) by listening to adults reading books aloud, and (c) by independent reading activities. This approach is based on the assumption that students will infer the meaning of unfamiliar words encountered while reading (NRP, 2000). Proponents of the indirect approach emphasize "literacy-rich" environments where children learn to read as a result of being exposed to and enjoying the written word. Such language- and word-rich environments, which contain both narrative and expository reading materials, are said to promote both incidental and intentional word learning and motivate students to learn more words on their own (Blachowicz et al., 2006). For indirect instruction to be effective, teachers need to engage students in conversations about word meanings and encourage students to use the new words in both oral and written forms. Although the benefits of wide reading include the incidental development of vocabulary knowledge, indirect approaches have some inherent shortcomings when teaching students with poor vocabularies and learning difficulties.

Indirect approaches fail to incorporate the teaching urgency needed for struggling readers to catch up to grade-level peers (Coyne, Simmons,

Kame'enui, & Stoolmiller, 2004; Musti-Rao & Cartledge, in press). That is, struggling readers and students at risk fail to engage in the volume of reading needed to make a significant difference in vocabulary growth and reading ability (Baker et al., 1998; Jitendra et al., 2004). With declining literacy levels nationwide, researchers and practitioners have begun to ask questions about the optimal approach to improve vocabulary knowledge. A direct approach to teaching word meanings provides the reader with strategies for deriving the meaning from words, as the words occur in context, independently.

Explicit and Direct Instruction

If the goal is to promote vocabulary development, then any instructional approach should ensure that students learn independent strategies for deriving the meaning from words they come across while reading (Anderson & Nagy, 1991). Direct instruction of strategies increases the likelihood that students will become better independent word learners. Research estimates on vocabulary growth suggest that students in the primary grades learn about 3,000 new words per year, or approximately 8 words per day (Baker et al., 1998). According to Stahl and Shiel (1999), students can be taught 300–400 new word meanings with direct and explicit instruction. Therefore, words selected for instruction should not only enhance comprehension but also provide functionality in using the words frequently in the future.

Direct instruction in word meaning should use the target word in context, providing the student with both contextual and definitional knowledge (Stahl, 1986). Students should be encouraged to engage in group discussions of the words and their meanings. Such active processing of meaning not only makes students more aware of words they encounter but also facilitates future vocabulary development. Finally, direct instruction in word meanings should include multiple exposures to the word beyond the teaching context. According to Stahl, both "drill and practice" (i.e., teaching definition of words repeatedly) and "breadth of knowledge" (i.e., teaching words in different contexts or settings) significantly improve vocabulary growth and comprehension.

Importance of Depth of Word Knowledge

An important factor to consider when designing vocabulary instructional programs is the depth of word knowledge. Based on short-term memory research, depth of word knowledge is based on the theory that "deep processing" of information results in better retention and recall than of information that is processed superficially. Stahl (1986) defined deep processing as "either making more connection between new and known information (or relating the word to more information than the student already knows) or spending more of one's mental effort on learning" (p. 664). Baker, Simmons, and Kame'enui (1998) contend that programs that address levels of word knowledge have the potential to emphasize a range of approaches that focus on individual words and their meaning.

Cronbach's 1942 work, as cited in Graves (1986), suggested five dimensions in describing the depth of word knowledge: generalization, application, breadth, precision, and availability. The most basic level of word knowledge is *generalization,* where the student knows the definition of the word. At the *application* level, the student is able to use the word appropriately in a given situation. *Breadth* of word knowledge requires the student to recall the different meanings of the word, and having *precision* requires the student to recognize situations in which the word does or does not apply. Finally, *availability* refers to retrieving the word and using it in discourse. Baumann and Kame'enui's (1991) simplified version of Cronbach's classification into three levels of word knowledge may help in determining the strategy to be used to facilitate improvement in vocabulary. The three levels of word knowledge are presented in Table 5.3.

TABLE 5.3   Levels of Word Knowledge

> - *Associative knowledge:* The student is able to connect a new word with a specific definition or a single context.
> - *Comprehension knowledge*: The student is able to use the definition of the word to find antonyms and classify words into categories.
> - *Generative knowledge:* The student is able to state the meaning of the word in his or her own words or use the new word in an original sentence (Baumann & Kame'enui, 1991).

RESEARCH-VALIDATED STRATEGIES FOR VOCABULARY INSTRUCTION

The decision of what strategy to use to teach vocabulary knowledge should depend on the goals of instruction. For example, if the goal is to teach specific words to facilitate comprehension of a given text, then strategies pertaining to individual word knowledge are needed. If the goal is to increase the students' generalized reading and comprehension, then students need to be taught independent strategies that help them analyze the word and derive meaning from context. Explicit vocabulary instructional methods that have shown to improve word knowledge and reading comprehension include (a) the key word method, (b) multiple exposures to vocabulary, (c) instruction across contexts, (d) preinstruction of vocabulary words, (e) computer-based instruction, and (f) restructuring the task.

The *key word method* is a mnemonic technique for learning new words. The students are taught a concrete key word that sounds like or makes up a part of the target word. The key word is used to create an interactive link between the target word and its definition. For example, for the word *cantankerous,* the key word would be *can,* and the interactive image would be an angry person crushing a can of soda. The key word method is known to strengthen the associative link between the word and its definition and has shown to enhance recall of information (NRP, 2000; Stahl & Fairbanks, 1986).

Mastery of vocabulary knowledge and maximization of vocabulary growth are enhanced by *multiple exposures to vocabulary* where students encounter words often and in many contexts. This approach includes repeated readings of a story or repeated exposures to target words in a story.

Vocabulary *instruction across contexts* extends beyond the language arts and includes activities and opportunities to encounter target words in various authentic contexts or settings. Vocabulary instruction in content areas can provide a richer context for building a broader vocabulary and aid in mastery of content area material.

Teaching of vocabulary words prior to having students read material containing the targeted words is known as *preinstruction* (Roberts, 1988; Ryder & Graves, 1994).

Students are explicitly taught target words and their definitions. Such instruction prior to reading makes the initial and subsequent readings smoother and easier to comprehend. Researchers have found that pre-teaching vocabulary improves both vocabulary acquisition and comprehension (cf. NICHD, 2000a, 2000b).

Although the research is still limited to a few studies, there is preliminary evidence that *computer-based instruction* can contribute to significant vocabulary gains (Davidson, Elcock, & Noyes, 1996; Heller, Sturner, Funk, & Feezor, 1993). Computer instruction can complement traditional instruction by providing additional practice opportunities for students. In addition, by offering multiple media, computer instruction may have significant positive effects on vocabulary development beyond those resulting from traditional instruction.

Restructuring and sometimes simplifying tasks is often necessary to ensure that students understand what they are required to do and to promote vocabulary learning. Methods may include substituting easier words for harder words, providing redundant information, and explicitly teaching how to identify and create a good definition (Kame'enui, Carnine, & Freschi, 1982; Schwartz & Raphael, 1985). Table 5.4 shows the characteristics of effective vocabulary instruction.

TABLE 5.4   Characteristics of Effective Vocabulary Instruction Across Grade Levels

---

- Vocabulary instruction is integrated within the context of the lesson with 20- to 30-minute weekly lessons for enrichment activities.
- Prior to the lesson, teachers provide explicit instruction of a limited number of new vocabulary words (such as technical vocabulary) that relate to the central ideas to be taught, using a brief definition, synonym, or association.
- Teachers create a verbal environment and provide students with multiple opportunities to use words in different contexts.
- Teachers provide instruction in both definitional and contextual knowledge of the word for determining word meanings.
- Teachers teach independent word-learning strategies and encourage and facilitate wide reading to develop vocabulary independently.
- Teachers model how to use semantic and syntactic clues to determine meanings of new words or concepts in sentences or paragraphs.

SOURCE: Adapted from University of Texas Center for Reading and Language Arts (2002). *Enhancing vocabulary instruction for secondary students* (rev.). Retrieved October 28, 2007, from www.texasreading .org/downloads/secondary/guides/2003enhancVocab_bw.pdf

ASSESSMENT OF VOCABULARY KNOWLEDGE ■

In contrast to the emphasis in the research on vocabulary development and instruction, there is relatively little to no discussion on reliable and valid ways to assess vocabulary growth. Since a person's receptive vocabulary is larger than his or her expressive vocabulary, any vocabulary assessment can only provide an estimate of vocabulary knowledge. An issue consistent in the research is the inability to document the effects of vocabulary instruction beyond text-specific comprehension gains to transfer measures (i.e., showing transfer of gains beyond the texts used for teaching the words to novel texts).

One explanation points to the inadequacy of the assessment measures that are used to assess vocabulary growth. With the various types of vocabularies (e.g., receptive, expressive, listening, reading, writing), what is it that we want to measure? There is a mismatch between what we teach and how we measure vocabulary and comprehension. For example, many of the vocabulary assessments emphasize the receptive dimension of vocabulary. Students are given a sentence or passage to read and asked to find a synonym or antonym of the italicized or underlined target word. In some cases, students are asked to match the word with its definition. In very rare instances is the productive aspect of vocabulary measured, where assessments measure the extent to which target words are used in speaking or writing (Pearson, Hiebert, & Kamil, 2007).

Vocabulary-matching tasks have been used as progress indicators in content areas. Researchers have found that vocabulary matching is a valid indicator of content area performance, especially at the middle school and high school levels (Espin & Deno, 1993, 1994–1995; Espin & Foegen, 1996).

Extending the research to an actual content area classroom, Espin, Shinn, & Busch (2005) found that performance on student-read vocabulary matching probes resulted in growth trajectories that were reliable and valid indicators of social studies performance. Vocabulary-matching tasks are one way to evaluate vocabulary knowledge that has some empirical support. In a matching task, the individual is required to identify the correct definition from several options for a particular stimulus word. In reverse, the individual could be asked to identify the correct word for the definition provided.

Pearson and colleagues (2007) suggest that the assessments used to measure vocabulary are insensitive to what we are trying to measure. Several issues compromise the reliability and validity of current assessment measures. First, the types of text used in assessment differ considerably from the types of text used during instruction. Second, words differ in meaning based on the context in which they are used. Therefore, measuring a student's understanding of isolated word meanings may not necessarily indicate the student's understanding of the meaning of the word when it is used in a different context. Third, a theoretical framework to guide the selection of words used in instruction and assessment does not exist. Finally, due to the inherent nature of the norm-referenced assessments, we gather information on how a student performs in relation to a comparative population rather than information on "any identifiable domain or corpus of words" (p. 288).

In an attempt to address several of these concerns that beset current assessments, the National Assessment of Educational Progress (NAEP) has proposed a framework for assessing vocabulary. Although this framework awaits empirical validation, the 2009 NAEP assessment proposes a systematic assessment of vocabulary with a potential for a vocabulary subscore. The assessment purports to measure *meaning vocabulary*, defined as the application of understanding word meanings as it relates to the comprehension of the passage. There will be sufficient items on the assessment to provide reliable and valid data for analysis. The NAEP framework acknowledges the differences in vocabulary present in different types of text and makes a distinction between vocabulary loads present in literary and informational texts.

■ TEACHING PRIMARY-LEVEL READERS FROM DIVERSE BACKGROUNDS

Vocabulary development begins as early as the first year of life, when infants and toddlers become more aware of their surroundings and begin to communicate with adults. There is a strong relationship between language development and literacy acquisition in school (Cohen & Byrnes, 2007). Just as children differ considerably in their understanding of the phonologic nuances of language, they also differ in the volume of vocabularies they bring to school. Vocabulary development becomes a critical factor in the school success of children from culturally and linguistically diverse homes. These students are less likely to speak standard English (Talbert-Johnson, 2004), and many children from culturally and linguistically diverse homes enter kindergarten with insufficient preliteracy experiences and oral language skills to facilitate classroom learning (Musti-Rao & Cartledge, in press).

In a longitudinal study, Hart and Risley (1995) found significant differences in the vocabulary development of economically disadvantaged children and their more affluent peers. It is documented that in a domain of 19,050 words, disadvantaged first graders knew half as many words (2,900 words) as middle-class first graders (5,800 words) (Graves, 1986). Children from economically disadvantaged homes begin the schooling process behind their affluent peers, evidencing a slower rate of vocabulary growth during the formative, primary years (Blachowicz et al., 2006). Chapter 2 of this volume highlighted the importance of explicit instruction in phonological development and the alphabetic principle. Vocabulary knowledge is also correlated to the development of other early literacy skills (e.g., phonemic awareness) and, hence, needs to be targeted for instruction as early as kindergarten or preschool (Coyne et al., 2004).

In a study of root word acquisition, Biemiller and Slonim (2001) estimated that children acquire about 5,200 root words at the end of Grade 2, or about 2.2 words per day starting from 1 year of age. In other words, most of the vocabulary differences among children occur before Grade 3. The importance of fostering vocabulary development in the preschool and early primary years cannot be overstated. Concerted efforts using a teacher-centered approach can increase vocabulary prior to Grade 2. To this end, the goal of vocabulary instruction in the primary grades should be to narrow the widening gap that exists between children with rich and poor vocabularies and to change vocabulary growth trajectories as early as possible.

Shared storybook reading provides a convenient forum for nonreaders to be exposed to new words within the context of the stories being read and from related oral language interactions between the adult and children (Coyne et al., 2004). In a seven-month study, Coyne and colleagues randomly assigned 96 kindergarteners to one of three intervention groups: storybook group, phonological and alphabetic skills group, and a control group that received instruction from a commercial reading program. Students in the storybook group received 108 half-hour lessons, with 120 target words selected from 40 children's storybooks. Primary analysis of the study indicated that students who received the storybook intervention that involved explicit vocabulary instruction showed greater growth on measures of vocabulary than did students in the other two groups. Particularly, the storybook intervention was found to be differentially more effective for students who started with smaller vocabularies than students in the control group. In summary, storybook reading activities that rely on students' learning new words incidentally are less effective than similar activities that are complemented with explicit instruction of word meanings within the context of the stories read. Table 5.5 describes some activities that make shared storybook readings more effective.

TABLE 5.5   Shared Storybook Reading Activities for Primary Grades

- *Use engaging books with relevance to students' cultures.* Select books with attractive pictures and appealing stories that will hold children's attention and interest.
- *Select target words for explicit instruction.* Select target words that will not only increase comprehension of the text but also build on students' prior knowledge.
- *Engage in rich dialogic discussion.* Scaffold instruction and students' understanding of the story by asking questions, adding information, and allowing students to share their own experiences. Encourage students to respond actively to the story elements and prompt them to increase the sophistication of their descriptions of the pictures or characters in the book.
- *Use clear and consistent wording.* Provide students with both definitional and contextual information on word meanings that is clear and unambiguous. Model the use of the target words in multiple contexts.
- *Reinforce new vocabulary learning.* Provide students with several opportunities to use the newly learned words during the lesson. Give them ideas and incentives to use the words in settings outside of the lesson in various contexts.
- *Read multiple times.* Revisit a previously read story by asking students to retell the story or parts of the story. Provide illustrations of the story and engage in discussions about the story with students.
- *Engage in performance-oriented readings.* Engage in little talk during book reading; rather, keep most of the talk before and after the reading. Start with an extended introduction to the book. Read the book with minimal interruptions. Engage in follow-up discussions where you either ask the students to reconstruct the story or relate the story to their own life experiences.
- *Read with smaller groups of students.* Arrange your classroom environment such that you are able to read to small groups of five to six students at one time. Solicit the help of an instructional assistant, reading teacher, parent, or adult volunteers to run similar reading groups or work on other activities with the rest of your students (Blachowicz et al., 2006; Coyne et al., 2004; Dickinson & Smith 1994; Whitehurst, Arnold, Epstein, Angell, Smith, et al., 1994).

For culturally and linguistically diverse (CLD) learners, it is especially important to use authentic stories that emphasize the students' backgrounds, interests, and experiences. Avoid making assumptions about the students' background knowledge. Many commonplace events or concepts may not be part of the experiential or language repertoire of CLD learners, particularly those from low-income families. Students need many opportunities to use these words, using them in context and personalizing the words in their personal stories, songs, games, and so forth.

Relatively simple interventions that employ explicit and direct instruction can improve reading outcomes for struggling readers. For example, word walls, consisting of high-frequency sight-words, are a common feature in many primary classrooms (i.e., K–3). Often teachers introduce as few as five sight words each week with limited connections made to words and their meaning in context. Children from vocabulary-impoverished backgrounds will need many opportunities to respond to these words within meaningful and varied contexts. One instructional format found effective for increasing the sight-word vocabulary of low-achieving CLD learners is peer tutoring (Al-Hassan, 2003; Kourea, Cartledge, & Musti-Rao, 2007). Peer tutoring, a research-based instructional strategy, is an effective teaching tool in which students are trained to serve as tutors and tutees and provide individualized instruction. Kourea and colleagues used total class peer tutoring with their urban learners and found that five of the six targeted students made substantial increases in their sight-word vocabularies as compared to their performance when participating in traditional teacher-led classroom instruction.

O'Donnell, Weber, and McLaughlin (2003) offered another model of systematic vocabulary instruction to improve the reading fluency and comprehension of a ten-year-old English language learner (ELL). The researchers selected key words in reading passages believed to be unfamiliar to the student or likely to be difficult for the student to define or pronounce. Prior to reading the passage, the researchers reviewed the definitions of the target words and asked the student questions to determine if the student understood the word meanings. The student also had the opportunity to ask questions about each of the words. Following this vocabulary instruction, the researcher read the passage to the student, and then the student read the passage aloud. Finally, the student answered comprehension questions about what was read. The researchers concluded this explicit vocabulary instruction to be a viable means for improving the reading performance of ELL students.

In another example, Burns, Dean, and Foley (2004) observed that explicit instruction of word meanings prior to reading a passage containing the targeted words increased the reading fluency and comprehension of third- and fourth-grade students with learning disabilities.

In addition to systematic, explicit instruction, the following are sample promising activities that teachers may use to enhance the vocabulary knowledge of primary-grade students.

- *Play "Bring a Word to School" game.* Ask children (in kindergarten and first grade) to bring a word that they heard while watching their favorite movie/TV show. Write down the word the student brings and ask if the student knows the meaning. Describe the meaning of the word to the rest of the students and ask them to use it in a sentence. Model the use of the words during instructional routines and activities throughout the day. For example, after watching the movie *The Lion King* several times at home, a kindergarten student brings the word *responsibility.* The teacher probes students' knowledge of the word's meaning, provides a simplified definition of the word, and uses the word several times during the day.

- *Use choral responding.* When introducing new words and their meanings, facilitate active student responding by asking students to repeat the word.
- *Engage in wordplay.* As students in primary grades develop awareness of sounds of letters and words (i.e., phonological awareness), engage in wordplay activities where students get the opportunity to provide words that rhyme, provide a synonym or antonym, and categorize words.

Some CLD learners may have difficulty with activities such as bringing to school novel words obtained from television or other such sources. Alternatively, teachers might use brief video clips that are attractive for children to watch and identify unknown words. The class would daily identify two or three new words, which are put into the class word bank. The words are projected with some type of mnemonic (e.g., the word *responsibility* might be accompanied by a picture of a child picking up toys to show the child being responsible). Each day, children would go through their bank of vocabulary words for which they have developed songs, sentences, and mnemonics.

TEACHING MIDDLE SCHOOL-LEVEL READERS FROM DIVERSE BACKGROUNDS

As students transition from the primary grades to middle school, the cognitive demands of the content areas increase at a rapid pace. Students are required to build a large repertoire of academic vocabularies to understand information provided in textbooks, often used as the primary instructional tool in most science, social studies, and mathematics classrooms. Content area textbooks have been criticized as being too difficult to read with too much information and as offering limited guidance for teachers (Hedrick, Harmon, & Linerode, 2004). Vocabulary instruction at the middle school level should not only focus on building students' definitional knowledge but also increase their conceptual knowledge by providing multiple exposures to word meaning within and outside of context (Stahl & Fairbanks, 1986).

A four-dimensional, empirically validated middle-grade vocabulary program, as recommended by Graves (2000), includes (a) independent reading to expand vocabulary knowledge, (b) instruction in individual words, (c) independent word-learning strategies, and (c) word consciousness. While some methods may be more effective than others, research generally supports the efficacy of using multiple strategies over any single strategy (Stahl & Fairbanks, 1986).

Baumann, Edwards, Boland, Olejnik, and Kame'enui (2003) studied the effects of morphemic and contextual (MC) analysis vocabulary instruction and textbook vocabulary (TV) instruction on 157 fifth-grade students. The interventions were integrated into the fifth-grade social studies curriculum, which included U.S. history. The TV group students received content-specific vocabulary instruction, whereas the MC group students received instruction in morphemic and contextual analysis strategies. The results of the study supported the efficacy of teaching multiple strategies that allow students to derive meaning from novel words in content area texts. Although the students in the TV group were more successful at learning words in the text-book, the MC group students were better able to infer meanings from novel words. There was no difference on comprehension or social studies learning between the two groups. Table 5.6 illustrates some steps teachers can use to teach students how to use morphemic analysis to learn word meanings.

TABLE 5.6   Steps in Morphemic Analysis for Teachers

1. Introduce the concept of breaking down words into morphemes (e.g., prefixes and suffixes). The teacher says, "Some words can be broken down into smaller parts that have meaning. These small parts are called morphemes. If you know the meanings of the smaller parts, then you can figure out the meaning of the whole word. For example, the word *interstate* can be broken down into *inter* and *state*. If you know that *inter* means 'between,' then you can figure out that *interstate* means 'between two states.'"

2. Introduce one morpheme and its meaning. For example, "The word *inter* means 'between.'"

3. Provide students with several examples of words containing the new prefix and "think aloud" about what the words mean. For example, "The word *international* can be broken down into two parts: *inter* and *national.* The word *national* means 'person of a specific country' or 'something from a specific country.' The word *international* means 'carried on between or among nations. '" Repeat this step with other words: *intersection, interchange,* and so on.

4. Provide students with several nonexamples of words containing the new prefix—that is, words that begin with the letters of the prefix but where the rule does not apply. Examples would be *interior* and *interest.* Discuss why these words cannot be used for morphemic analysis.

5. Encourage students to find new words in their various readings that contain the newly introduced prefix and ask them to maintain a word bank.

6. Periodically review the words students have collected and revisit previously learned morphemes.

Many words have multiple meanings, and it becomes a daunting task for a teacher to teach every single word and its meaning. Teaching students multiple meanings to words increases the students' word consciousness—that is, the awareness that words have multiple meanings and that the meanings can change from one context to another (Blachowicz et al., 2006). In an attempt to study the effects of contextually based multiple-meaning vocabulary instruction, Nelson and Stage (2007) randomly assigned 238 third- and fifth-grade students to two groups. One group received contextually based multiple-meaning vocabulary instruction embedded in the regular language arts instruction, and the other group received the standard language arts instruction (i.e., nonspecific treatment group). The contextually based multiple-meaning intervention included a systematic multiple-step, two-day lesson sequence in which 36 words as well as 3 related words per meaning were taught over a four-month period. Students with low initial vocabulary and comprehension achievement who received the intervention showed statistically significant gains in both vocabulary knowledge and reading comprehension skills in comparison to students with average to high initial achievement in both dependent measures. The study highlighted the difference in effects of vocabulary instruction as a result of varying ability levels among students.

Strategies and tips for vocabulary development for CLD learners at the middle school level include the following.

- *Teach multiple meanings of words.* In the case of words with multiple meanings, introduce the different meanings of the word that fall into different semantic categories (e.g., verb, noun, adjective) based on context.
- *Teach use of dictionaries.* Although this is a more traditional method to increasing vocabulary knowledge, teach students how to use dictionaries and other references aids to understand the meaning of words. Particularly, teach students how to use dictionaries available on the Internet, providing students with endless possibilities to learn new words. For example, Web sites like Dictionary.com (http://dictionary.reference.com) allow for word searches that result in multiple meanings, antonyms and synonyms, and use of the word in a sentence, providing a context to understanding the meaning.
- *Engage students in reciprocal peer tutoring.* After explicit instruction on target vocabulary words, allow students to practice the words and their meanings using the peer-tutoring strategy. Students assume roles of tutor and tutee and instruct each other on the meaning of the word and how the word can be used in a sentence. Refer to Cartledge and Lo (2006) for a more detailed description on how to set up and train students in peer tutoring. Figure 5.1 illustrates the flash cards used for peer tutoring.

FIGURE 5.1   Peer Tutoring Flash Cards for Vocabulary Practice

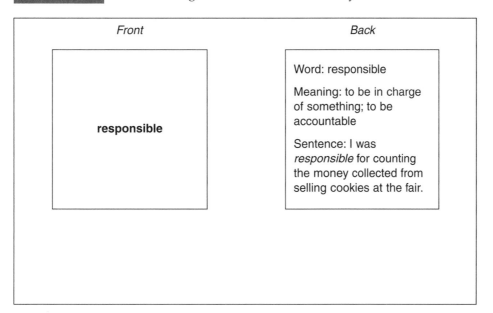

■ TEACHING HIGH SCHOOL-LEVEL READERS FROM DIVERSE BACKGROUNDS

The need for vocabulary development becomes an even more critical issue at the high school level when students need to acquire the content of the secondary curriculum. Many students from CLD backgrounds who read below grade level tend not to read in sufficient volume to enable them to bridge existing racial and socioeconomic vocabulary gaps. Increasing their academic and technical vocabularies for content area knowledge requires that students understand word origins (e.g., Greek, Latin) and their meanings and derivatives (e.g., prefixes, root words, suffixes).

Formal curriculums for vocabulary development at the secondary level are rare. One exception is the Reading is FAME remedial curriculum implemented at Girls and Boys Town, which incorporates many different evidence-based instructional strategies to improve the vocabulary knowledge and reading comprehension of struggling adolescent readers (Curtis & Longo, 2001). Vocabulary words are taught both in isolation (e.g., prereading vocabulary activities) and in context (e.g., applying word meanings to understand reading material). Students are provided multiple, repeated exposure to the words in a variety of contexts and engage in a variety of tasks promoting mastery of target words (e.g., reading, writing, answering questions, expanding definitions).

The research dealing with vocabulary instruction at the high school level is limited. Many of the evidence-based strategies described earlier in this chapter and strategies that have been effective with middle school students also are likely to improve the vocabulary knowledge and comprehension of high school students. For example, Terrill, Scruggs, and Mastropieri (2004) investigated the effects of teaching high school students with learning disabilities mnemonic strategies to learn new vocabulary words. The results indicated that students mastered more words under the mnemonic strategy condition than under a more traditional instructional condition.

■ REVISITING JASMINE

One of the strategies Jasmine's teachers decided to employ was to expand her vocabulary through increased reading. They reasoned that they should begin with culturally specific and authentic literature that would be particularly attractive to Jasmine. The teachers learned that Jasmine really enjoyed Sharon Draper's books, so they began with the award-winning and popular *Copper Sun* (Draper, 2006), one of Draper's more recent books. Although the book is about slavery, the main character is a person about Jasmine's age, and she was motivated to read it. To make the reading more engaging for Jasmine, at least three other students elected to read this book as well. The students read one chapter every two or three days. They were given approximately 15 minutes during the class period to meet with each other to share the vocabulary words that they identified, the definition of the words, and how they could use the words in sentences. The students then discussed the chapter and were expected to use the new words in their discussions. The words were also put into their word banks. Once a week, when the students met, they were to review and use all the words that had been identified for that chapter while discussing the chapter events. The students also were scheduled to participate in brief periods of reciprocal tutoring of the vocabulary words.

To give Jasmine and her classmates even more practice with the vocabulary words and to help them increase their spoken vocabulary, the teachers organized debate teams within the classroom. Hooley (2007) offers that debate participation can lead to improvements in critical thinking skills as well as academic achievement. Although schoolwide and national debate participants are often selected because of their superior language and thinking skills, there is good reason to believe that this format, on a much smaller scale, would be effective in helping language-deficient students improve their vocabulary, thinking, and literacy skills. Special rules were set up for the debates that included the use of formal, not informal, language; the use of newly acquired vocabulary words; and the number of new or different points made during the debate. Debates took place weekly based on the content of the books students were reading at that time. For example, in reading *Copper Sun,* students could debate the pros and cons of runaway slaves attempting to escape by running south rather than north. This meant that the students had to do some research on the topic of runaway slaves and the most effective escape routes.

The long-term strategy for Jasmine, and her classmates, was to increase gradually the quantity of reading she was required to complete and, as she progressed, to expect her to master increasingly difficult words. The diversity of the books also would increase so that, although initially the choice of books would emphasize cultural and personal interests, eventually she would read the full array of books expected of high school students. Jasmine and the other students would be expected to become increasingly independent in their vocabulary development, using strategies such as online dictionaries and personal journals as vehicles for improving meaningful vocabularies and reading comprehension.

MOVING ON ■

Given the importance of vocabulary knowledge in reading acquisition and development of comprehension, we concur with colleagues in the field on several key points. First, any vocabulary instruction is better than no instruction. Second, direct instruction increases the probability that students will become better independent word learners. Finally, instruction should be sequential and comprehensive by increasing both definitional and contextual word knowledge. For CLD learners, a successful vocabulary program can bridge the well-documented vocabulary gap that only widens throughout schooling. Traditional vocabulary instruction for these students can be enhanced through the use of culturally specific materials and activities. For example, much vocabulary instruction focuses on the reading of literature, which should reflect the backgrounds and interests of these students to increase motivation. Although teachers should not make assumptions about what students already know, they also should not underestimate the students' capacity to learn, nor should they fail to capitalize on the students' special abilities or talents.

6

Improving Comprehension

Jeffrey P. Bakken

CHAPTER OBJECTIVES

In this chapter we will

- establish the importance of comprehension to developing and becoming a competent reader;
- identify research related to comprehension difficulties; and
- provide examples of culturally and linguistically responsive comprehension practices important to primary, middle school, and high school readers.

NOT MAKING IT IN HIGH SCHOOL

Emmanuel Jackson, an African-American student, is enrolled in a large, inner-city school district in Chicago, Illinois. His high school consists of students from the 9th through 12th grades with approximately three thousand total students. The typical school day runs from 8:00 AM to 3:00 PM. Emmanuel is a tenth grader and receives about 75 percent of his instruction in general education classes and the other 25 percent in a special education placement. Emmanuel's high school is very typical, in that students attend eight

50-minute class periods throughout the school day, with each period covering a different topic or content area. The classes he is taking include English, basic algebra, biology, physical education, drama, music, reading, and a study hall. Emmanuel is educated with peers with and without disabilities for all of his classes except for reading and his study hall. For reading, he is instructed in a separate class by the special education teacher with other peers who have reading difficulties and Individualized Education Programs (IEPs). His study hall is also with the special educator to provide a much smaller environment than the normal study hall in the commons area with over 200 students. Here he can also receive support for his other classwork if needed, whereas there is no opportunity for assistance in the general education study hall.

Emmanuel's inclusion classes include from 25 to 33 students; in his special education classes, the number is considerably lower with only 12 to 15 students. In his inclusion classes, there are typically at least five to eight other students with identified specific learning disabilities, emotional/behavioral disabilities, developmental disabilities, or visual impairments. Each class has a full-time content area teacher as well as a paraprofessional. In the reading class and study hall are students identified with specific learning disabilities, emotional/behavioral disabilities, and developmental disabilities, and these two classes have a full-time special educator and a full-time paraprofessional.

Emmanuel was referred for a multidisciplinary evaluation at the end of third grade as a result of continuing difficulties reading in this grade as well as in previous years. Over the years, Emmanuel has improved significantly with the help of many dedicated teachers and his mother, but he still struggles in reading with comprehension. He can verbally read out loud or to himself but has difficulty remembering what he has read. His time spent in special education environments has focused on strategies to help him improve his comprehension skills. Currently, he is receiving training on comprehension strategies from his special education teacher in hopes he will apply them in his general education classes.

In addition to reading comprehension difficulties, Emmanuel's mother has a concern about his future after high school. She is worried he will not have the reading skills to be successful when he is on his own. As a single parent with six other children, and having reading difficulties herself, she knows she cannot give the attention needed to help her son with reading comprehension. She also works at a restaurant as a second-shift employee, so when she is at work, Emmanuel, her oldest child, is responsible for his siblings at home. He does not mind watching his siblings, but this takes time away from working on schoolwork. On the positive side, Emmanuel is a very hard worker and wants to do well. He knows he has difficulties in the area of reading comprehension and is trying to improve his skills. On the negative side, Emmanuel has a hard time deciding what strategy to implement in his other content area classes. Often he wastes a lot of time just trying to decide what strategy to use. Since comprehension in the content area classes is so important, his ability to choose appropriate strategies will be a focus this year and next.

WHAT IS READING COMPREHENSION? ■

Reading comprehension is the process of understanding and constructing meaning from a piece of text. Connected text is any written material involving multiple words that forms coherent thoughts. Phrases, sentences, and paragraphs are examples of connected text where reading comprehension is necessary. Reading difficulties are most apparent when students are unable to grasp the meaning from text. Reading comprehension may be affected by the vocabulary words used in the text, the difficulty of the text, and the student's familiarity with the subject matter, among other factors. Reading comprehension skills tend to separate skilled and unskilled readers. Skilled readers interact with the text and predict what will happen next in a story using clues presented in the text. They may also clarify parts of the text that have confused them and connect the events in the text to prior knowledge or experiences. Unskilled readers read the text but do not interact with it, causing possible comprehension difficulties (Time for Learning, n.d.).

Skilled reading comprehension involves the use of a number of cognitive skills. At a lower cognitive level, skilled readers automatically recognize letters and words, and they automatically activate the meanings of words when they read them. Unskilled readers are unable to do this and are not automatic, many times focusing so much on the individual letters, letter sounds, and words that comprehension is compromised. Skilled reading comprehension also involves higher-level cognitive processes, such as relating what one reads to what one already knows and creating inferential bridges to span between things that are written and things that one's experience says must be true. We must recognize that students will not spontaneously implement strategies to help them with their comprehension and that teachers must teach them appropriate strategies and give them opportunities to practice these strategies in a group as well as independently. Six key strategies that teachers can implement to help plan lessons, which are accessible to a range of students, include (a) vocabulary and language development; (b) guided interaction; (c) metacognition and authentic assessment; (d) explicit instruction; (e) the use of meaning-based context and universal themes; and (f) modeling, graphic organizers, and visuals (Alliance for Excellent Education, 2005).

Teaching Reading Comprehension

Vocabulary and Language Development

Teachers introduce new concepts by discussing vocabulary words key to that concept. Not knowing vocabulary words is detrimental to successful reading comprehension. The more words a child knows, the better he or she will understand the text. Classroom strategies include the following:

- *Preteach vocabulary:* Before doing an activity, teaching content, or reading a story, the teacher preteaches the vocabulary words needed for comprehension by playing "Block Words." For example, when introducing a story about Native Americans, the teacher selects key vocabulary words from the story introduction—*tepee, chief, tribe,* or *headdress*—and gives each reader some blocks. Readers place blocks from left to right for each vocabulary word in the sentence as it is repeated aloud. The teacher then reviews meanings of each word prior to initial reading.

- *Scaffold:* The teacher provides support for students as they learn new skills or information. Examples include using a graphic organizer, putting up a word wall, or labeling pictures and drawings. For instance, as the teacher and students read a story about Martin Luther King, Jr., words that are uncommon or unfamiliar to the students, such as *freedom, dream,* and *demonstration,* are placed on the wall to be practiced and as a resource for reading and literacy development.

- *Focus on cognates:* Cognates are words in different languages that are derived from the same original word, or root (e.g., *family* and *familia*). For example, a teacher who has Hispanic students can use words from Spanish to learn the English words. Activities can be developed, a word wall can be used, and objects in the classroom can be labeled. Some examples include *bank* and *banco, decorate* and *decorar, mark* and *marca,* and *teapot* and *tetera.*

- *Audio books:* These build vocabulary as the student hears and sees the word in context at the same time. For example, students who have English as a second language can listen to books on tape as they read along in the text. If they do not understand something the first time, they can rewind the tape and listen to it again. Teachers must remember they still need to check for understanding of the reading selection, and this can be done orally, in writing, or some other way.

- *Computer programs:* These proven supplements to instruction help build vocabulary skills individually or with a peer. There are many programs available that reinforce comprehension skills. Programs can be chosen that relate to students' areas of interest and can monitor their comprehension performance over time.

Guided Interaction

Teachers structure lessons so that students work together to understand what they read by listening, speaking, reading, and writing collaboratively about the academic concepts in the text. Students are placed in groups and collaboratively work to understand the meaning of the reading selection with guidance from the teacher. For example, the teacher can structure student groups so the diversity of the classroom is represented in each group (if possible). This way, each student can offer his or her unique perspective on how they understand and interpret the text and can see how students with different ethnic backgrounds can sometimes draw different conclusions based on their backgrounds and experiences.

Metacognition and Authentic Assessment

Teachers model and explicitly teach thinking skills crucial to learning new concepts. With authentic assessments, teachers use a variety of activities to check students' understanding, acknowledging that students learning a second language need a variety of ways to demonstrate their understanding of concepts that are not totally reliant on advanced language skills. For example, a teacher may be discussing how different the early 1900s were as compared to today. At the end of the unit, students are required to do a project. Choices they might have to show their understanding of the content could be writing a research paper, developing a PowerPoint presentation, designing a Web page, or even making some type of model or artifact. This would give students the opportunity to choose something that interests them, and they could focus on a skill at which they are proficient to express their knowledge of the subject matter to the teacher.

Explicit Instruction

Explicit instruction is the direct teaching of concepts, academic language, and reading comprehension strategies needed to complete classroom tasks. Teachers pick specific strategies and teach these directly to the students in the classroom. Teachers interact with students, providing feedback on performance and working towards independent strategy implementation for the student. For example, the teacher can teach the students to look over the questions they are to answer prior to reading. This way, students have more of a purpose during the reading process and know what is important to focus on learning while they read.

The Use of Meaning-Based Context and Universal Themes

Teachers use something meaningful from the students' everyday lives as a springboard to interest them in academic concepts. Teachers must consider the ethnic and cultural backgrounds of all students in the classroom and use this information to promote classroom learning. Making a connection with the students will aid both the teacher and students when working on reading skills. Students will also learn about different perspectives from other students, based on their heritage and cultural background.

Modeling, Graphic Organizers, and Visuals

The use of a variety of visual aids, including pictures, diagrams, and charts, helps all students and, especially, ELL students. Visuals make both the language and the content more accessible to students. For example, when reading through a story, the teacher can implement a story map that has sections for the main character, setting, action, problem, and conclusion. After the story is read, the students fill in the appropriate information in each space. When everyone has completed the task, the teacher could interact with the students and review to make sure they have the correct answers. It is important to note that these techniques will not be effective unless the teacher instructs the students on how to use them. The teacher must model to the students how and when to implement these types of strategies (see Table 6.1 for specific examples) and discuss why they are important to use (Alliance for Excellent Education, 2005).

TABLE 6.1   Key Strategies and Specific Examples

Key Strategy	Specific Examples
Vocabulary and language development	Word analysis (e.g., dissecting words into their parts of prefix, root, and suffix)
	Vocabulary journals, A-B-C books, word webs, and word walls
	Interactive editing, cloze paragraphs, dictation, and subject-specific journals
Guided interaction	Partner interviews, class surveys, think-pair-share, numbered heads together, four corners
	Poster projects and group presentations
	Readers' theater
Metacognition and authentic assessment	Guided reading, completing chapter prereading guides, reciprocal teaching, directed reading thinking activity (DRTA), and anticipation guides
	Think-alouds, K-W-L, and learning logs/journals
Explicit instruction	Reading directions, sentence starters, teaching essay formats, using pattern drills, or completing a story map
	Teaching specific reading comprehension skills for completing task procedures, answering questions, working word problems, and understanding text and graphics
Using meaning-based context and universal themes	Quick-writing responses or recording students' responses to visuals, current event stories, real-life models, video clips, thematic prompts, role-plays and comparing language uses for similar contexts
	Identifying and analyzing different perspectives and language references
Modeling, graphic organizers, and visuals	Venn diagrams, story maps, main idea + supporting detail schematics, double-entry journals, and semantic attribute matrixes

IMPROVING COMPREHENSION IN ELEMENTARY SCHOOL ■

Culturally responsive curriculum (CRC) is authentic, child centered, and connected to the child's real life. It employs materials from the child's own culture and history to help illustrate the principles and concepts they are to learn (Chion-Kenney, 1994). Helping CLD students at the primary level is important, and making sure they get off to a successful start in literacy instruction is essential. Academic early reading programs concentrate on the direct teaching of specific language and reading skills in which the teacher presents stimuli designed to elicit language responses. Integrating specific language activities that encourage student involvement is critical for early intervention in language development, especially for students who have limited opportunities to experience literacy outside the classroom. Skill activities associated with direct, explicit instruction are considered the sole focus of these types of programs. Skills are taught throughout the school day by engaging students in meaningful language that focuses on the acquisition of each language goal (Nichols, Rupley, Webb-Johnson, & Tlusty, 2000).

Word Recognition Skills

Building word recognition skills can also improve reading comprehension skills. Building word recognition skills means increasing the number of words that a student can recognize effortlessly and without thought. Words that can be recognized effortlessly and without thought are words that that student can recognize automatically. A competent reader at the college level can have a sight vocabulary in excess of thousands of words. The logic behind building automatic word recognition skills is based on the idea that recognizing words by thinking about them makes reading a laborious process. This can cause increasingly greater difficulties as a student moves into junior and senior high school, where the reading load in subject matter areas such as science, math, and social studies greatly increases. If word recognition for a large number of words can be made automatic, then reading will be easier, and a student will be more likely to keep up with peers as reading load increases. A reader with a large sight vocabulary will be able to identify words instantly without having to sound them out. Instant word recognition by sight greatly increases reading fluency and reading comprehension. Students whose native language is not English would benefit from instruction that focuses on the sight words, as well as content-specific words, needed to comprehend different reading selections.

Predictable Reading Materials

Another way to provide students with positive literacy experiences in early reading programs is to use predictable reading materials that involve choral reading. Choral reading has also been used successfully in promoting language learning for CLD students. The benefits of using choral reading to enhance children's acquisition of a second language are that it (1) creates a low-anxiety environment, (2) provides repeated practice, (3) is based on comprehensible input, and (4) incorporates drama (McCauley & McCauley, 1992). Choral reading involves the whole class reading a passage at the same time. This allows good readers to read freely and those who do not consider themselves to be good readers to participate as much as they can without fear of being put in front of everyone reading independently. This type of activity also allows the students to hear unfamiliar words, which aids in the comprehension process. This should not be the only form of reading, as it is still important for the student and the teacher to assess reading skills of students individually as well to monitor progress.

Patterned Books

Patterned books, which have stories with predictable features, such as rhyming and repeated phrases, can be implemented to promote language development (Norton, 1995). Patterned books frequently contain pictures that may facilitate story comprehension as well. Books with a patterned structure can provide modeling as a reading strategy, challenge students' current level of linguistic competence, and provide assistance in comprehending difficult concepts. When using these materials, teachers must remember to take into consideration their students' prior knowledge and experiences as they create lessons. They need to be responsive to individual students, their cultures, and their communities. They can also focus attention on prior knowledge by using the senses to focus attention, particularly at the beginning of a lesson when directions and objectives are presented (Schmidt, 2005).

Simple Sentence Patterns

Comprehension through the repetition of a simple sentence pattern can motivate second-language learners to continue trying to learn to read. These fully illustrated stories repeat simple patterns that second-language learners can use to begin the reading process. Reading is a difficult process, and the self-esteem of readers is important in their overall success. Using simple sentence pattern materials can help students be successful from the very beginning and help to promote continued efforts in the reading process as they try to develop their reading skills.

Integrated Basal and Literature-Based Reading Programs

Morrow (1992) conducted research in second-grade classrooms on how an integrated basal and literature-based reading program positively affected the literacy achievement of CLD children. The features of her integrated program included (a) literacy centers within each classroom providing students access to a variety of books and literacy materials, such as multiple genres of children's literature, comfortable seating, and manipulatives (e.g., felt stories, roll movies, and taped stories); (b) teacher-guided activities helping students understand what they could do and should do; and (c) independent reading and writing periods to allow students to choose between working alone or with others and to select from a variety of activities, ranging from retelling to dramatizing stories. Activities included teachers' use of modeling and scaffolding, directed reading-thinking activities (DRTA), and retellings using both books and props (e.g., felt stories, puppets, and roll movies). The combination of these activities produced improvements in the literacy achievement of CLD children.

Repeated Readings

Research has also documented that repeated readings can help with the comprehension of students with disabilities. Although much of the research documents how repeated readings influence the fluency of the reader, they also help the reader with comprehension. In a meta-analysis on fluency and comprehension gains as a result of repeated readings, Therrien (2004) found that students with and without learning disabilities not only improved their fluency but also their comprehension. The optimal number of times to read a passage to improve fluency was seven; to improve reading comprehension, three.

Retellings

Last, retellings can help to improve reading comprehension. Students read a selection and, immediately upon completion, retell what they remember from the passage. Five steps recommended by Irwin and Mitchell (1991) for using retellings include (a) teacher modeling (the teacher reads a story to children or children read a story silently and the teacher models retelling), (b) small-group oral retelling (following the reading of the story, children take turns retelling in a small-group format), (c) partner retelling (two children participate in a retelling after they read a story, and the listener gives feedback), (d) individual oral retellings (children retell individually to someone else or into a tape recorder, and if the listener has not read the same text, then the listener only asks clarifying questions or gives comments), and (e) individual written retellings (students write everything they can remember about the text). Teachers will want to focus on students learning to summarize what they have read and realizing that when they cannot develop a summary, they have to reread the selection. This activity can be done individually, in pairs, or in cooperative groups. See Table 6.2 for sample activities for elementary school students.

TABLE 6.2   Activities for Improving Comprehension in Elementary School

- *Preteach vocabulary.* Identify words from a story with which diverse students in the classroom might not be familiar. Create sentences with those words in them, with the actual words missing from the sentences. Using a word bank (a list of all the words to be put in the blanks), students read each sentence and fill in the word that best completes it.

- *Teach sight words.* Use the card game Bang. Put sight-word cards in a can. The student picks a card and reads it out loud. If the student is correct, she keeps the card, and it is the next student's turn. The object is to have the most cards at the end of the game. "Bang" is written on some cards. When a student draws a card saying "Bang," he has to read "BANG!" in a nice loud voice and put *all* of his cards back in the can.

- *Use sight-word bingo.* Develop bingo cards with sight words on them. Read one word at a time. Students need to identify the word on their card correctly if they have it. Once a bingo is established, the winner must orally read all of her words in the bingo.

- *Use predictable reading materials.* Choose stories and reading materials that are predictable. If possible, use multicultural reading materials. The teacher can read the story out loud, and then the class can read it out loud together. Practice numerous times until students are proficient.

- *Use patterned books.* Choose beginning-level reading materials that have predictable features, such as rhyming and repeated phrases. Books written by Dr. Seuss are a good resource and are typically enjoyed by most beginning readers.

- *Use integrated basal and literature-based reading programs.* Literacy centers within each classroom provide students access to a variety of books and literacy materials, such as multiple genres of children's literature, comfortable seating, and manipulatives (i.e., felt stories, roll movies, and taped stories); retellings using both books and props (i.e., felt stories, puppets, and roll movies); and independent reading and writing periods to allow students to choose between working alone or with others and to select from a variety of activities ranging from retelling to dramatizing stories.

- *Use retellings.* Choose a multicultural reading selection (if possible) at an appropriate reading level and have students read the story. After they have read the story, have students retell it in their own words.

- *Use authentic assessment.* After reading a biography of their own choosing, students are allowed a choice of the project they will complete to explain the book. Students could write a written summary, complete a time line, create a mobile, act out the story, or complete various other activities. This approach allows each student to use his or her strengths and interests to complete the assignment.

IMPROVING COMPREHENSION SKILLS IN MIDDLE SCHOOL ■

In addition to the previously mentioned activities for students at the primary level, some additional activities can be implemented at the middle school level. One strategy is to incorporate literature that has a connection with the students and their cultures or heritages. For our country to develop an understanding and acceptance of others, we must become educated about the cultural heritages of many groups. One of the most effective ways to accomplish this task is to incorporate multiethnic and multicultural literature into our classrooms (Nichols et al., 2000). Not only will this be motivating, but teachers can then learn more about their students. Teachers can also engage students during class in forms of discourse and joint activities characteristic of informal social interactions to discuss what was read. By permitting students to express their thoughts freely, teachers can create better communication channels. Such channels are vital and can be effective avenues for developing students' language and literacy skills and for conveying curricular knowledge (Tharp & Gallimore, 1988).

Concept Maps and Graphic Organizers

When students see connections among the content areas, learning seems more relevant. Concept maps and other graphic organizers can demonstrate connections with other content areas (Vacca & Vacca, 2005). Sometimes the text is not enough to comprehend the material. In this case, it is suggested that a visual representation of the to-be-learned material be developed. This will allow students to see similarities as well as differences between various knowledge and concepts. Examples include Venn diagrams, cause-and-effect diagrams, sequencing diagrams, and main idea and details diagrams.

Venn Diagram

A Venn diagram is used to show the relationship between two sets of information. This technique was developed by British mathematician John Venn. Typically, it uses circles to represent sets, with the position and overlap of the circles indicating the relationships between the sets. It could be implemented in reading to show a reader, for example, the similarities and differences between characters in a story. This information can later be studied or reviewed to help with comprehension.

Cause-and-Effect Diagram

A cause-and-effect diagram shows the relationship between an action or event and another, resulting event. This diagram helps students see the relationship between an action that is taken and the outcome that is produced. For example, it could be used to show what happened to a character as the result of some action that character performed. This information can later be studied or reviewed to help with comprehension.

Sequencing Diagram

A sequencing diagram shows the order of events and how they fit with each other. For students with memory difficulties, this diagram may help them to organize the information that was previously read. For example, this type of chart could be used to show the steps of the water cycle. Typically, students can be prompted with words like *first, second, third,* etc., and then they can fill in the appropriate information to study later to help with comprehension.

Main Idea and Details Diagram

A main idea and details diagram helps the student organize what the important concept is and the details that support that main concept. It is important to find the main ideas when reading, as they help readers remember important information. For example, the main idea of a paragraph tells the topic of the paragraph, and the topic tells what all or most of the sentences are about. This information can later be studied or reviewed to help with comprehension.

See Figure 6.1 for visual depictions of the above examples.

FIGURE 6.1   Commonly Used Types of Graphic Organizers

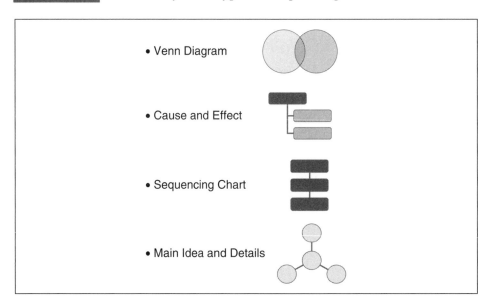

Cooperative Learning

CRC often incorporates strategies that utilize cooperative learning and whole-language instruction, includes self-esteem building, and recognizes multiple intelligences and diverse learning styles (Association for the Advancement of Health Education, 1994). Cooperative learning allows the teacher to plan carefully who works in groups and to assign student roles based on student strengths so that all students can be contributing members of the group. It also gives the teacher the opportunity to have students with diverse backgrounds in different groups and students working with peers with whom they might not work of their own choosing. This process will help to promote how different people can have different views/ideas based on their unique individual experiences and cultural backgrounds.

The group should focus on one common goal, and all students need to work together to be successful. It is suggested that groups consist of no more than four students. It is also important to remember that students must exhibit acceptable social skills for the groups to function effectively. If these social skills are not at acceptable levels, some instruction in this area might be warranted before cooperative learning groups begin. Examples of cooperative learning can be seen in Table 6.3.

TABLE 6.3   Examples of Cooperative Learning

Example	Description
Think-pair-share	Students each think of their answers, then discuss them with partners, and then share their combined responses with the class.
Roundtable	A single piece of paper is systematically passed around a small group on which each student responds to a question.
Corners	Different aspects of a topic are posted in each corner of the room. The students move to the corner that represents their feelings on the topic and discuss why they chose that corner with the other students there. Finally, each group reports their responses to the class.
Graffiti	Each small group is given a large piece of paper and a marker, and they respond to a question or topic by writing words and phrases on the paper.
Learning together	Small groups of students work together to prepare one team product.
Jigsaw	Members of a small group each become "experts" on a different aspect of a topic and then teach one another in the group.
Group investigation	Students plan and carry out a project or plan of study within a small group. The group decides what to investigate, how each member will contribute, and how the information will be communicated to the class.

Literature-Based Reading Instruction

Teachers can also integrate a social action approach into the curriculum by using literature-based reading instruction. Literature-based instruction for CLD students can feature stories from various cultures and languages displayed around the classroom; writings of students covering the walls like ribboned wallpaper; portfolios showing drafts of creative writing pieces, such as journals of all kinds, letters, and poetry; and field notes of student activities. Integrating multiethnic literature into a school curriculum for second-language learners helps students realize that all ethnic groups have roots in the past and a strong heritage that is a part of their culture (Bieger, 1996). For example, if a classroom had students that were Caucasian, African-American, Hispanic, and Korean, there could be stories from those cultures and languages featured around the room. In addition, the teacher could have students from the different ethnic groups orally share stories (maybe their favorites) from their culture with others in the class.

Student Team Literature

Student Team Literature (STL) was designed to enhance middle school students' motivation to learn while improving their reading comprehension and understanding of good literature. Student Team Literature is an adaptation of Student Team Reading (Stevens & Durkin, 1992).

STL uses award-winning novels, higher-order thinking activities, and cooperative learning to create a motivating environment for reading. STL teachers introduce novels with discussions of relevant background knowledge, genre, and vocabulary. Students work in cooperative learning teams as they read. Activities include (a) partner reading (students first read silently, then take turns reading orally with a partner), (b) treasure hunts (higher-order questions guide student reading, requiring them to search and think to generate text-supported answers), (c) word mastery (students practice saying new vocabulary words with their partners, then use those words in writing "context clue" sentences), (d) story retelling (students summarize stories in their own words), (e) story-related writing (students write in response to prompts about their reading), (f) extension activities (students complete cross-curricular research, fine arts, dramatics, and media activities as they explore themes in the books), (g) tests (students take tests on complete cross-curricular research, fine arts, dramatics, and media activities as they explore themes in the books), and (h) explicit instruction of comprehension strategies (teachers model and guide students in comprehension and metacognitive self-checking strategies). Giving students different opportunities and activities can break the monotony of always just doing the same things and can challenge different students in many different ways. See Table 6.4 for sample activities for middle school students.

TABLE 6.4   Activities for Improving Comprehension Skills in Middle School

- *Use multiethnic and multicultural literature.* Choose literature that reflects different cultures in your classroom. Make a list of choices and let students choose the reading selection. Choosing relevant reading selections will increase the motivation and learning of students from different cultural backgrounds.

- *Use a sequencing chart.* After reading a short story or culturally relevant historical selection, have students use a sequencing chart or time line to help them organize the events of the selection. Students can read the selection and fill it in as they go, wait till the end, work independently, or work in groups. Once the activity is complete, the students then have a study guide.

- *Use a main idea and details chart.* After reading a speech from Abraham Lincoln about slavery, have students fill in a main idea and details chart. After the activity is complete, the students will see the main points of the essay and how Lincoln supported his ideas. The class can then discuss Lincoln's ideas and compare and contrast the information with their own.

- *Use a learning together cooperative group.* In this activity, a group (typically 3–4 students) works together to prepare one team product. Groups can be multicultural, and projects can be chosen so that students can use their strengths and interests to complete the project. For example, there may be some very artistic students in your class. Place these students in different groups throughout the class and prepare a project that has a drawing component (e.g., What might a home have looked like in 1860?).

- *Use a roundtable cooperative group.* A single piece of paper is systematically passed around a small group on which each student responds to a question regarding something that was read. Groups can be multicultural, and questions can be very general or specific. For example, the question posed may be related to a reading on Germany: Should the Berlin Wall have been torn down? After all students respond, answers are read and discussed within the group. This activity creates a lot of discussion and allows students to hear and think about different perspectives.

- *Use literature-based reading instruction.* After reading about different types of poetry, have students write a sonnet (a poem of 14 lines that follows a strict rhyme scheme and logical structure) about their family. Allow students to write in their native language if they would like. Display the poems around the room or in a center. Each day, have one or two students read their sonnet and translate to the class if necessary.
- *Use student team literature.* Choose a novel to read that relates to one or more students in your class. An example could be *Make a Wish, Molly* (a girl from Russia learns about unfamiliar traditions in the United States) by Barbara Cohen (1994). The teacher introduces the novel with discussions of relevant background knowledge, genre, and vocabulary. Students work in cooperative learning teams as they read, and classroom discussions are held to summarize and hear viewpoints from others in the class.

IMPROVING COMPREHENSION SKILLS ■ IN HIGH SCHOOL

All students need some type of activity to help them with comprehension, and high school students are no different. Each young adolescent is unique with a particular, experiential, and personal background and a distinctive array of learning styles, interests, talents, and skills. No single teaching method works for every student; in fact, no single method will work for any one student every day. Instead, research points to the positive impact on students' achievement of using varied and appropriate strategies for learning and teaching (Cawelti, 1995; Epstein & Mac Iver, 1992; Russell, 1997). Activities previously listed may be beneficial at this level as well. See Table 6.5 for a list of possibilities.

TABLE 6.5   Culturally Responsive Activities to Improve Comprehension

Activity	*Citation*
Decide how and what to study, because students learn best when they have some control over their learning.	Wiggins & McTighe (1998)
Enhance and accommodate diverse skills, interests, abilities, and talents.	Tomlinson (1999)
Establish a culturally responsive classroom environment in which students and teachers understand the diverse cultural backgrounds represented in the classroom; communicate acceptance and positive attitudes about cultural diversity; and build on cultural diversity through day-to-day teaching and learning activities to promote pride and motivation and improve parents' perceptions of the school.	Gay (2000); Shumow & Harris (1998); Villegas (1991)
Connect new learning to prior knowledge and understanding.	Bruning, Schraw, & Ronning (1999)
Engage in hands-on activities in meaningful contexts.	Eggen & Kauchak (2001); Needels & Knapp (1994)

(Continued)

TABLE 6.5   (Continued)

Activity	Citation
Integrate literacy across the curriculum, using strategies applicable across content areas to enhance learning from texts and using content-specific strategies to improve comprehension.	Gay (2002)
Collaborate with other teachers across areas of expertise to adapt instruction and learning approaches to students' needs.	Schmidt (2000)
Communicate and collaborate with families, because students benefit from that cooperation, demonstrating higher rates of attendance, improved academic achievement, and an increased willingness to do homework.	Cameron & Lee (1997); Lopez & Scribner (1999)

Listening

When students have opportunities to listen and talk, they can write and read more easily. Listening to others in the group promotes learning. Talking about what they are learning helps them think and write. When they read what they have written, they have opportunities to rethink, edit, and revise. They hear their own and others' errors and significant ideas, thus developing critical eyes and ears. Students actively involved in the small groups and pairs also experience less anxiety and are better able to practice their literacy learning (Schmidt, 2005). This in turn helps them with their comprehension and understanding of what was read.

They can also learn that, depending on one's background and experiences, different conclusions can be drawn from the same reading selection. For example, after a unit on World War II, a teacher might have students write about how Japanese Americans might have felt when they were placed in relocation camps. The teacher could then have students read their written work aloud to others, which would help them practice their reading skills while others in their group could focus on the comprehension of the passage being read. Through this activity, all students work on important skills needed in the comprehension process, and after all writings have been read, a discussion could follow that addresses the different perspectives that culturally diverse students in the classroom have on this topic.

Social Identities

High school students' relationships to curriculum are also very much influenced by their social identities. *Social identity* is an individual's sense of self in relation to others. People identify with some groups and distance themselves from others. They internalize their group's understanding about what they can or ought to hope for economically, politically, and personally (Steinitz & Solomon, 1986). And they display their identity by looking and acting in ways deemed appropriate by group members.

Students are more willing to learn in class when pedagogies take into account their social identities. Culturally responsive teachers who acknowledge students' social identities generally meet with more success than those who do not (Hemmings, 1994). By having opportunities to discuss and defend their ideas with others, students come to complex understandings. Instead of lecturing and transmitting material, teachers facilitate the learning process by encouraging cooperation among students. While cooperative learning is appropriate for all students, it is critical for CLD students who may face socioeconomic disadvantages. Through collaborative practices, they can develop the social skills and intergroup relationships essential to academic success. For example, a teacher could implement cooperative groups (discussed previously) which would focus on completing an academic task but would also focus on social skill development within the group. This strategy might also allow students to work with those with whom they would normally not associate and see that different people have different ideas and viewpoints based on their experiences and cultural background.

Cognitively Guided Instruction

Cognitively guided instruction emphasizes learning strategies that enhance students' metacognitive development. It focuses on the direct teaching and modeling of cognitive learning strategies and giving students opportunities to practice them while teachers monitor that practice. Through explicit instruction, students learn how to monitor their own learning by tapping various strategies to accelerate their acquisition of English or academic content (Waxman, Padrón, & Knight, 1991). One example of effective cognitively guided instruction is reciprocal teaching, a procedure in which students are instructed in four specific reading comprehension-monitoring strategies: (1) summarizing, (2) self-questioning, (3) clarifying, and (4) predicting. These cognitive skills can increase reading achievement and help students master their school-based knowledge (Padrón, Waxman, & Rivera, 2002).

Summarizing

Summarizing is how we take larger selections of text and reduce them to their smallest units: the gist, the key ideas, the main points that are worth noting and remembering. This is one of the hardest strategies for students to grasp and one of the hardest strategies to teach. The teacher must repeatedly model it and give students ample time and opportunities to practice it, but it is a very valuable strategy and competency. Can you imagine your students succeeding in school or the community without being able to break down content into manageable, small, succinct pieces? We ask students to summarize all the time, but we often neglect to teach them good ways to do this! This strategy is truly about equipping students to be lifelong learners.

- After students have used selective underlining (underlining with a goal or purpose) on a selection, the teacher has them close the reading selection or handout packet and attempt to create a summary paragraph of what they can remember of the key ideas in the piece. They should only look back at their underlining when they feel stumped. They can go back and forth between writing the summary and checking their underlining several times until they have captured the important ideas in the article in a single paragraph. For example, the teacher can photocopy a selection the students will be reading and have them underline the important information. (Remember, first they must be taught to do this.) Then they write a summary paragraph based on the information they identified in the reading selection as important. This can also be done in pairs or groups before students do it independently, which will give them more opportunities to practice this activity before doing it on their own.

- The teacher uses the "newspaper theme": students use the key words or phrases to identify Who, What, When, Where, Why, and How. For example, given a story about a family involved in the Mexican Revolution, they could answer questions about the reading and then discuss their answers with a peer.
- Students write successively shorter summaries, constantly refining and reducing their written pieces until only the most essential and relevant information remains. They can start off with half a page, then try to get it down to two paragraphs, then one paragraph, then two or three sentences, and ultimately a single sentence.
- The teacher takes articles from the newspaper and cuts off their headlines. Students practice writing headlines for (or matching the severed headlines to) the "headless" stories.
- The teacher takes a comic strip or comic book page and deletes some of the dialogue. Students try to fill in the missing information so it still makes sense.

Self-Questioning

Self-questioning is the ongoing process of the reader asking questions before, during, and after reading to understand text. The questions are based on clues that are found in the text and are generated to spark curiosity that focuses the reader's attention on investigating, understanding, and connecting to the text. A self-questioning strategy is a set of steps that a student follows to generate, think about, predict, investigate, and answer questions that satisfy curiosity about what is being read. Struggling readers may need instruction and practice in surveying text and generating questions before they read; other students may need instruction and practice in using self-questioning as they read; others might use self-questioning as a way of summarizing or studying. Regardless of when the self-questioning process is used, the basic components of the strategy are the same.

If students do not know or use self-questioning as an ongoing strategy during reading, they are likely to have trouble with before and after use of the strategy.

- *The before-reading self-questioning strategy:* This strategy focuses on teaching students to use the self-questioning process as a way of previewing text before reading begins and creating a set of guiding questions to check comprehension during reading. For example, if the reader was reading a chapter on the Holocaust, he could be taught to look at the title of the reading selection, major headings, pictures and captions, and tables and charts and create questions that would help guide his reading and improve comprehension.

- *The during-reading self-questioning strategy:* This strategy focuses on teaching students to use a self-questioning process as they read paragraphs and sections of text. For example, while reading, the student can be taught to ask herself, "Did I understand what I just read?" after each paragraph or page. If she cannot answer yes, she should be taught to read it over again.
- *The after-reading self-questioning strategy:* This strategy focuses on teaching students to generate questions and answer questions after they have read the text. This strategy is usually used for studying and self-testing information that should have been gained from the text (Special Connections, n.d.). Teachers can also give students questions to answer when they are first learning this strategy, until they become proficient at coming up with questions on their own.

Clarifying

Clarifying is an activity that is particularly important when working with students who have a history of comprehension difficulty. These students may believe that the purpose of reading is saying the words correctly; they may not be particularly uncomfortable that the words and, in fact, the passage are not making sense. Their focus is on reading the words correctly, not comprehending their overall meaning. When the students are asked to clarify, their attention is called to the fact that there may be many reasons why text is difficult to understand (e.g., new vocabulary, unclear reference words, and unfamiliar and perhaps difficult concepts). They are taught to be alert to the effects of such obstacles to comprehension and to take the necessary measures to restore meaning (e.g., reread, use context clues, ask for help). For example, given any reading task, the teacher could place a laminated note card (see Figure 6.2) on the desk of each student who has different steps to go through when text is unclear or not understood.

FIGURE 6.2   Sample Note Card of Steps to Go Through When Text Is Unclear

1. Reread the text.
2. Sound it out (if it is an unclear word).
3. Use context clues.
4. Ask a peer for help.
5. Ask the teacher for help.

Predicting

Predicting occurs when students hypothesize what the author will discuss next in the text. To do this successfully, students must activate the relevant background knowledge that they already possess regarding the topic. Students with disabilities typically do not do this independently. Teachers must teach and practice this skill with them so the process becomes automatic. The students have a purpose for reading: to confirm or disprove their hypotheses. Furthermore, the opportunity has been created for the students to link the new knowledge they will encounter in the text with the knowledge they already possess.

The predicting strategy also facilitates use of text structure, as students learn that headings, subheadings, and questions imbedded in the text are useful means of anticipating what might occur next. For example, when reading a selection together as a class, the teacher can stop after every page and have students verbally explain what they have read so far and then make predictions based on current knowledge as to what they think will happen next. After the next page or two, they can affirm or reject their prediction based on what they have read. Students would then formalize a new prediction, continuing this process through the entire selection. After enough practice as a class and in groups, students should be able to perform this task independently. The importance of being able to perform this task is that the reader becomes involved with the text, which aids in the comprehension of the material.

Cognitive Learning Strategies

Cognitive strategies provide a structure for learning that actively promotes the comprehension and retention of knowledge through the use of engaging strategies. Some examples of cognitive learning strategies include rehearsal, elaboration, organization, comprehension monitoring, and affective techniques. For all of these strategies, teachers must remember to explain the purpose of each, show students how to perform them, and give students opportunities to practice until they become proficient.

- *Rehearsal:* Rehearsal is the act of practicing the material being learned. Examples of different types of rehearsal are repetition, copying, listing, and underlining. For example, students could be instructed how to underline the major (main) ideas and supporting details in a reading selection to put them later into an outline to use for studying about the reading selection.
- *Elaboration:* Elaboration is the ability to associate a new piece of information with information already learned. Examples of different types of elaboration include forming mental images, paraphrasing, summarizing, forming analogies, and relating new information to known information. Paraphrasing, for example, is a person's own rendition of essential information and ideas expressed by someone else. Paraphrasing material (see Figure 6.3) makes it easier to remember because it is in the reader's own words, which are more familiar and can be recalled more readily.

FIGURE 6.3   Steps for Effective Paraphrasing

1. Reread the original passage until you understand what it means.

2. Put the original aside and write your paraphrase on a note card.

3. Jot down a few words under your paraphrase to remind you of the content later when using this material.

4. At the top of the note card, write a phrase to indicate the subject of your paraphrase.

5. Check your paraphrase with the original to make sure everything is accurate.

- *Organizing:* Organizing is the ability to arrange material into a well thought-out and meaningful framework. Examples of different types of organizing include grouping, outlining, categorizing, and diagramming. For example, after reading a selection, students can be instructed to make a topical outline that organizes the text. First the topic needs to be identified. Next, the main categories under the topic need to be identified. Finally, subcategories with examples (if possible) should be provided under each category. Once this is completed, the student can use this outline to study about the reading or for an exam.
- *Comprehension monitoring:* Comprehension monitoring is the ability to monitor learning progress and select alternative strategies if necessary. Examples of comprehension monitoring include self-questioning (to check for understanding) and goal setting. For example, one can teach students to ask themselves if they understood what they read and to reread the selection again if they do not understand it.
- *Affective:* Affective techniques make the student aware of the learning environment. Examples of affective strategies include maintaining attention, time management, and reducing anxiety. Students can be taught to monitor their own performance and to focus on the task of reading. They can also be taught to predict how long it will take them to read a selection based on the topic, length, and difficulty, which will help them in their planning and time management.

Multimedia and Technology

Instead of delivering knowledge, teachers are facilitators of learning through the use of multimedia and other technology (Padrón & Waxman, 1999). Web-based picture libraries can promote CLD students' comprehension in content-area classrooms (e.g., science and mathematics). Multimedia can facilitate auditory skill development by integrating visual presentations with sound and animation (Bermudez & Palumbo, 1994). Digitized books are effective tools that allow CLD students to request pronunciations for unknown words, request translations of sections, and ask questions. Technology-enriched instruction also helps students connect learning in the classroom to real-life situations, thereby creating a meaningful context for teaching and learning (Means & Olson, 1994). For example, in a science lesson on the states of matter (i.e., solid, liquid, and gas), the teacher can locate pictures, simulations, and video clips from the Web to show students how different materials change depending on the environment. Through the use of technology, the students will get a better understanding of these concepts, and this will help them with the comprehension of the material. See Table 6.6 for sample activities for high school students.

REVISITING EMMANUEL ■

Emmanuel's teachers worked together to support his learning of new content. For example, his inclusion teacher regularly prepared lists of key concepts for each chapter in his social studies textbook and reviewed them with him. She also shared the lists with other students in Emmanuel's class

TABLE 6.6   Activities for Improving Comprehension Skills in High School

- *Use predicting.* While reading a story about the life of Don Quixote, for example, the teacher stops at every page and has students predict what they think will happen next. After each page, the class confirms or discounts what was predicted and makes a new prediction. If this is done as a group activity, all students should be allowed an opportunity to participate.

- *Use underlining.* When reading a selection on Adolph Hitler, for instance, the teacher copies the selection for students to read along. Students underline important information while reading. After each major section, the class discusses the text to make sure students have underlined important information. The students create an outline from the underlined information to study at a later date.

- *Use summarizing.* While reading a selection on Chih-Kung Jen (a Chinese physicist who emigrated to the United States and participated in some of the 20th century's major scientific, political, and social developments in both the United States and China), students write a summary sentence, in their own words, after each page. Once the selection is complete, they combine sentences to create one concise summary statement. As this can be a difficult process, students must be taught through modeling and guided practice how to do this.

- *Use topical outlines.* While reading a selection on Harriet Tubman, the teacher has students create a topical outline. As they read about major themes (typically identified as major headings), students should write down important points/concepts under each theme. Once the exercise is complete, the student has a passage summary in the form of an outline.

- *Use self-questioning.* While reading a selection on the Native American Geronimo, the teacher has students ask themselves, "Did I understand what I just read?" after each paragraph. If they did not, they should be taught to reread the selection again to aid them in comprehension.

- *Use multimedia presentations.* After reading about the Hawaiian culture, the teacher creates a multimedia presentation (e.g., video and audio clips, pictures, simulations) to help students understand what was read. Students can also make multimedia individually or in groups to help with their comprehension.

- *Use Web-based picture libraries.* When reading about Japanese samurai, the teacher incorporates Web-based picture libraries, using pictures of traditional clothing, weapons, housing, etc. to aid students in becoming familiar with what they are reading and better comprehend the material. Teachers can also have students do the research, find the information and pictures, and present the information to the class.

and, whenever possible, paired one of them with Emmanuel for content review sessions. His science teacher distributed illustrations of experiments being discussed in class and projected the steps for completing them while students worked on them. Emmanuel's inclusion teacher worked closely with her colleagues to develop these and other materials and to review them with him. To give sustained practice with understanding what he was learning in content area classes, his inclusion teacher also taught Emmanuel to use effective strategies to review and generate questions before reading, to use self-questioning as he was reading, and to prepare a simple summary after reading an assigned chapter. She also modeled how to summarize the content of each chapter in *The Americanization of Ben Franklin* and *Behind You,* which he was reading in his English class.

The primary strategy for Emmanuel was to increase his participation greatly in content area instruction by improving his understanding of core vocabulary with regular practice. Teaching comprehension strategies that he could generalize across his different classes also increased the efficiency and effectiveness of the plan his teacher put in place.

MOVING ON ■

When working with CLD students to improve reading comprehension, one must adopt an integrated approach to instruction. This involves contextualizing learning and respecting the assets that children bring to the classroom, as well as teachers systematically and explicitly evaluating instructional techniques. Much of the literature on effective instruction for CLD students has indicated the necessity of providing instruction that contextualizes learning in meaningful and relevant ways and builds on these students' cultural and linguistic strengths (García & Ortiz, 2004). Teachers must also build trusting relationships with students and parents (Kalyanpur & Harry, 1999). When teachers have trusting relationships with their students and their students' parents, good faith is built that can help overcome conflicts. When students know their teacher cares about them and their learning, they are much more likely to take risks in the educational process (Gay, 2002).

Developing a working relationship with students' families is key to successful implementation of culturally responsive instruction (Edwards, Danridge, McMillon, & Pleasants, 2001). Families in impoverished areas often feel uncomfortable about coming to school because they may have negative memories regarding their own educational experiences. Therefore, since the teacher is in a position of power, it is believed that the teacher has a responsibility to blur the boundaries between home and school (Edwards, 2004). A teacher who makes the effort to communicate with families is demonstrating a respect for family involvement (Schmidt, 2000).

Therefore, to get the most from students, teachers must plan instruction for the diverse populations in their classes and make learning relevant to motivate students to do their best. It seems clear that high expectations require active involvement, engagement, and support from students, teachers, and parents (Dale, 2005).

This approach allows teachers to learn more about individual students and frees them to help those who need special attention. It also demonstrates that the teachers believe their students are capable of learning with carefully planned direction. It demonstrates that the teacher trusts the students to share and discuss information gained and completed in the assigned work. The teacher as facilitator can then circulate and assess individual, paired, and group learning (Schmidt, 2005).

As was mentioned, there are activities that teachers can implement when working with primary-level, middle school-level, and high school-level students to improve reading comprehension skills. Although specific activities are listed within each category of students, it is important to remember that the activities can cross the boundaries of the three levels of students. Teachers must assess current performance levels of students and problems they are experiencing and choose an appropriate activity they think will benefit the student or students. To see if it is effective or not, data should be collected on performance, and then decisions about effectiveness can be made.

7

Culturally Responsive Literacy Instruction for All

Festus E. Obiakor and Darren J. Smith

CHAPTER OBJECTIVES

In this chapter, we will

- discuss the rationale for culturally responsive literacy for all learners;
- provide methods for promoting culturally responsive instructional learning communities; and
- propose the premise that culturally responsive instructional learning communities are necessary in all grade levels and school programs to maximize the potential of learners.

ONE SIZE AND ONE WAY FOR ALL?

"Good afternoon class, I hope you enjoyed the mystery meatloaf you had for lunch today. I am always too scared to eat it, so I hopped into my car and went to Eat and Run and ordered from the dollar menu. My lunch sure was good!" said Mr. Jones, one of four fifth-period language arts and English classroom teachers, after all 24 students were in their seats waiting for class to begin. The students sat in four rows of six students per row in alphabetical order.

"Today, we are going to pick up where we left off yesterday, so please write down the objectives for today's class." Without saying a word, it was clear that all but one student understood what Mr. Jones expected of them. In unison, they took out their red notebooks and waited for him to write down the objectives of the day. William, one of the students, kept himself busy shuffling papers between two notebooks, one red and one blue. He did not comply with Mr. Jones's directive.

"William, why do I have to tell you everyday to organize your papers on your own time and not on my time? You are preventing your classmates from paying attention and from doing their work."

"Mr. Jones, it ain't my fault everybody likes watching me instead of listening to you, and ...," explained William, but before he could finish his answer, Mr. Jones jumped in and said," Okay William, go to the principal's office. They'll know what to do with you."

At this time, William became upset. With his right hand, he pushed all of his books and folders on the floor, causing the papers he was trying to organize to spill out all around him. Students were watching with expressions on their faces that suggested that the exchange between Mr. Jones and William was nothing new, so they multitasked by copying the objectives of the day into their red folders while keeping an eye on William as he stomped out of the room to go to the principal's office. Bang! The door made a loud noise when he slammed it behind him.

Without showing signs of frustration, Mr. Jones gave a hand signal to two of the students sitting near William, and they understood it to mean to stop what they were doing and pick up William's books, folders, and papers and place them all under his desk inside the tray there. After the two students quickly cleaned up the mess, they resumed copying the course objectives of the day. By now, Mr. Jones was done writing the last objective of the day on the board and began reading each objective aloud. He requested that each student repeat each objective aloud, assuming that if they could repeat what he said, they could somehow learn it better.

"Objective number one: The subject and verb of any sentence must agree; singular subjects require singular verbs, and plural subjects require plural verbs. The plural subjects will have an s at the end of the word to indicate plural, and the verb will not have an s to indicate plural. As an example, 'The girls are going to the park to play volleyball immediately after school ends.' (The subject is plural and the verb is plural—both indicate more than one.)"

The classroom lesson continued until the bell rang to signal the end of the period and the start of the next period. Each class was conducted in this way until it came to the period devoted to teacher prep-time, student organizational meetings, and special sessions for students in need of extra help to understand and complete the day's class. Fifteen minutes before the end of the school day, students reported to their homeroom, the same class where each school day began, to receive special last-minute announcements in response to events that developed after the 8:15 AM morning announcements were piped throughout the school on the general public address system.

On any given day, if anyone were to walk inside a traditional public school classroom from Grades 1 to 12, he or she will witness events similar to those described in the above situation. Clearly, the teacher taught from a traditional framework, while students responded to the various stimuli articulated by their teacher. To a great degree, in the above learning community, teachers are seen as stewards of knowledge charged with the task of transmitting that knowledge to novice students, who are supposedly in their appropriate grade level based on chronological age more than their cognitive ability.

Of course, most classrooms are comprised of students covering a wide range of academic abilities, a wide range of emotional maturity, and a wide range of cultural sensibilities, even when by outward appearance all or most students appear to be a homogenous population. In spite of these differences, teachers follow a generic lesson plan format; hence, every teacher opens each class period by writing the objective(s) for the day on the board for everyone to copy into his or her preselected classroom folder. Some call this traditional form of instruction *direct instruction* (DI), some call it *going back to the basics,* and others call it *explicit instruction.* In all cases, there are clear guidelines for teachers to follow, and there are also clear expectations of what students are expected to do and learn.

As articulated above, the typical sequence of events in the classroom involves stating of the objective; providing explicit, teacher-directed examples to match the objective of the day; and providing follow-up examples to the entire class so students can demonstrate mastery of the course objective(s). As usual, procedural steps are outlined in the teacher's manual provided to all teachers to accompany the required subject area textbooks. This routine is not culturally responsive, in part because all that takes place inside each classroom is teacher driven and centered on the notion of one size, one way for all.

The teacher is in charge, and students are supposedly passive learners. Both parties have been conditioned to behave in rather prescribed ways, and both parties understand that learning is based on high-stakes tests designed by in-house and outside experts. Everyone is held accountable to someone for something that is sometimes less than relevant to teaching and learning. In spite of current demographic changes in society, the quality and type of education experienced by persons going to public school falls short of being culturally responsive and instructionally rigorous enough to ensure that once finished, high school graduates will have functional life options, from postsecondary school to professional schools and in the real world (Obiakor, 2004, 2007; Utley, Obiakor, & Kozleski, 2005).

In *Those Who Can, Teach,* Ryan and Cooper (1998) suggested that 20th-century American schools should embark on providing culturally responsive literacy instruction for all. The *Brown v. Board of Education, Topeka* case of 1954 was supposed to open the gates for equitable education. Today, researchers such as Kozol (2005) have noted that schools are more segregated now than in previous years. In point of fact, the location of schools defines the kind of literacy that prevails in them, and language capabilities are clearly linked to the socioeconomic status of school demographics. Yet some education commentators, like Hirsh (1987), continue to favor the Eurocentric, literacy-informed educational foundation. Not surprisingly, this thinking is visible in all facets of public education, including textbooks, curricula frameworks, and school personnel. This is the reason why a culturally responsive literacy instructional milieu must be compulsory for America to live up to its goal of providing all its citizenry with a quality educational experience. This is the focus of this chapter.

RECOGNIZING AND REDUCING TENSION WHEN BUILDING CULTURALLY RESPONSIVE LITERACY SCHOOLS AND COMMUNITIES

For all practical purposes, since the beginning of American civilization, its immigrant inhabitants have used public education to forge a new literacy in a new place to achieve social, political, and economic prosperity. Our literacy development is psycho- and socioculturally derived, and each immigrant community develops its own literacy for the sake of successfully communicating with one another and across ethnic groups. And since the beginning of public schools for all, there has been tension and clashes between the literacy created in each ethnic community and the literacy promoted inside schools. Zimmerman (2002) referred to these conflicts as cultural wars, emphasizing the jockeying of different ethnic groups for position second to that of the majority, European population, which tends to dominate all aspects of the goings-on in many public schools. For example, literacy experiences of culturally diverse people are frequently viewed as substandard, inferior, and totally inappropriate for expressing oneself and communicating learned knowledge in school. It is not a historical surprise that today's teachers teach the same material in the same way over the same period of time and evaluate students' success or failure in the same manner.

Even though it is known that teachers and students are different, and that they bring competing and complementary literacy histories to any and all classrooms, what happens inside most classrooms is uniform. Gone are the days when it was presumed that all students inside any classroom had the same literacy history, especially if the people in question looked alike and shared the same ethnic origin. Afferbach (1990), Cummins et al. (2005), and Edwards (2001) argued that to a certain degree, the success that students and teachers experience in class is born out of welcoming, knowing, and celebrating different literacy histories. Clearly, the literacy history debate gets magnified when the persons in question have different ethnic origins, like African-American, Latino, or Asian-American (Gay, 2000).

Nonetheless, little to no attention is given to the notion that students may have had different literacy experiences from birth to their first day of public schooling. Families within the lower socioeconomic category spend less money on reading materials and spend even less time reading to their children the supposed "classic" children stories that all students are presumed to know before entering preK or any primary grade. In addition, students born into lower socioeconomic status families continue to manifest traits of nonstandard English, in part because they do not have consistent and regular practice speaking or hearing others speak in a manner closely similar to the standard English taught in schools. Thus, students in a nonculturally responsive classroom have a more difficult time transitioning into the routines of school, because they are entering into a world where the language may sound familiar but is substantively different from that which they know and use at home.

For schools to be called culturally responsive, they must readdress the competing literacy histories that students already possess as they enter schools. Creating educational environments or experiences that are culturally responsive requires dispelling the myth or clearing up the misconception that all persons in a particular academic grade studying the same subject possess an equal amount of prior knowledge on all fronts. People are different from one another, yet many educators still try to box people into the same mold and insist on treating them the same. Save for sharing the same chronological age, most students who happen to be in the same grade do not enter school with identical backgrounds, literacy, or other knowledge and skills (Manzo, Manzo, & Thomas, 2005). The simple but complicated truth is that students enter schools with a wide range of different literary experiences, thus making it extremely hard for teachers, who also have different histories, to cater to learning needs and styles of all students (Lessen & Dejong, 2001; Smith, 1999). For instance, Lessen and Dejong concluded that students may have difficulty reconciling very different ways to acquire literacy. As a result, educators must effectively manage their classroom instruction in culturally responsive ways.

Today's teachers are called upon to be referees as they get all students to value and support each other's desire to excel in school. The problem remains that other versions of English are viewed as wrong, incorrect, bad, and improper and are devalued and silenced by persons in power in schools. While it is unrealistic for public schools to adopt and promote culturally responsive literacy for every child, schools can do a much better job of accepting the unique culture each person brings to school. They should accommodate differences in cultures by showcasing their similarities and differences, without favoring one over the other. Proclaiming the different literacy history of students and teachers translates into acknowledging that the literacy we develop and use is not a set of unchanging universal skills or knowledge operating in a vacuum or in the abstract. What truly counts depends on factors such as location, governing body, purpose, period in history, culture, socioeconomic situation, and power relations!

To reduce educational tensions, educators and service providers must value different literacy histories unfolding in schools. And to facilitate an accepting attitude about the different literacy histories that everyone brings into any classroom, educational professionals must welcome the exchange of different autobiographical literacy histories into the classroom community. Without the use of autobiographic recollection and exploration, the roles of students and teachers may remain one-dimensional, with students receiving the information that teachers are narrowly prepared to offer. With autobiographies in the curriculum, however, students become teachers and teachers become students, and learning becomes transactional, depending on the nature of the subject and assignment, with all participants discovering new perspectives about self vis-à-vis others.

Freire (1970) was right in his book *Pedagogy of the Oppressed,* when he stressed that the surest way for people to expand and grow beyond traditional roles is by self-interrogating their own lived experiences. Such self-interrogations are culturally based self-reflections about how people have come to be who they are. In addition, self-reflections foster respect and acceptance of the different literacy histories that students and teachers bring to schools. As an example, students can be invited to use pictures of families and familiar locations in their immediate and extended surroundings as the bases for writing activities; this may lead to a picture dictionary with thesaurus component to reflect the unique and common vocabulary and general language rules and patterns used by people within and across ethnic or homogeneous groups. Another example could be the use of a modified treasure hunt that reflects a literacy theme to encourage students and teachers to collect things that best reflect who they are in terms of literacy experiences and/or capabilities. Year to year, they can take turns doing show and tell or guessing what collected items belong to whom based on hints and clues. Creative teachers can foster literacy development and grants in their classrooms by inviting students to author language experience stories, whereby they write original stories or dictate sentences to a capable writer and later review and practice reading the original story to build a strong language base. At various grade levels, teachers and service providers can foster and enhance the literacy of all, consequently creating a culturally responsive learning community.

The irony is that schools have continued to try literacy assimilation based on selective membership by imposing the conventional, standard English that is adopted as the official language of the public education system. Of course, the version of English still used by many African Americans and other culturally and linguistically diverse people does not always mirror its parent English, and therein lies the problem. This imposition leads to assimilation, not accommodation, thus making it difficult for students to survive the intricacies of schooling (i.e., teaching, learning, testing, labeling, categorizing, and placing). According to Flood and Anders (2005), today's schools are insensitive to the dialectal nuances—nonconventional forms of English—displayed in different communities. For instance, while linguistically informed researchers like Smitherman (2001) and Jenkins (2006) have made strong cases about the validity and use of Black English in schools, many teachers continue to hold steadfast to the stereotype of perceiving Black English and other alternative versions as inappropriate or unpolished for school. These teachers forget that language dexterity is greatly influenced by the diversity of human contacts. The mastery of various language domains—phonological, vocabulary, and comprehension—affect how we perceive ourselves and affect how well we will succeed or how often we may fail when learning and communicating with each other in school. To a large extent, each of us begins to form our literacy identity inside our mother's womb and continue with each stage of development until birth; we subconsciously train ourselves to lock into a specific language (i.e., sound and frequency). Our immediate family and community relations play a major role in how we develop our literacy identity.

FORM AND CONTENT, NOT FORM OVER CONTENT, IN LITERACY ACQUISITION

Humans have the innate capability to form social relations with others for survival and social purposes, and it is by different literacy acts that people are who they are and that they are different from others. Our literacy modes of expression are different yet rooted in the same base English. These acts enable us to negotiate how we deal with life's challenges, life's surprises, and life's new developments alone and with others. In addition, our culturally derived language is a psychosocial, contextually derived creation that each human may develop partially or completely and, in most cases, differently from others. The stages of literacy development are (a) decoding knowledge, (b) vocabulary knowledge, (c) syntactic knowledge, (d) discourse knowledge, (e) metacognitive knowledge, and (f) fluency. The following subsections discuss these stages.

Decoding Knowledge

Decoding knowledge encompasses phonological development and deals with letter-sound manipulation and phonemic awareness of consonant and verb articulation. Consonants and verbs may involve one-, two-, or three-letter combinations.

Vocabulary Knowledge

Vocabulary knowledge deals with word creation and the realization that words are made up of prefixes, suffixes, cognates, and borrowed parts from different ethnic populations. It is also important to realize that all that we do and know is culturally informed; thus, language has become a primary means by which people and cultures develop and coexist. Once a language begins to diminish, the culture runs the risk of dying out in due time.

Syntactic Knowledge

Syntactic knowledge deals with creating sentences and ideas by stringing a series of words together in a rule-governed manner. It enables people to distinguish themselves from one another. Sentences can be simple or complex, and the ability to manipulate words to convey ideas is what separates humans from other forms of life.

Discourse Knowledge

Discourse knowledge deals with creating larger ideas in the context of different subject domains and stylistic variations; it is the means by which ideas are organized to suit different subject domains and literary styles. Every aspect of who we are is manifested through the means that make our lives available for others to experience; thus, we tend to have an affinity for certain styles of expression and subject domains over others. That is, some people have a greater literacy in math over English versus the arts or the kinesthetic literacy domains, to name a few.

Metacognitive Knowledge

Metacognitive knowledge deals with how well people understand their cognitive and literary capabilities. It also deals with people being aware of all that they do in clarifying where they are on the language continuum. Interestingly, all language learners go through similar paths to become completely fluent. In spite of the differences between standard, conventional English versus alternative forms, each stage on the language continuum is a part of the process. Teachers and service providers who see standard, conventional English as correct, proper, and good view all alternative versions of English as incorrect, improper, and bad. Such a stance is neither respectful of nor sensitive to the inevitable differences in how each ethnic American creates and re-creates literacy domains for the expressed purpose of learning and communicating ideas with peers, community members, and outsiders. All versions of English are uniquely rule governed, although they may be different from one another. It is necessary to examine what makes standard, conventional English different from the literacy style of others.

THE LACK OF ABSOLUTENESS OF LANGUAGE AND GOING BEYOND KNOWN ALPHABETS ■

The critical question is, Can one go beyond the 26 known alphabetic letters in literacy and/or language mastery? The phonemic sounds that correspond with the 26 letters of the American alphabet system are held captive to the Anglo, mid-Western way of expression. The standard, conventional English, spoken and written, that has been accepted as universal maintains it core essence; but as different people begin to experience and acquire it over time, the modes of expression change to reflect the diversity of its users. The debate continues to return to how different the literacy acts are from the standard, conventional version adopted as the form to master. For instance, some of the features of African-American literacy modes of expression that continue to differ from mainstream, conventional, standard English are described below (see Williams, 1975):

- The lack of contrast between *pin* and *pen* so as to pronounce them as homonyms, especially in Southern speech acts
- The /e/ becoming /i/ so that the word is *hin* rather than *hen* and *limon* rather than *lemon*
- Omitting /r/ in words like the person's name *Ca'ol* rather than *Carol*
- Simplification of final consonant clusters so that a word like *cold* becomes *cole* and a word like *left* becomes *lef*
- The zero copula; that is, the omission of the "to be" verb expressive form, wherein you get a sentence to read, "He busy," rather than, "He is busy."

As Williams pointed out, there are many noticeable differences between African-American literacy expression and the standard version promoted in schools, namely the following:

- Initial and final sounds of the phoneme /th/ read /d/ in words like *dat* and *dese* rather than *that* and *these*.
- Medial or final /r/ and /l/ deletion to read like *hip* and *des* rather than *help* and *desk*.
- Subject and verb disagreement to read, "We was there," rather than, "We were there," and, "Is you crazy?" rather than, "Are you crazy?"
- Possessive deletion to read "the girl dress" rather than "the girl's dress"

As it appears, the phonological issues that were prevalent many years ago are still prevalent in today's spoken and written forms of expression at all grade levels. It is imperative that teachers develop the skills to compare and contrast the competing versions of English; the objective should not be to stress that one version of English is better than the other but to stress that the versions are different from each other. To denote superiority of one form of English over another is a gross misrepresentation of the facts (Flint, 2008). Teachers and service providers may have an easier time getting students to understand the utility of both versions if they use the inductive mode of analysis to show common and dissimilar things about the two versions of English. Then it becomes critical to remind students that there may be appropriate times and places for all versions of English without having to choose one outright over all others.

This notion of using alternative versions of English for communicative purposes is not something new. From birth, we know that children respond to different people differently, via language acts, to show a greater affinity with some people more than others. For instance, the late Martin Luther King, Jr. altered his language style depending on the audience and purpose of his speaking engagement—he used a more conventional, standard style of English to address the Nobel Peace Prize audience and used a more unconventional style of English to address the garbage workers worried about needing a modest pay raise to maintain an acceptable lifestyle. Delpit (1995) argued that teachers and service providers should help students to determine the appropriate time and place to use one version of English over the other, as they embrace the rich qualities of this different language and use it as a bridge to master the conventional English and the norms and mores embedded within.

Without getting into the linguistic underpinnings of language, sound production (i.e., language) is not (and never will be) an absolute, organically derived, correct, proper, and right mode of expression easily learned by all. Although it is something that we have the innate capacity to develop, it can be based on whom we associate ourselves with as we grow into adulthood. Without human contacts, we may not develop our literacy capabilities to the degree that we otherwise would—it is by human contact that we grow into our literacy sensibilities. What is not given enough thought or attention is the fact that we have taken so much for granted in terms of how we develop our initial literacy. For example, the notion of learning to create the sounds associated with spoken and written English is more than the simple task of listening to someone and repeating verbatim what was heard. It is taken for granted and assumed that people hear sounds in the same manner and that they evolve into literacy skills in the same manner. The truth is that people hear, produce, and reproduce sounds in different ways from how others hear, produce, and reproduce sounds. As similar as the two versions may be, if they are analyzed closely, it will become clear that no two people communicate in the same manner.

Our spoken language capabilities are as unique as our fingerprints. Understanding such literacy shades of gray can play an instrumental role in how teachers and service providers facilitate the language development of students. The naïve understanding that teachers have about language and literacy formation and transmission has resulted in many students opting not to learn how to read, spell, and speak. For example, "Black English," something that has proven to be highly controversial, is not only a culturally derived, rule-governed entity, but it has a linguistic origin. That is, to produce the /th/ sound as /d/ rather than /th/ is about how one person uses the human instrument, the mouth, differently than those who speak the conventional way. Whether an individual is African-American or Anglo-American is less of an issue than the mere fact that each sound he or she produces is created in a unique way by how the mouth, lips, and tongue are manipulated vis-à-vis how he or she inhales and exhales, and whether or not sounds are produced with a vibration of air. A logical extension is that if students truly experienced learning literacy in a culturally responsive manner, the linguistic underpinning of speech (i.e., sound formation) would be addressed.

It is common knowledge that promoting literacy begins with introducing students to the alphabet song and making sure they can repeat the alphabet song with 100 percent accuracy. The task then shifts to associating each letter with a concrete object and specific sound. For example, students learn in a primary grade reading classroom that the letter *a* sounds like the /a/ in apple, the letter *b* sounds like the /b/ in ball, the letter *c* sounds like the /c/ in cat, and so on. Within a culturally responsive instructional setting, the learning of alphabets and sounds that correspond with each consonant and verb would be inductively taught. Perhaps the starting place would be writing each student's name on the overhead or board and saying each name aloud to determine what letter sounds are heard and to what degree and, conversely, what letter sounds are not heard and why. The discussion would then continue with stressing that there may not be a one-to-one correspondence to each letter of the alphabet—this will dispel the grand naïve assumption that learning the 26 sounds of each letter of the alphabet is enough to ensure complete literacy development.

In the same dimension, in a culturally responsive instructional setting, teachers would know that vowels are very iffy sounds to master, because they are easily influenced by the letters that come before or after them. So it would be counterproductive to start teaching students the sounds that correspond with the letters of the alphabet by starting with the letter *a,* a vowel. Instead, teachers may start with the letter *m,* for it is an easier sound to produce and one that most readily master at the earliest of ages.

In addition, it would be instructive to stop saying, "Sound it out," when a student comes to a letter sound or sound combination that has not been mastered. Instead, teachers and service providers may tell students to be cognizant that to produce the short /a/ sound, as in the word *sat,* a person must widely spread the mouth as if trying to produce a big smile, and it is necessary to pay attention to the position of the tongue, for it should be positioned low in the mouth. To get a student to utter the /a/ sound, the teacher may say something to the effect of asking a student to cry like a baby for emphasis purposes. Apparently, sounding letters out does not help students to learn how to match sounds with alphabets.

Such linguistic awareness constitutes cultural responsiveness, especially in working with exceptional students who have severe speech problems or who are considered English-language learners. Allen (1991, 1994) and O'Brien (1973) clarified methods and materials teachers and service providers should use to support the literacy development of English-language learners. To help these learners to master standard, conventional English, general and special educators must understand the phonological differences between English and the language involved. For example, educators of students with Spanish as a first language should know the following:

- There are fewer vowel sounds in English than in Spanish—no short /a/ as in *hat* and no short /i/ as in *fish.*
- Some high-frequency phonemic sounds that might cause confusion for speakers of Spanish origin are /b/ pronounced with a /p/, in changing *cab* to *cap;* /j/ becoming /y/, changing *jet* to *yet;* /ch/ becoming /sh/, changing *chin* to *shin;* /a/ becoming /e/, changing *bat* to *bet;* and /v/ becoming /b/, changing *vote* to *bote.*
- Morphological speaking, the Spanish *de* ("of"), used to show possession, means that the expression usually read as "Joe's pen" becomes "the pen of Joe." And *mes* ("more"), used to show comparison, means that a comparative word like "faster" becomes "more fast."

- Syntactically speaking, Spanish uses *no* for *not* so one would read, "He no do his homework."
- Having no *s* to make plurals means one says, "my two friend."
- Singular-plural agreement between adjectives and nouns and having adjectives follow nouns means one reads, "the elephants bigs."

Clearly, linguistic differences between Spanish literacy expression and standard, conventional English should be recognized by educators (Cummins, 1994; Cummins et al., 2005). Educational professionals must confess their shortcomings about being monolingual and thereafter become more open to learning from students elements of whatever second language they are confronted with. The *Lau v. Nichols* (1974) case should have crystallized this fact. A logical extension is that *Lau v. Nichols* mandated school districts to take positive and proactive steps to overcome the educational barriers experienced by students who do not speak English. Sadly, many people, including teachers and service providers, continue to advocate an "English-only" law of the land. As more and more teacher education programs begin to inform their preservice teachers about the reality of culturally derived languages, this trend may change! Hopefully, it will become clearer that culturally responsive literacy should be promoted and developed across the academic grade levels and across ethnic boundaries.

■ INSTRUCTION MATTERS IN LITERACY

We are a product of our life experiences. Moreover, we are a product of the people with whom we identify as having the most influence on us growing up. When it comes to teaching and instructional practices, we tend to use the same reasoning. So most teachers teach in the manner in which they were taught. On the one hand, few teachers can articulate a sound theoretical principle to support why they teach in a particular fashion. On the other hand, many teachers say that they teach the way they do because that is how they were taught. In retrospect, the "good old days" may represent when all of what teachers did proved to be effective for all. At times, we wonder if the "good old days" is a code phrase that refers to days gone by when schools were segregated and students did not question authority figures in schools; they simply did what they were told! If they failed, it was deserved; if they passed, it was due to the hard work of the teacher. This romantic recollection and fantasy has had everyone falling into line and getting whatever lesson, objective, or goal planned for any given instructional day.

These days, one cannot talk about effective instruction without talking about the 2001 No Child Left Behind Act, another federally charged directive supposedly created to make our schools good and leave no child behind. A particularly interesting aspect of this federal initiative is that lots of money has been allocated to incorporate scientifically researched best practices to ensure that all students inside public schools become literate. Yet the law is still poorly funded, especially when it comes to responding to the unique needs of culturally and linguistically diverse learners.

Unlike in yesteryear, it is not enough to use fond memories of days gone by to justify current teaching or instructional practices. Today, the driving strategy is direct instruction, also known as deductive or explicit instruction. Ironically, direct instruction is based on the premise of one size, one way suits all. As we understand it, within a direct instruction classroom community, the cultures of students and teachers have no factor on whether or not teachers are effective teachers and on whether or not students learn. This is evident in the steps of direct instruction, namely the following:

1. State the goal.

2. Show concise and lucid examples to suit the desired goal.

3. Provide some guided practice.

4. Provide independent time on-task to replicate the guided practice.

5. Return to Step 1 if the previous steps were unsuccessful.

6. Move on to a new task once the objective has been mastered.

If time runs out, blame resides with students if they failed to get it. As it appears, these procedural steps promote assimilation and not cultural responsiveness. In a typical traditional classroom, the following are true:

- The teacher seems always prepared and has the correct answer to every question provided during the lesson.
- Students are asked to listen to peers read and eventually get a chance to read aloud.
- The best readers are those who read fast and with the most accuracy.
- Teachers ask questions that have readily identifiable answers within the pages of the assigned reading.
- The "bad" readers are those who read slowly, mispronounce words, and cannot follow instructions. These "bad" readers are viewed as "bad" students, since they have questions when it is time to do independent seatwork.
- The "good" students are underchallenged, and the "bad" students are easily distracted and cause behavior problems.

In direct instruction, the goal or task is usually predetermined by some external expert through a prepackaged curriculum consisting of "basal" materials designed to follow a particular scope and sequence. On rare occasions, teachers are allowed to choose their own curricular materials; this mostly happens when their students perform well above the national average on high-stakes tests. As regards literacy formation, it is often decided in advance that the first order of business is to start with phonics and work toward fluency. But no consideration is given to what (phonic) knowledge students may have already mastered prior to entering school. So regardless of who students are and what knowledge they already possess, teachers must start at the beginning and work their way to a pre-established end. This pattern of selecting goals and tasks is the same in all areas. Thus, in this light, direct instruction may not be culturally responsive, because it breaks the most important rule of a culturally responsive literacy instructional community: *know your students and what knowledge they already have and what knowledge they may need to learn*. Afferbach (1990) suggested that having this prior knowledge would avoid wasting time reteaching knowledge students may already know or introducing knowledge beyond students' capabilities. Imagine what the students are thinking if they are told that they must devote valuable instructional time revisiting knowledge they already know and, worse, learn knowledge that may be so disconnected from their cultural knowledge base as to be incomprehensible.

To be more culturally responsive, teachers and service providers should give more attention to the inherent value of students' prior knowledge. And most importantly, attention should be given to the best mode of instruction to facilitate among students a desire and will to learn about any subject area. Once inside school, students intuitively begin to assess how closely the language they bring into school resembles what is passed on as standard, conventional English. They do not need to be told that they sound or communicate differently than what they are taught in school. The problem is not knowing what accounts for these differences.

For most Americans, the home language is different enough from the language in school that learning is compromised. That is, the degree to which people speak and write to mimic conventional, standard English is in direct proportion to how well they were nurtured prior to starting formal schooling. In addition, the differences between the communicative acts of persons from lower socioeconomic situations and affluent persons are dramatic enough that the person from a lower socioeconomic background may struggle in school if he or she does not develop an understanding of the school language and how it differs from the language developed at home. Gutiérrez (2005) and Rueda (2005) acknowledged that students born into a literacy community of low socioeconomic status have problems communicating in standard conventional English due to school-related and non-school-related problems. For instance, some parents may spend little time communicating with their children except to reply to requests for help; thus, these students have a difficult time participating in a dynamic teacher-and-student question-and-answer exchange.

For many idealists, becoming literate is as natural as learning to walk and talk without any explicit instruction. For literacy development to be culturally responsive, it has to be centered around authentic learning events that people can imagine themselves doing, even if they never have the benefit of formal education. Regardless of the name, the core is realizing that learning does not occur in a vacuum by robots filled with predetermined knowledge for others to access and memorize. Teachers and service providers must understand that they have the freedom and power to do the following:

- Initiate learning tasks.
- Survey students, informally and formally.
- See what background knowledge students have about a given topic.
- Survey materials that may be used to facilitate learning.
- Create the manner in which learning will be determined if students understand the topics under review.

Within an inclusive teaching framework, teachers and service providers might consider introducing a literature discussion about banned books to evaluate if they are harmful to the mental and moral development of students. Also, within a more inclusive teaching setting, lectures may be replaced by offering students a host of learning and reading strategies that are inseparable from the level at which they choose to engage themselves. New strategies may be used because teachers and service providers are no longer be held captive by the literacy police. The ultimate goal is to create a culturally responsive school where all students can feel accepted and nurtured equitably (Bazron, Osher, & Fleischman, 2005).

Logically, a culturally responsive school creates a more culturally responsive instructional learning community, as advocated by Winzer and Mazurek's (1998) book, *Special Education in Multicultural Contexts;* Obiakor's (2001) book, *It Even Happens in "Good" Schools: Responding to Cultural Diversity in Today's Classrooms;* Delpit and Dowdy's (2002) book, *The Skin That We Speak: Thoughts on Language and Culture in the Classroom;* Jenkin's (2006) book, *What's Missing in the Education of African-American Children: The Real Reasons Behind the Gap;* and Obiakor's (2007) book, *Multicultural Special Education: Culturally Responsive Teaching.*

REVISITING WILLIAM ■

In the introductory case, William was a student who actually enjoyed daily struggles with his teacher who, in turn, enjoyed "getting rid of" him. The lack of placidity in William's class was caused by both him and his teacher. Apparently, William enjoyed getting on the teacher's nerves, while the teacher enjoyed excluding William from instruction. The problem, however, was that the teacher's instructional strategy was mundane, traditional, boring, uncreative, and uninteresting to many of his students, including William. In other words, his instruction was not necessary for *all* his students. Based on his dealings with William, he failed to comprehend issues of learning styles, multiple intelligences, and intraindividual and interindividual differences. More than two decades ago, DeBruyn (1984) concluded that "if we adopt a 'get rid of' attitude, we violate a basic tenet of education: that each student is an individual, and that our instruction and curriculum must try to make allowances for individual differences" (p. 1).

To teach students like William is to know and value them! Teachers and service providers must go beyond tradition to reach different students who learn and interact differently. The goal must be to provide literacy instruction in least-restrictive environments that allow *all* students to bloom. Teachers and service providers must understand and value the wide range of academic abilities, multiple intelligences, multiple voices and personalities, and cultural sensibilities that students bring to classrooms. They need to shift their literacy instructional paradigms and modify and adapt their classroom activities to be inviting to their students. Hilliard (1992) argued that teachers and service providers must develop *real pedagogical power.* As he concluded,

> Real pedagogical power means that all children reach a high level of achievement on criterion-based standards. It means that all children who may have disabilities receive sophisticated, valid service that causes them to do better than they would have done if they had not received special services at all. (p. 168)

■ MOVING ON

This chapter has focused on how to provide culturally responsive literacy instruction for all students, their race, culture, socioeconomics, and national origin notwithstanding. We have argued that literacy instruction cannot be divorced from language and cultural valuing. Our premise is that language is an integral part of culture. No language is better than the other, but languages are different from each other. As a result, teachers and service providers must recognize the linguistic packages that students bring to school. This recognition will help them to design instructional packages that meet the unique needs of students. Teachers and service providers can build on already acquired frames of reference and extend them to new knowledge.

Denying people's languages is to deny their humanity. There is a connectivity between how culturally prepared or unprepared teachers are and how they teach those from different cultures. Clearly, teachers and service providers must get out of their comfort zones to reach the "unreachable" and teach the "unteachable." In the end, we must acknowledge that what goes on in the classroom must be connected to what goes on in communities. For culturally responsive literacy instruction to meet the needs of all students, teachers and service providers must create culturally responsive environments that nurture culturally related activities.

Appendix A

Glossary

Acoustic-visual cognition: Understanding that written spellings systematically represent phonemes of spoken words.

Adult-reader reading: The adult reads a passage first, providing the reader with a model of fluent reading. Then the reader rereads the same passage aloud to the adult, with the adult providing assistance and encouragement.

Affective techniques: Techniques that make readers aware of learning environments by cueing them to maintain attention, use time management, and reduce anxiety.

After-reading self-questioning strategy: A strategy that teaches readers to self-generate questions and self-respond to questions after reading a passage.

Alliteration: Occurrence in a phrase of two or more words having the same initial sound.

Alphabetic principle: Knowledge and skills involved when a reader learns to map speech to print. Effective use of the alphabetic principle requires proficiency in letter recognition, sound-letter relationships, and spelling skills.

Automaticity: Fast, accurate, and effortless identification of words in isolation or in lists. It entails an unconscious use of a skill quickly and without error.

Basic assumptions of literacy development: People hear, produce, and reproduce sounds differently than others hear, produce, and reproduce sounds. No two people communicate in the same manner.

Before-reading self-questioning strategy: A strategy that teaches readers to use self-questioning as a way to preview a passage before initiating and creating a set of guiding questions to check comprehension during reading.

Black English: A culturally derived, rule-governed entity with a linguistic origin.

Blending: A skill in which readers combine individual phonemes to form words.

Building word recognition skills: Skills related to increasing the number of words that a reader can recognize effortlessly and without thought.

Cause-and-effect diagram: A visual representation of the to-be-learned material, allowing a reader to see the relationship between an action and event and how that relationship will produce a certain response to the action in the form of another event.

Choral reading: An instructional strategy in which readers read along as a group with another fluent reader or readers.

Clarifying: An activity whereby readers are cued to attend to text difficulty and are taught to use reading strategies to restore meaning.

Cognitive strategies: A set of strategies that provides a structure for learning. Such strategies actively and explicitly cue readers to comprehend and retain acquired information by activating and using self-engaging strategies.

Cognitively guided instruction: Instruction that emphasizes learning strategies to enhance metacognition. Such strategies help the instructional process by focusing on direct teaching and explicit modeling of cognitive learning strategies and enhancing readers' practice opportunities.

Comprehension: The purpose for reading; understanding what is read.

Comprehension instruction: Instruction in comprehension that helps readers to understand what they read, remember what they read, and communicate effectively with others about what they read.

Comprehension monitoring: The ability to monitor learning progress and to select alternative strategies as necessary.

Concept maps and graphic organizers: Visual representations of the to-be-learned material, allowing readers to see similarities and differences between and among subject matter and concepts.

Connected text: Any written material involving multiple words that results in coherent discourse and thoughts. Phrases, sentences, and paragraphs are examples of connected text that can be recognized, recalled, and retained where comprehension is necessary.

Cooperative learning strategies: A set of learning strategies that allows the teacher to plan literacy groups and/or execute individual or group assignments.

Cultural wars: Tension and clashes between the literacies created in each ethnic community and with literacy promoted inside traditional schools.

Culturally responsive curricula: Curricula that are authentic, child centered, and connected to readers' lives.

Culturally responsive literacy instruction: Literacy instruction in a community of learners whereby teachers and other adults guide and facilitate diverse learners' linguistic underpinnings of speech; understand, value, and respect diverse learners' unique and individual sound formations and prior knowledge, motivations, and authentic literacy events; and explicitly and directly facilitate literacy opportunities. Such instruction enhances diverse learners' contributions to their own and others' behavioral, cultural, ethnic, linguistic, literate, and social identities. Such instruction encourages teachers and learners to accept, nurture equitably, and value their own and others' self-worth as human beings in, and as contributors to, our world.

Culturally responsive schools: Schools that address competing literacy histories that readers already possess upon school entry, welcoming the exchange of different autobiographical literacy histories into classroom communities.

Culturally responsive teachers: Teachers possessing knowledge, skills, and dispositions that respect and value diverse learners' interests, experiences, and backgrounds when planning, managing, delivering, and evaluating their teaching of these skills.

Culturally responsive literacy teaching: A pedagogy that acknowledges the significance of including readers' cultural preferences in all aspects of learning, providing a connection between culture and curriculum, home and school, while promoting socioemotional wellness and academic achievement.

Decoding: Result of sounding out letters, words, phrases, and sentences by using an understanding of the relationships between graphemes and phonemes.

Decoding knowledge: Knowledge that encompasses phonological development and deals with letter-sound manipulation and phonemic awareness of consonant and verb articulation.

Delivering instruction: A component of effective instruction that involves presenting content, monitoring student learning, and adjusting the teaching-learning process.

Dialectal nuances: Nonconventional forms of English, as displayed in different communities.

Discourse knowledge: Knowledge that seeks to create larger ideas in the context of different subject domains and stylistic variations; the means by which ideas are organized to suit different subject domains and literary styles.

During-reading self-questioning strategy: A strategy that teaches readers to use the self-questioning process as they read paragraphs and sections of passages.

Dysfluency: Lack of ability to decipher known words, process text meaning, decode unknown words, and read phrases and sentences automatically and rapidly.

Elaboration: The ability to associate and expand on a new piece of information with information already learned.

Evaluating instruction: A component of effective instruction that involves the process by which teachers decide whether the methods and materials they are using are appropriate, as based on students' performances.

Explicit instruction: Direct teaching of literacy concepts, academics, linguistics, language, and reading comprehension strategies needed to complete academic tasks and learning requirements.

Fluency: The ability to project the natural pitch, stress, and juncture of the spoken word on written text, automatically and at a natural rate, coupled with the ability to group words quickly to gain meaning from what is being read.

Formative evaluation: Evaluation that occurs during the process of instruction such that a teacher collects data during instruction and uses data to make informed, instructional decisions.

Frustration reading level: The level measured by an assessment device at which a reader is completely unable to read the material with adequate word identification or comprehension.

Grapheme: The smallest part of written English language that represents a phoneme in the spelling of a word.

Guided interaction: Interaction in which teachers structure lessons so that readers work together to understand what they read by listening, speaking, reading, and writing collaboratively about concepts.

Independent reading level: The level measured by an assessment device at which a reader reads successfully without assistance.

Instructional reading level: The level measured by an assessment device at which a reader reads with assistance from a teacher.

Listening activities: Activities in which readers have opportunities to listen to and talk with others, facilitating their knowledge, skills, and dispositions in writing and reading skills.

Listening vocabulary: Vocabulary that includes the words we need to know to understand what we hear.

Literature-based reading instruction: Instruction that features stories from various cultures and languages displayed in classrooms; readers' writings, portfolios, poetry, and/or field notes.

Main idea and details diagram: A visual representation of the to-be-learned material, allowing a reader to organize important concepts and details that support main concepts.

Managing instruction: A component of effective instruction that involves getting ready for teaching, using time productively, and creating a positive environment.

Meaning-based context and universal theme: Something meaningful from readers' everyday lives that can be used as a springboard to interest readers in academic concepts.

Metacognition and authentic assessment: Assessment in which teachers model and explicitly teach thinking skills crucial to learning new concepts.

Metacognitive knowledge: Knowledge related to how well people understand their own cognitive and literary capabilities; learning about what people do and how they learn; clarifying where people are on the language continuum.

Modeling, graphic organizers, and visuals: Use of a variety of visual aids, including pictures, diagrams, and charts.

Morphemes: Smallest meaningful units of language to speak or write. These include prefixes, suffixes, and inflected endings.

Morphology knowledge: Knowledge related to understanding the makeup of words, including word base and word units.

Multimedia and technology: Media and technology that include Web-based picture libraries, media, digitized books, and other technology-enriched instruction.

Oral vocabulary: Vocabulary that refers to words one uses when speaking or listening.

Organizing: The ability to arrange material into a well-thought-out and meaningful framework.

Paraphrasing: One's own rendition of essential information and ideas expressed by someone else.

Partner reading: A reading strategy in which paired readers take turns reading aloud to each other. More fluent readers are often paired with less fluent peers.

Patterned books: Books containing stories with predictable features, such as rhyming and repeated phrases. Often used to promote language development.

Phoneme addition: Making a new word by adding a phoneme to an existing word.

Phoneme blending: Listening to a sequence of separately spoken phonemes, then combining the phonemes to form and write a word.

Phoneme categorization: Recognizing the word in a set of three or four words that has the "odd" sound.

Phoneme identification: Recognizing the same sounds in different words.

Phoneme isolation: Recognizing the individual sounds in a word.

Phoneme manipulation: Working and playing with phonemes in words.

Phoneme segmentation: Breaking a word into its separate sounds and saying each sound as tapped out or counted.

Phoneme substitution: Replacing one phoneme for another to make a new word.

Phoneme: The smallest part of sound in a spoken word that makes a difference in the word's meaning; individual sounds that make up words.

Phonemic awareness: Understanding that sounds make words and that sounds of spoken language work together to make words. Such awareness includes the insight that every spoken word can be conceived of as a sequence of phonemes.

Phonemic detection: Recognizing the word that remains when a phoneme is removed from another word.

Phonics: Understanding the relationships between the letters (graphemes) of written language and the individual sounds (phonemes) of spoken language. Includes sound structure skills.

Phonological processing: Process of identifying sounds and subsequently identifying the words that the sounds combine to make.

Planning instruction: A component of effective instruction that involves making instructional decisions, including what to teach and how to teach it, and communicating realistic expectations.

Pragmatics: Functional language use.

Predicting: An activity whereby readers hypothesize what an author will discuss next in the text such that readers can confirm or disprove hypotheses by linking new knowledge encountered in the text with prior knowledge.

Prerecorded tape-assisted reading: A tactic in which readers read together as they listen to a fluent reader, then reread the passage aloud on audiotape.

Reader-centered instruction: Instruction that encourages learning to be cooperative, collaborative, and community oriented.

Readers' theater: A tactic in which readers rehearse and perform a play for peers or others.

Reading comprehension: The process of understanding and constructing meaning from written text.

Reading vocabulary: Vocabulary that a reader recognizes or uses in print.

Rehearsal: The act of practicing the material being learned.

Repeated readings: A reading strategy that enhances comprehension and fluency whereby a reader is cued to read a passage multiple times to increase accuracy and read with fewer errors.

Retellings: A means of enhancing reading comprehension whereby the reader reads a passage and, immediately upon completion, retells what he or she remembers from the passage.

Rhyme knowledge: Understanding the similarity of word endings.

Segmenting: Breaking words into their individual phonemes.

Self-interrogating own lived experiences: Culturally based self-reflections about how people come to be who they are. Such experiences imbue the different literacy histories that readers and teachers bring to schools with recognition, regard, acceptance, and valuing.

Self-questioning: The ongoing process of asking oneself questions before, during, and after instruction to enhance retention and recall, as well as speed and accuracy.

Semantics knowledge: Understanding the meaning or content of words and word combinations.

Sequencing diagram: A visual representation of the to-be-learned material, allowing a reader to see the order of events and how events fit with each other.

Simple sentence patterns: A teaching tactic of enhancing reading comprehension through the repetition of a simple sentence pattern.

Social identity: An individual's sense of self in relation to others.

Speaking vocabulary: Vocabulary that includes the words we use when we speak.

Structural analysis of words: One's ability to add prefixes, suffixes, or other meaningful word units to a base word, sometimes referred to as morphemic analysis.

Structural knowledge analysis: An analysis involving word recognition and word attack skills.

Student team literature: Use of award-winning novels, higher-order thinking activities, and cooperative learning to create a motivating literate environment for reading.

Student-adult reading: A literacy opportunity in which the reader reads one-on-one with an adult.

Summarizing: A tactic wherein readers reduce large selections of text to their smallest units to enhance comprehension.

Summative evaluation: Evaluation that occurs at the end of instruction whereby the teacher administers a test or formal assessment to determine whether readers have met instructional objectives.

Syllabication knowledge: Knowledge related to an understanding that letters in a word correspond approximately to a syllable of spoken language.

Syllable knowledge: Understanding of a unit of spoken language that is comprised of one or more vowel sounds alone, a syllabic consonant alone, or any of these with one or more consonant sounds.

Syntactic knowledge: Knowledge related to the act of creating sentences and ideas by stringing a series of words together in a rule-governed manner.

Syntax: Order and relationship between words and other structural elements in phrases and sentences.

Tape-assisted reading: A tactic whereby readers follow the passage as they hear a fluent reader read the passage on an audiotape.

Teachers' competence in comparing and contrasting competing versions of English: The knowledge, skills, and dispositions that teachers and other adults working with diverse learners must have when comparing and contrasting competing versions of English; recognizing and acting on the belief that one version of English is not better than others but stressing that behavioral, cultural, ethnic, linguistic, and social versions of English (and other languages) are different from each other.

Teaching: The systematic presentation of content assumed necessary for mastery within a general area of knowledge; the process by which teachers explicitly and directly demonstrate, guide, arrange practice opportunities, and reflect such that learners learn.

Venn diagram: A visual representation of the to-be-learned material that allows a reader to see the relationship between two sets of information.

Vocabulary knowledge: Knowledge related to word creation and the realization that words are made up of prefixes, suffixes, cognates, and borrowed parts from different behavioral, cultural, ethnic, linguistic, and social populations. All that a people do and know is culturally informed; language is a primary means by which people and cultures develop and coexist.

Vocabulary: An understanding that words have meanings and that knowing the meaning of new words is important for reading higher-level passages. Critical for comprehension, vocabulary is the words we must know to communicate effectively.

Word typography: Visual appearance of printed characters on a page.

Writing vocabulary: Vocabulary that includes the words we use in writing.

Zero copula: An omission in the African-American literacy tradition of the "to be" verb expressive form.

Appendix B

Additional Suggested Readings on Cultural Diversity

Banks, J., Cookson, P., Gay, G., Hawley, W., Irvine, J., Nieto, S., et al. (2001). Diversity within unity: Essential principles for teaching and learning in a multicultural society [Electronic version]. *Phi Delta Kappan, 8*(3), 196–203. Retrieved October 11, 2003, from Academic Search Premier

Bowman, B. (1994). *Cultural diversity and academic achievement.* (Order No. UMS-CD094). Oak Brook, IL: Urban Education Program. (ERIC Documentation Reproduction Service No. ED382757)

Connelly, F., & Clandinin, D. (1990). Stories of experience and narrative inquiry. *Educational Researcher, 19*(5), 2–14.

Cotton, K. (1991). School improvement research series: Fostering intercultural harmony in schools; Research finding (Contract RP91002001). Portland, OR: Northwest Regional Educational Laboratory. Retrieved October 1, 2003, from www.nwrel.org/scpd/sirs/8/topsyn7.html

Cummins, J. (1995). Empowering minority students: A framework for intervention. In L. Weis & L. Delpit. *Other people's children: Cultural conflict in the classroom.* New York: The New Press. (Reprinted from *Harvard Educational Review, 1986, 56*(1), 18–36)

Delpit, L. (2003). Educators as "seed people" growing a new future. *Educational Researcher, 32*(7), 14–21.

Dimitriadis, G. (2001). *Performing identity/performing culture: Hip hop as text, pedagogy and lived practice.* New York: Peter Lang Publishing.

Freeman, C., Scafidi, B., & Sjoquist, D. (2002). *Racial segregation in Georgia public schools 1994–2001: Trends, causes and impact on teacher quality* (Fiscal Research Program Report #77). Atlanta, GA: Andrew Young School of Policy Studies. Retrieved August 15, 2008, from http://aysps.gsu.edu/frc/files/report77.pdf

García, E. (1999). *Student cultural diversity: Understanding and meeting the challenge* (2nd ed.). Boston: Houghton Mifflin.

Gee, J. (1999). Literacy, discourse, and linguistics: Introduction. *Journal of Education, 171,* 5–17.

Greene, M. (1995). *Releasing the imagination: Essays on education, the arts, and social change.* San Francisco: Jossey-Bass.

Grieco, E., & Cassidy, R. (2001). *Overview of race and Hispanic origin: Census 2000 brief.* Washington, DC: U.S. Department of Commerce, Economics and Statistics Administration, U.S. Census Bureau. Retrieved October 6, 2003, from http://www.census.gov/prod/2001pubs/cenbr01-1.pdf

Hale, J. (2001). *Learning while Black: Creating educational excellence for African American children.* Baltimore, MD: Johns Hopkins University Press.

He, M. F. (2002). A narrative inquiry of cross-cultural lives: Lives in China. *Journal of Curriculum Studies, 34*(3), 301–321.

Howard, T. C. (2003). Culturally relevant pedagogy: Ingredients for critical teacher reflection [Electronic version]. *Theory into Practice, 42*(3), 195–202. Retrieved October 5, 2003, from Academic Search Premier

Josselson, R. (Ed.). (1996). *The narrative study of lives: Vol. 4. Ethics and process in the narrative study of lives.* Thousand Oaks, CA: Sage.

Klug, B., & Whitfield, P. (2002). *Widening the circle: Culturally relevant pedagogy for American Indian children.* New York: RoutledgeFalmer.

Meadows, D. H. (1990). *State of the village report.* Hartland, VT: Sustainability Institute. Retrieved August 5, 2008, from http://www.sustainer.org/dhm_archive/index.php

Ladson-Billings, G. (1994). *The dreamkeepers: Successful teachers of African American children.* San Francisco: Jossey-Bass.

Ladson-Billings, G. (1995). But that's just good teaching! The case for culturally relevant pedagogy [Electronic version]. *Theory into Practice, 34*(3), 159–165. Retrieved October 5, 2003, from Academic Search Premier

Lipka, J. (2002). *Schooling for self-determination: Research on the effects of including Native language and culture in the schools* (Report No. ED-99-CO-0027). Charleston, WV: Clearinghouse on Rural Education and Small Schools. (ERIC Document Reproduction Service No. ED459989)

Morrison, T. (1970). *The bluest eye.* New York: Lume.

Mullen, L. (2002, January). Review note: Sarah Pink (2001). [Review of the book *Doing ethnography: Images, media and representation in research*]. *Forum Qualitative Sozialforschung/Forum: Qualitative Social Research, 3*(1). Retrieved October 10, 2003, from http://www.qualitative-research.org/fqs-texte/1-02/1-02review-mullen-e.htm

Nieto, S. (2000). *Affirming diversity: The sociopolitical context of multicultural education* (3rd ed.). New York: Longman.

Nussbaum, M. C. (1997). *Cultivating humanity: A classical defense of reform in liberal education.* Cambridge, MA: Harvard University Press.

Ohanian, S. (1999). *One size fits few: The folly of educational standards.* Portsmouth, NH: Heinemann.

Palmer, P. (1998). *The courage to teach.* San Francisco: Jossey-Bass.

Perry, T., & Delpit, L. (1998). *The real Ebonics debate: Power, language, and the education of African-American children.* Boston: Beacon Press.

Phillion, J. (2002). Narrative multiculturalism. *Journal of Curriculum Studies, 34*(3), 265–279.

Salzer, J. (1998, February). Regents board says little is expected from poor, minority students. *Online Athens: Athens Banner Herald.*

Steele, C. M. (1992, April). Race and the schooling of Black Americans. *The Atlantic Monthly, 269*(4). Retrieved August 26, 2003, from http://www.theatlantic.com/politics/race/steele.htm

Townsend, B. L. (2002). Leave no teacher behind: A bold proposal for teacher education [Electronic version]. *International Journal of Qualitative Studies in Education,15*(6), 727–738. Retrieved October 5, 2003, from Academic Search Premier

Villegas, A. M. (1991). *Culturally responsive pedagogy for the 1990s and beyond.* Washington, DC: ERIC Clearinghouse on Teacher Education.

Weis, L., & Fine, M. (Eds.). (2005). *Beyond silenced voices: Class, race, and gender in United States schools* (rev. ed.). Albany, NY: State University of New York Press.

West, C. (2001). *Race matters* (2nd ed.). New York: Vintage.

Appendix C

*Sources for Reviews of
Multicultural Literature for
Children and Adolescents*

http://www.eastern.edu/publications/emme/

The *Electronic Magazine of Multicultural Education* (EMME) is a free-access e-journal published twice a year for international scholars, practitioners, and students of multicultural education. EMME provides a forum for the exchange of ideas to strengthen the theories and practices of multicultural education. Each issue of EMME contains themed and specific articles dealing with broad topics in multicultural education, instructional activities, and reviews of books and multimedia materials. EMME is an excellent source for reviews of books for young readers (see example below).

Cole, Babette. (1997). *Prince Cinders.* New York: Putnam Publishing Group. (32 pp.)

This new twist on the original Cinderella story will delight boys and girls of all ages. Cinders, the runt of the family, is relegated to cleaning up beer cans and macho magazines after his three big, masculine older brothers, who spend their time at the Palace Disco with their princess girlfriends. Finally one night, as Cinders is doing a load of his brothers' dirty socks, a fairy drops down the chimney and tries to improve the plight of poor Cinders. Unfortunately, most of the spells go wildly amok as the fairy gives Cinders a swimsuit in her attempts to create a fashionable suit and accidentally turns him into an ape when trying to give him a more "buff," masculine look. Nonetheless, Cinders looks in the mirror and thinks he looks dashing; he jumps in a little red sports car (the one item the fairy got right) and heads off to the Palace Disco. The remaining events of the night result in Cinders meeting Princess Lovelypenny on the public transit system and the loss of his pants (not glass slippers) as the princess tries to find out his name. Ending in the happy union of Cinders with Princess Lovelypenny, this book will help children realize that love goes beyond being skin deep and gives an alternate view of princes and princesses.

SOURCE: http://www.eastern.edu/publications/emme/2002fall/book_reviews.html

http://ijme-journal.org/index.php/ijme

The *International Journal of Multicultural Education* (IJME) is the successor to EMME as a peer-reviewed, open-access journal for scholars, researchers, practitioners, and students of multicultural education. Its editors are committed to promoting educational equity, cross-cultural understanding, and global aware-ness in all levels of education. IJME publishes a variety of writings, such as research reports, typically of a qualitative orientation; literature-based, scholarly articles addressing theories and scholarship of multicultural education; essays describing successful multicultural education programs or practical instructional ideas and strategies; and reviews of visual arts, professional and children's books, and multimedia resources. Registration is required to access the journal.

http://www.isomedia.com/homes/jmele/homepage.html

The Multicultural Book Review Homepage (MBRH) is an annotated collection of multicultural literature for teachers and other professionals working with children and adolescents in grades K–12. The books are grouped in the following sections: African-American Literature, Asian-American/Pacific Islander Literature, Latino and Latina Literature, Native American and Eskimo Literature, Jewish, Middle Eastern or East Indian, Titles in English From Other Countries, Textbooks, and Multiple Ethnicities. Many of the reviews are contributed by practicing profes-sionals, and each includes the following information (see examples below):

- Author and title, publisher, year of publication, whether or not there are illustrations, the culture or ethnicity dealt with in the book, whether the protagonist is male or female, and brief information about the type of book (e.g., fiction, autobiography)
- A short annotation about the content and purpose of the book
- An indication of the most suitable age group (K–3, 4–6, middle school/junior high, or high school) for the book
- A grade for the book (A+ to F).

Invisible Man. Ralph Ellison, Vintage Books, 1947.

African-American, male, fiction. The classic novel of the experience of African-Americans who are caught between what white society expects and what black society sees of them. Beautifully written, strong, moving, emotional. For older students who can under-stand its subtleties. Longish book. Suitable for high-school upper classmen. Grade: A

Honor and Duty, Gus Lee, Ivy Books, 1994.

Chinese-American, male, fiction. The follow-up to Lee's first book *China Boy,* [this] fol-lows Kai Ting through his ordeals at West Point as the only Chinese-American in the school. Only caution: the book is long. Suitable for high school. Grade: B+

SOURCE: http://www.isomedia.com/homes/jmele/joe.html

http://www.mcreview.com/

MultiCultural Review (MCR) is a subscription-based resource for finding materials to add to your library collections or to assist in classroom instruction. MCR is dedicated to providing information to enhance understanding of diversity. It focuses on differences in ethnicity, race, spirituality, religion, disability, and language and contains reviews of new English-language or bilingual books and nonprint materials in the Reviews section of each issue.

Appendix D

Other Resources

100 Best Books

A list of best books for kids selected by the National Education Association, grouped by age level, is posted on the TeachersFirst.com Web site. There are also links to other literacy resources. http://www.teachersfirst.com/100books.htm

A to Z Teacher Stuff

This Web site provides teachers with lesson plans, thematic units, reproducible materials, and other resources. An active discussion forum allows teachers to exchange ideas and give advice on a variety of issues. http://atozteacherstuff.com

ReadWriteThink

Teachers share lessons that have been successful with English-language learners on this Web site. The materials include relevant research support and everything needed for implementation, including step-by-step instructional plans, applicable resources, and appropriate assessment techniques. http://www.readwritethink.org

OTHER HELPFUL WEB SITES ON DIVERSITY ■ AND MULTICULTURAL SUPPORT

Diversity Calendar

Monthly listings of ethnic, national, and religious days. From the University of Kansas. http://www3.kumc.edu/diversity/

Diversity Web

This resource hub for higher education is part of an initiative designed to create new pathways for diversity collaboration and connection via the World Wide Web and more traditional forms of print communication. It is a component of a larger communications initiative entitled Diversity Works. http://www.diversityweb.org

Educating Teachers for Diversity

This article addresses the critical issue of preparing future teachers to promote "meaningful, engaged learning for all students, regardless of their race, gender, ethnic heritage, or cultural background." From North Central Regional Educational Laboratory (NCREL). http://www.ncrel.org/sdrs/areas/issues/educatrs/presrvce/pe300.htm

Equity and Diversity Resources

Articles, self checklists, stories, and more on the issues of equity and diversity in the classroom. From the Eisenhower National Clearinghouse. http://www.goenc.com

Multicultural Education and Ethnic Groups: Selected Internet Sources

A mix of Web resources on multicultural education and diversity, including background articles, Web sites for K–12 teachers, bibliographies, biographies, ethnic cooking, religion, and more. From the California State University—Stanislaus Library. http://www.library.csustan.edu/lboyer/multicultural/main.htm

Reading Resources: Celebrate It Through Reading 365 Days a Year— Multicultural Web Resources

These Web resources promote multiculturalism through literature. They provide a window on the world for your students. From the National Education Association. http://www.nea.org/webresources/readmulticult 0509.html

Teaching Tolerance: Resources for Educators

This Web site (a project of the Southern Poverty Law Center) encourages people from all walks of life to fight hate and promote tolerance. Two free classroom resources are available:

- *Teaching Tolerance* magazine subscription (one copy per issue)
- *Responding to Hate at School* booklet (available in bulk)

http://www.tolerance.org/teach/index.jsp

Appendix E

Audio Clips

Dr. Julie Wood: Girls and Technology

Dr. Wood explains the phenomenon of girls losing interest in math, science, and computers and offers ideas on how to counter the trend. http://real.playstream.com:8080/ramgen/sinc/TeacherRadio/tr76_20010307_wood5.smi

Wynton Marsalis: Jazz for Young People Curriculum

World-renowned trumpeter and music educator talks about the inspiration for his new Jazz for Young People curriculum. http://real.playstream.com:8080/ramgen/sinc/teacherradio2/tr14_20020204_marsalis.smi

Appendix F

National Reading Panel

In 1997, Congress asked the National Institute of Child Health and Human Development (NICHD), through its Child Development and Behavior Branch, to work with the U.S. Department of Education in establishing a National Reading Panel that would evaluate existing research and evidence to find the best ways of teaching children to read. The 14-member panel considered roughly 100,000 reading studies published since 1966 and another 10,000 published before that time; from this pool, the panel selected several hundred studies for its review and analysis.

A brief summary of the panel's findings is described below, revealing that a combination of techniques is effective for teaching reading:

- **Phonemic awareness**: Knowledge that spoken words can be broken apart into smaller segments of sound known as phonemes. Readers who are read to at home—especially material that rhymes—often develop the basis of phonemic awareness. Readers who are not read to will probably need to be taught that words can be broken apart into smaller sounds.
- **Phonics:** Knowledge that letters of the alphabet represent phonemes and that these sounds are blended together to form written words. Readers who are skilled in phonics can sound out words they haven't seen before, without first having to memorize them.
- **Fluency:** Ability to recognize words easily; read with greater speed, accuracy, and expression; and understand better what is read. Readers gain fluency by practicing reading until the process becomes automatic; guided oral repeated reading is one approach to helping readers become fluent readers.
- **Guided oral reading:** Reading out loud while getting guidance and feedback from skilled readers. The combination of practice and feedback promotes reading fluency.
- **Teaching vocabulary words:** Teaching new words, either as they appear in text or by introducing new words separately. This type of instruction also aids reading ability.

SOURCE: Adapted from National Reading Panel. (2001). *About the National Reading Panel: Charge to the NRP.* Retrieved January 7, 2008, from http://www.nationalreadingpanel.org/NRPAbout/Charge.htm

- **Reading comprehension strategies:** Techniques for helping readers to understand what they read. Such techniques involve having readers summarize what they've read to gain a better understanding of the material.

The panel's findings, released in April 2000, and other reading research provided the basis for the No Child Left Behind Act, which was signed by the president in December 2001. The Act calls upon states to set basic reading standards for local school systems and to test students to ensure that they have met those standards. To find out more about the work of the National Reading Panel, visit its home page at www.nationalreadingpanel.org and/or download copies of the following reports:

- *Report of the National Reading Panel: Teaching Children to Read—Summary Report.* http://www.nationalreadingpanel .org/Publications/summary.htm
- *Report of the National Reading Panel: Teaching Children to Read—Reports of the Subgroups.* http://www.nationalreadingpanel.org/Publications/subgroups .htm

Other Sources of Information Available From the National Reading Panel

- Put Reading First: The Research Building Blocks for Teaching Children to Read. http://www.nationalreadingpanel.org/Publications/researchread .htm
- Put Reading First: Helping Your Child Learn to Read. http://www.nation alreadingpanel.org/Publications/helpingread.htm

Other Sources of National Reading Panel Information

National Reading Panel. (2000). *Teaching children to read: An evidence-based assessment of the scientific research literature on reading and its implications for reading instruction* (NIH Publication No. 00–4769). Bethesda, MD: National Institute of Child Health and Human Development. Available at http://www.nationalreadingpanel.org/Publications/ publications.htm

National Reading Panel. (2000). *Teaching children to read; Reports of the subgroups* (NIH Publication No. 00-4754). Bethesda, MD: National Institute of Child Health and Human Development. Available at http://www.nichd.nih.gov/publications/nrp/ report.cfm.

References

CHAPTER 1

Algozzine, B., & Ysseldyke, J. E. (2006). *Effective instruction for students with special needs*. Thousand Oaks, CA: Corwin Press.

Algozzine, B., Ysseldyke, J. E., & Elliott, J. (1997). *Strategies and tactics for effective instruction* (2nd ed.). Longmont, CO: Sopris West.

Armbruster, B. B., Lehr, E., & Osborn, J. (2003). *Putting reading first: The research building blocks of reading instruction* (2nd ed.). Jessup, MD: National Institute for Literacy.

Au, K. (1993). *Literacy instruction in multicultural settings*. Orlando, FL: Harcourt Brace College Publishers.

Flint, A. S. (2008). *Literate lives: Teaching reading and writing in elementary classrooms*. Hoboken, NJ: John Wiley & Sons.

Flood, J., & Anders, P. L. (2005). *Literacy development of students in urban schools: Research and policy*. Newark, DE: International Reading Association.

Guthrie, J. T., & Wigfield, A. (2000). Engagement and motivation in reading. In M. Kamil, P. Mosenthal, P. D. Pearson, & R. Barr (Eds.), *Handbook of reading research: Vol. III* (pp. 403–424). Mahwah, NJ: Lawrence Erlbaum Associates.

Hannaway, J. (2005). Poverty and student achievement: A hopeful review. In J. Flood & P. L. Anders (Eds.), *Literacy development of students in urban schools: Research and policy* (pp. 3–34). Newark, DE: International Reading Association.

Holiday, B. G. (1985). Towards a model of teacher-child transactional processes affecting black children's academic achievement. In M. B. Spencer, G. K. Brookins, & W. R. Allen (Eds.), *Beginning: The social and affective development of black children* (pp. 117–130). Mahwah, NJ: Lawrence Erlbaum Associates.

Hoosain, R., & Salili, F. (2005). *Language in multicultural education*. Greenwich, CT: Information Age.

Lee, C. D. (2005). Culture and language: Bidialectical issues in literacy. In J. Flood & P. L. Anders (Eds.), *Literacy development of students in urban schools: Research and policy* (pp. 241–274). Newark, DE: International Reading Association.

Manzo, A. V., & Casale, U. D. (1985). Listen-read-discuss: A content reading heuristic. *Journal of Reading, 28,* 732–734.

Manzo, A. V., Manzo, U. C., & Thomas, M. N. (2005). *Content area literacy: Strategic teaching for strategic learning*. Hoboken, NJ: John Wiley & Sons.

National Reading Panel. (2000). *Teaching children to read: An evidence-based assessment of the scientific research literature on reading and its implications for reading instruction* (NIH Publication No. 00–4769). Bethesda, MD: National Institute of Child Health and Human Development. Available August 5, 2008, at http://www.nationalreadingpanel.org/Publications/publications.htm

Nichols, W. D., Rupley, W. H., Webb-Johnson, G., & Weaver, L. R. (1996). *Embracing cultural and linguistic diversity: Culturally responsive reading instruction*. (ERIC Document Reproduction Service No. ED409 550)

Obiakor, F. E. (2003). *The eight-step approach to multicultural learning and teaching* (2nd ed.). Dubuque, IA: Kendall/Hunt.

Obiakor, F. E. (2007). *Multicultural special education: Culturally responsive teaching*. Upper Saddle River, NJ: Pearson Merrill/Prentice Hall.

Obiakor, F. E., & Smith, D. J. (2005). Understanding the power of words in multicultural education and interaction. In R. Hoosain & F. Salili (Eds.), *Language in multicultural education* (pp. 77–92). Greenwich, CT: Information Age.

Ornstein, A. C., & Levine, D. U. (1993). *Foundations of education* (5th ed.). Boston: Houghton Mifflin.

Raphael, T. (1986). Teaching question-answer relationships, revisited. *Reading Teacher, 39*(6), 516–520.

Schmidt, P. R. (2005). *Culturally responsive instruction: Promoting literacy in secondary content areas*. Naperville, IL: Learning Point Associates.

Stahl, S. A. (1990). Riding the pendulum: A rejoinder to Schickedanz and McGee and Lomax. *Review of Educational Research, 60,* 141–151.

Trueba, H. (1984). The forms, functions, and values of literacy: Reading for survival in a barrio as a student. *Journal of the National Association for Bilingual Education, 9,* 21–38.

Utley, C. A., Obiakor, F. E., & Kozleski, E. B. (2005). Overrepresentation of culturally and linguistically diverse students in special education in urban schools: A research synthesis. In J. Flood & P. L. Anders (Eds.), *Literacy development of students in urban schools: Research and policy* (pp. 314–344). Newark, DE: International Reading Association.

CHAPTER 2

Adams, G., & Engelmann, S. (1996). *Research on direct instruction: 25 years beyond DISTAR.* Seattle: Educational Achievement Systems.

Adams, M. (1990). *Beginning to read: Thinking and learning about print.* Cambridge, MA: MIT Press.

Adoff, A. (with Steptoe, J., ill.). (1982). *All the colors of the race: Poems.* New York: William Morrow.

Algozzine, B., & Ysseldyke, J. E. (2006). *Effective instruction for students with special needs.* Thousand Oaks, CA: Corwin Press.

Al Otaiba, S., & Fuchs, D. (2002). Characteristics of children who are unresponsive to early literacy intervention. *Remedial and Special Education, 23*(5), 300–316.

Alvermann, D. E., & Moore, D. W. (1991). *Handbook of reading research.* Mahwah, NJ: Erlbaum.

Archer, A. L., Gleason, M. M., & Vachon, V. (2000). *REWARDS: Reading excellence; Word attack and rate development strategies.* Longmont, CO: Sopris West.

Ball, E., & Blachman, B. A. (1991). Does phoneme awareness training in kindergarten make a difference in early word recognition & developmental spelling? *Reading Research Quarterly, 26,* 49–66.

Bear, D., Invernizzi, M., Templeton, S., & Johnston, F. (1994). *Words their way: Word study for phonics, spelling and vocabulary development.* Upper Saddle River, NJ: Prentice Hall.

Benner, G., & Nelson, J. R. (2005). Improving the early literacy skills of children with behavioral disorders and phonological processing deficits at school entry. *Reading and Writing Quarterly, 21,* 105–108.

Benner, G., Nelson, J. R., & Gonzalez, J. (2005). An investigation of the effects of a prereading intervention on the early literacy skills of children at risk of emotional disturbance and reading problems. *Journal of Emotional and Behavioral Disorders, 13*(1), 3–12.

Biancarosa, G., & Snow, C. (2004). *Reading next: A vision for action and research in middle and high school literacy—A report to Carnegie Corporation of New York.* Washington, DC: Alliance for Excellent Education.

Blachman, B. A. (1989). Phonological awareness and word recognition assessment and intervention. In A. Kamhi & H. Catts (Eds.), *Reading disabilities: A developmental language perspective* (pp. 138–158). Needham Heights, MA: Allyn & Bacon.

Blachman, B. A. (1991). Early intervention for children's reading problems: Clinical applications of the research in phonological awareness. *Topics in Language Disorders, 12,* 51–65.

Boehner, J. (2002). *President Bush's Reading First initiative ensuring that every child learns to read by third grade.* Retrieved September 16, 2005, from http://edworkforce.house.gov/issues/107th/education/nclb/factsheetreadingfirst.htm [no longer available online]

Brady, S., Fowler, A., Stone, B., and Winbury, N. (1994). Training Phonological Awareness: A study with inner-city Kindergarten children. *Reading Research Quarterly, 24,* 46–66.

Brown, T. (1995). *Konnichiwa! I Am a Japanese-American Girl.* New York: Henry Holt.

Bruchac, J. (1993). *First strawberries: A Cherokee story.* New York: Dial Books/Penguin.

Cartledge, G., & Lo, Y. (2006). *Teaching urban learners: Culturally responsive strategies for developing academic and behavioral competence.* Champaign, IL: Research Press.

Catts, H. W. (1991). Facilitating phonological awareness: Role of speech-language pathologists. *Language, Speech, and Hearing Services in Schools, 22,* 196–203.

Chall, J. (1996). *Stages of reading development* (2nd ed.). Orlando: FL: Harcourt Brace.

Chard, D., Jackson, B., Paratore, J., & Garnick, S. (2000). An early intervention supporting the literacy learning of children experiencing substantial difficulty. *Learning Disabilities Research & Practice, 14*(4), 254–267.

Christie, J., Richgels, D., & Roskos, K. (2003). The essentials of early literacy instruction. *Young Children, 17,* 52–62.

Ehri, L. (1996). Development of the ability to read words. In R. Barr, M. Kamil, P. B. Mosenthal, and P. D. Pearson (Eds.), *Handbook of reading research: Vol. II* (pp. 383–418). Mahwah, NJ: Lawrence Erlbaum.

Engelmann, S., Johnson, G., Carnine, L., Meyer, L., Becker, W., & Eisele, J. (1999). *Corrective reading decoding strategies B2.* Columbus, OH: SRA.

Flood, J., & Anders, P. L. (2005). *Literacy development of students in urban schools: Research and policy.* Newark, DE: International Reading Association.

Gaskins, I. (1995). Classroom application of cognitive science: Teaching poor readers how to learn, think and problem solve. In K. Gilly (Ed.), *Integrating cognitive theory and classroom practice* (pp. 129–154). Cambridge, MA: MIT Press.

Goswami, U., & Bryant, P. E. (1990). *Phonological skills and learning to read.* London: Erlbaum.

Grace, K. (2005). *Phonics and spelling through phoneme-grapheme mapping.* Longmont, CO: Sopris West.

Greenberg, D., Fredrick, L. D., Hughes, T. A., & Bunting, C. J. (2002). Implementation issues in a reading program for low reading adults. *Journal of Adolescent & Adult Literacy, 45,* 626–632.

Greenman, G., Schmidt, R., & Rozendal, M. (2002). Reading instruction in the inclusion classroom. *Remedial and Special Education, 23*(3), 130–140.

Gregory, A., & Schmitt, M. (2005). The impact of an early intervention: Where are the children now? *Literacy Teaching and Learning, 10*(1), 1–20.

Grossen, B. (2002). *Direct instruction model for secondary schools: The research base for the REACH system.* New York: Center for Applied Research in Education. (ERIC Document Reproduction Service No. ED481390)

Grossen, B. (2004). Success of a direct instruction model at a secondary level school with high-risk students. *Reading & Writing Quarterly, 20,* 161–178.

Harvard Civil Rights Project. (2001). *Racial inequity in special education.* Retrieved December 3, 2002, from http://harvardscience.harvard.edu/directory/programs/civil-rights-project

Haviland, V. (with Chambliss, M., ill.). (1994). *Favorite fairy fales told in England: Retold from Joseph Jacobs.* New York: Beech Tree Books.

Hiebert, E. H. (2005). State reform policies and the reading task for first graders. *Elementary School Journal, 105,* 245–266.

Hoover, M., Dabney, N., & Lewis, S. (1990). *Successful black and minority schools.* San Francisco: Julian Richardson.

Howard, E. F. (1991). *Aunt Flossie's hats (and crab cakes later).* New York: Clarion.

Jacobs, H. (Ed.). (1973). *Cajun Night Before Christmas by "Trosclair."* Gretna, LA: Pelican.

Jitendra, A. K., Cole, C. L., Hoppes, M. K., & Wilson, B. (1998). Effects of a direct instruction main idea summarization program and self-monitoring on reading comprehension of middle school students with learning disabilities. *Reading & Writing Quarterly, 14,* 379–396.

Justice, L., & Pullen, P. (2003). Enhancing phonological awareness, print awareness, and oral language skills in preschool children. *Young Children, 6,* 39–47.

Kim, T., & Axelrod, S. (2005). Direct instruction: An educators' guide and plea for action. *Behavior Analyst Today, 6,* 111–120.

Kozol, J. (1991). *Savage inequalities.* NY: Trumpet Club.

Leake, D., & Black, R. (2005). *Cultural and linguistic diversity: Implications for transition personnel.* Minneapolis: National Center on Secondary Education and Transition, University of Minnesota.

Lenz, B. K., & Hughes, C. A. (1990). A word identification strategy for adolescents with learning disabilities. *Journal of Learning Disabilities, 23*(3), 149–158, 163.

MacIver, M. A., & Kemper, E. (2002a). The impact of direct instruction on elementary students' reading achievement in an urban school district. *Journal of Education for Students Placed at Risk, 7,* 197–220.

MacIver, M. A., & Kemper, E. (2002b). Research on direct instruction in reading. *Journal of Education for Students Placed at Risk, 7,* 107–116.

McCollin, M., & O'Shea, D. J. (2005). Increasing reading achievement of students from culturally and linguistically diverse backgrounds. *Preventing School Failure, 50*(1), 41–44.

McCollin, M., & O'Shea, D. J. (2006). Improving literacy skills of students from culturally and linguistically diverse backgrounds. *Multiple Voices, 9*(1), 92–107.

McQuiston, K., O'Shea, D. J., & McCollin, M. (2007). Improving literacy skills of adolescents from culturally and linguistically diverse backgrounds. *Multicultural Learning and Teaching, 2*(2), 1–13.

Moats, L. C. (2001). When older students can't read. *Educational Leadership, 58*(6), 36–40.

Moore, D. W., Bean, T., Birdyshaw, D., & Rycik, J. (1999). *Adolescent literacy: A position statement.* Newark, DE: International Reading Association.

National Institute of Child Health and Human Development. (2000a). *Put reading first: The research building blocks for teaching students to read.* Washington, DC: U.S. Department of Education.

National Institute of Child Health and Human Development. (2000b). *Report of the National Reading Panel. Teaching students to read: An evidence based assessment of the scientific research literature on reading and its implications for reading instruction* (NIH Publication No. 00-4769). Washington, DC: Government Printing Office.

National Reading Panel. (2000). *Teaching children to read: An evidence-based assessment of the scientific research literature on reading and its implications for reading instruction* (NIH Publication No. 00–4769). Bethesda, MD: National Institute of Child Health and Human Development. Available August 5, 2008, at http://www.nationalreadingpanel.org/Publications/publications.htm

National Research Council. (2002). *Minority students in special and gifted education.* Washington, DC: National Academy Press.

Obiakor, F. E., & Wilder, L. K. (2003). Disproportionate representation of culturally diverse students in special education: What principals can do. *Principal Leadership, 4*(2), 16–21.

Perie, M., Grigg, W., & Donahue, P. (2005). *The nation's report card: Reading 2005* (NCES 2006–451). Washington, D.C.: U.S. Department of Education, National Center for Education Statistics. Available August 4, 2008, at http://nces.ed.gov/pubsearch/pubsinfo.asp?pubid=2006451

Schmidt, P. R. (2005). *Culturally responsive instruction: Promoting literacy in secondary content areas.* Naperville, IL: Learning Point. Retrieved July 30, 2006, from http://www.learningpt.org/literacy/adolescent/cri.pdf

Shankweiler, D. (1999). Words to meaning. *Scientific Studies of Reading, 3,* 113–127.

Share, D. L. (1995). Phonological recoding and self-teaching: Sine qua non of reading acquisition. *Cognition, 55,* 151–218.

Shippen, M. E., Houchins, D. E., Steventon, C., & Sartor, D. (2005). A comparison of two direct instructional reading programs for urban middle school students. *Remedial & Special Education, 26,* 175–182.

Snow, C. E., Burns, M. S., & Griffin, P. (Eds.). (1998). *Preventing reading difficulties in young children* [Electronic version]. Washington, DC: National Academy Press. Retrieved August 4, 2008, from http://books.nap.edu/html/prdyc/

Stanovich, K. E. (1994) Romance and reality. *The Reading Teacher, 47*(4), 456–459.

Sulzby, E., & Teale, W. (1991). Emergent literacy. *Handbook of Reading Research, 2,* 727–757.

Swanson, H., Hoskyn, M., & Lee, C. (1999) *Interventions for students with learning disabilities: A meta-analysis of treatment outcomes.* New York: Guilford Press.

Torgesen, J. K., Wagner, R. K., & Rashotte, C. A. (1999). *Test of word reading efficiency.* Austin, TX: PRO-ED.

Van Kleeck, A., Stahl, S. A., Bauer, E. B. (Eds.). (2003). *On reading books to children: Parents and teachers.* Mahwah, NJ: Lawrence Erlbaum Associates.

Vaughn, S., Bos, C. S., & Schumm, J. S. (2005). *Teaching exceptional, diverse, and at-risk students in the general education classroom* (IDEA 2004 update ed.). Upper Saddle River, NJ: Pearson Education.

Yamate, S. S. (with Tohinaka, J., ill.). (1992). *Ashok by any other name.* Chicago: Polychrome.

Yopp, H. (1988). The validity and reliability of phonemic awareness test. *Reading Research Quarterly, 23,* 159–177.

CHAPTER 3

Adams, G., & Engelmann, S. (1996). *Research on direct instruction: 25 years beyond DISTAR.* Seattle: Educational Achievement Systems.

Adams, M. (1990). *Beginning to read: Thinking and learning about print.* Cambridge, MA: MIT Press.

Algozzine, B., & Ysseldyke, J. E. (2006). *Effective instruction for students with special needs.* Thousand Oaks, CA: Corwin Press.

Alvermann, D. E., & Moore, D. W. (1991). *Handbook of reading research.* Mahwah, NJ: Erlbaum.

Armbruster, B. B., Lehr, E., & Osborn, J. (2003). *Putting reading first: The research building blocks of reading instruction* (2nd ed.). Jessup, MD: National Institute for Literacy.

Bear, D., Invernizzi, M., Templeton, S., & Johnston, F. (1995). *Words their way: Word study for phonics, spelling and vocabulary development.* Upper Saddle River, NJ: Prentice Hall.

Burns, M. S., Griffin, P., & Snow, C. E. (Eds.). (1999). *Starting out right: A guide to promoting children's reading success* [Electronic version]. Washington, DC: National Academy Press. Available August 5, 2008, at http://www.nap.edu/html/sor/

Bursuck, W. D., & Damer, M. (2007). *Reading instruction for students who are at risk or have disabilities.* Boston: Pearson.

Carnine, D. W., Silbert, J., Kame'ennui, E. J., & Tarver, S. G. (2004). *Direct instruction reading.* Upper Saddle River, NJ: Pearson Education.

Catts, H. W. (1991). Facilitating phonological awareness: Role of speech-language pathologists. *Language, Speech, and Hearing Services in Schools, 22,* 196–203.

Chall, J. (1996). *Stages of reading development* (2nd ed.). Orlando, FL: Harcourt Brace.

Delpit, L. (1995). *Other people's readers: Cultural conflict in the classroom.* New York: The New Press.

Delpit, L. (2003). Educators as "seed people" growing a new future. *Educational Researcher, 32*(7), 14–21.

Ehri, L. (1996). Development of the ability to read words. In R. Barr, M. Kamil, P. B. Mosenthal, & P. D. Pearson (Eds.), *Handbook of reading research: Vol II* (pp. 383–418). Mahwah, NJ: Lawrence Erlbaum.

Goswami, U., & Bryant, P. E. (1990). *Phonological skills and learning to read.* London: Erlbaum.

Grace, K. (2005). *Phonics and spelling through phoneme-grapheme mapping.* Longmont, CO: Sopris West.

Grossen, B. (1997). *A synthesis of research on reading from the National Institute of Child Health and Human Development.* Retrieved August 4, 2008, from http://www.nrrf.org/synthesis_research.htm

Hecht, S., Burgess, S., Torgesen, J., Wagner, R., & Rashotte, C. (2000). Explaining social class differences in growth of reading skills from beginning kindergarten through fourth grade: The role of phonological awareness, rate of access, and print knowledge. *Reading and Writing: An Interdisciplinary Journal, 12*(1–2), 99–127.

Ladson-Billings, G. (1995). But that's just good teaching! The case for culturally relevant pedagogy. *Theory into Practice, 34*(3), 159–165.

Lenz, B. K., & Hughes, C. A. (1990). A word identification strategy for adolescents with learning disabilities. *Journal of Learning Disabilities, 23*(3), 149–158, 163.

Liberman, I. Y., & Shankweiler, D. (1985). Phonology and the problems of learning to read and write. *Remedial and Special Education, 6*(6), 8–17.

Liberman, I. Y., Shankweiler, D., & Liberman, A. M. (1989). *The alphabetic principle and learning to read.* Bethesda, MD: National Institute of Child Health and Human Development. (ERIC Document Reproduction Service No. ED427291)

Lyon, G. R. (1998). Why reading is not a natural process. *Educational Leadership, 55*(6), 14–19.

Lyon, G. R., & Moats, L. C. (1997). Critical conceptual and methodological considerations in reading intervention research. *Journal of Learning Disabilities, 30,* 578–588.

Mathes, P., Howard, J., Allen, S., & Fuchs, D. (1998). Peer-assisted learning strategies for first grade readers: Responding to the needs of diverse learners. *Reading Research Quarterly, 33*(1), 62–95.

McQuiston, K., O'Shea, D. J., & McCollin, M. (2007). Improving literacy skills of adolescents from culturally and linguistically diverse backgrounds. *Multicultural Learning and Teaching, 2*(2), 1–13.

Moats, L. C. (2001). When older students can't read. *Educational Leadership, 58*(6), 36–40.

National Institute of Child Health and Human Development (NICHD). (2000). *Put reading first: The research building blocks for teaching children to read.* Washington, DC: U.S. Department of Education.

National Reading Panel. (2000). *Teaching children to read; An evidence-based assessment of the scientific research literature on reading and its implications for reading instruction* (NIH Publication No. 00-4769). Bethesda,

MD: National Institute of Child Health and Human Development. Available August 5, 2008, at http://www.nationalreadingpanel.org/Publications/publications.htm

Perie, M., Grigg, W., & Donahue, P. (2005). *The nation's report card: Reading 2005* (NCES 2006–451). Washington, D.C.: U.S. Department of Education, National Center for Education Statistics. Available August 4, 2008, at http://nces.ed.gov/pubsearch/pubsinfo.asp?pubid=2006451

Snow, C. E., Burns, M. S., & Griffin, P. (Eds.). (1998). *Preventing reading difficulties in young readers.* Washington, DC: National Academy Press.

Teale, W. H., & Sulzby, E. (1987). *Emergent literacy: Writing and reading.* Norwood, NJ: Ablex.

Tompkins, G. E. (2004). *Literacy for the 21st century.* Upper Saddle River, NJ: Pearson/Merrill-Prentice Hall.

Torgesen, J. K., & Mathes, P. G. (1998). *What every teacher should know about phonological awareness.* Tallahassee: Florida Department of Education.

Vaughn, S., Bos, C. S., & Schumm, J. S. (2005). *Teaching exceptional, diverse, and at-risk students in the general education classroom, IDEA 2004 update edition.* Upper Saddle River, NJ: Pearson Education.

Vaughn, S., Bos, C. S., & Schumm, J. S. (2007). *Teaching students who are exceptional, diverse, and at risk in the general education classroom, fourth edition.* Upper Saddle River, NJ: Pearson Education.

CHAPTER 4

Adams, M. (1990). *Beginning to read: Thinking and learning about print.* Cambridge, MA: MIT Press.

Artiles, A. J., Kozleski, E. B., Dorn, S., & Christensen, C. (2006). Learning in inclusive education research: Remediating theory and methods with a transformative agenda. *Review of Research in Education, 30,* 65–108.

Bailey, C., & Boykin, A. W. (2001). The role of task variability and home contextual factors in academic performance and task motivation of African-American elementary school children. *The Journal of Negro Education.* Retrieved May 5, 2007, from http://findarticles.com

Banks, J. A., Cookson, P., Gay, G., Hawley, W., Irvine, J. J., Nieto, S., et al. (2001). Diversity within unity: Essential principles for teaching and learning in a multicultural society. *Phi Delta Kappan, 83*(3), 196–198.

Bear, D. R., Invernizzi, M., Templeton, S., & Johnston, F. (1996). *Words their way: Word study for phonics, vocabulary and spelling instruction.* Englewood Cliffs, NY: Prentice-Hall.

Begeny, T., & Martens, R. (2006). Assisting low-performing readers with group based reading fluency instruction. *School Psychology Review, 35*(1), 91–107.

Brady, S., & Moats, L. (1997). *Informed instruction for reading success.* Baltimore, MD: International Dyslexia Association.

Carnine, D. W., Silbert, J., Kame'enui, E. J., & Tarver, S. G. (2004). *Direct instruction reading.* Upper Saddle River, NJ: Pearson Education.

Carnine, D. W., Silbert, J., Kame'enui, E. J., Tarver, S. G., & Jungjohann, K. (2006). *Teaching struggling and at-risk readers: A direct instruction approach.* Upper Saddle River, NJ: Pearson Education.

Chall, J. (1996). *Stages of reading development* (2nd ed.). Orlando, FL: Harcourt Brace.

Chapman, A. (Ed.). (2001). *Black voices: An anthology of African-American literature.* New York: Signet Classic. (Original work published 1968)

Chard, D. J., Vaughn, S., & Tyler, B. J. (2002). A synthesis of research on effective interventions for building reading fluency with elementary students with learning disabilities. *Journal of Learning Disabilities, 25,* 386–406.

Clay, M. M. (1993). *An observation survey of early literacy achievement.* Portsmouth, NH: Heinemann.

Crew, L. (1989). *Children of the river.* New York: Delacorte.

Cummins, J. (1986). Empowering minority students: A framework for intervention. *Harvard Educational Review, 56,* 18–36.

Cunningham, P. M. (2000). *Phonics they use: Words for reading and writing* (3rd ed.). New York: Longman.

Cunningham, P. M., Hall, D. P., & Defee, M. (1998). Nonability-grouped, multilevel instruction: Eight years later. *Reading Teacher, 51,* 652–664.

Darling-Hammond, L. (1997). *The right to learn: A blueprint for creating schools that work.* San Francisco: Jossey-Bass.

Dunbar, Paul Laurence. (1993). *The collected poetry of Paul Laurence Dunbar* (J. M. Braxton, Ed.). Charlottesville: University Press of Virginia. ("We Wear the Mask" originally published 1895)

Ellison, R. (1995). *The invisible man* (2nd ed.). New York: Vintage Books. (Original work published 1947)

Foorman, B., Francis, D., Winikates, D., Mehta, P., Schatschneider, C., & Fletcher, J. (1997). Early interventions for children with reading disabilities. *Scientific Studies of Reading, 1*(3), 255.

Foster, M., Lewis, J., & Onafowora, L. (2003). Anthropology, culture, and research on teaching and learning: Applying what we have learned to improve practice. *Teachers College Record, 105*(2), 261–277.

Fuchs, L. S., Fuchs, D., Hosp, M. K., & Jenkins, J. R. (2001). Oral fluency as an indicator of reading competence: A theoretical, empirical, and historical analysis. *Scientific Studies of Reading, 5,* 239–256.

Fuchs, L. S., Fuchs, D., & Kazdan, S. (1999). Effects of peer-assisted learning strategies on high school students with serious reading problems. *Remedial and Special Education, 20,* 309–319.

Gay, G. (2000). *Culturally responsive teaching: Theory, research and practice.* New York: Teachers College Press.

Good, R. H., & Kaminski, R. A. (2002). *DIBELS: Dynamic Indicators of Basic Early Literacy Skills* (6th ed.). Eugene, OR: Institute for the Development of Educational Achievement.

Hintze, J. M., Callahan, J. E. III, Matthews, W. J., Williams, S. A. S., & Tobin, K. G. (2002). Oral reading fluency and prediction of reading comprehension in African-American and Caucasian elementary school students. *School Psychology Review, 31,* 540–553.

Hirsch, E., & Moats, L. (2001). Overcoming the language gap. *American Educator, 25*(2), 4–9.

Hirschfelder, A. B., & Singer, B. R. (Eds.). (1992). *Rising voices: Writings of young Native Americans.* New York: Ballantine.

Ikpa, V. (2004). Leaving children behind the racial/ethnic achievement gap. *Research for Educational Reform, 9*(2), 3–13.

Jacob, I. (Ed.). (2002). *My sisters' voices: Teenage girls of color speak out.* New York: Henry Holt.

Kame'enui, E. J., & Simmons, D. C. (2001). Introduction to this special issue: The DNA of reading fluency. *Scientific Studies of Reading, 5,* 203–210.

Kogawa, J. (1992). *Itsuka.* New York: Viking.

Kuhn, M., & Stahl, S. (2003). Fluency: A review of developmental and remedial practices. *Journal of Educational Psychology, 95,* 3–21.

Ladson-Billings, G. (1994). *The dreamkeepers.* San Francisco: Jossey-Bass.

Ladson-Billings, G. (1995). But that's just good teaching! The case for culturally relevant pedagogy. *Theory into Practice, 34*(3), 159–165.

Lee, C. (2001). Is October Brown Chinese? *American Educational Research Journal, 38*(1), 97–142.

Lyon, G. R. (1998a). Why learning to read is not a natural process. *Educational Leadership, 55*(6), 14.

Lyon, G. R. (1998b). Why reading is not a natural process. *Educational Leadership, 55*(6) 14–19.

Lyon, G. R., Alexander, D., & Yaffe, S. (1997). Progress and promise in research in learning disabilities. *Learning Disabilities: A Multidisciplinary Journal, 8,* 1–6.

Lyon, G. R., & Moats, L. C. (1997). Critical conceptual and methodological considerations in reading intervention research. *Journal of Learning Disabilities, 30,* 578–588.

Mathes, P., Howard, J., Allen, S., & Fuchs, D. (1998). Peer assisted learning strategies for first grade readers: Responding to the needs of diverse learners. *Reading Research Quarterly, 33*(1), 62–95.

McCollin, M., & O'Shea, D. (2005). Increasing reading achievement of students from culturally and linguistically diverse backgrounds. *Preventing School Failure, 50*(1), 41–44.

McCormick, S. (2003). *Instructing students who have literacy problems.* Upper Saddle River, NJ: Merrill/Prentice Hall.

McQuiston, K., O'Shea, D. J., & McCollin, M. (2007). Improving literacy skills of adolescents from culturally and linguistically diverse backgrounds. *Multicultural Learning and Teaching, 2*(2), 1–13.

Meltzer, J. (2002). *Adolescent literacy resources: Linking research and practice.* Providence, RI: Lab at Brown University.

Mercer, C. D., Campbell, K. U., Miller, M. D., Mercer, K. D., & Lane, H. B. (2000). Effects of a reading fluency intervention for middle schoolers with specific learning disabilities. *Learning Disabilities Research & Practice, 15,* 179–189.

Miccinati, J. (1985). Using prosodic cues to teach oral reading fluency. *Reading Teacher, 39*(2), 206–212.

Moats, L. (2001). When older kids can't read. *Educational Leadership 58*(6), 36–40. Retrieved August 5, 2008, from http://www.scoe.org/reading/docs/older_091103.pdf

Moll, L. C., Amanti, C., Neff, D., & Gonzalez, N. (1992). Funds of knowledge for teaching: Using a qualitative approach to connect homes and classrooms. *Theory Into Practice, 31*(2), 132–141.

Myers, W. D. (1988). *Fallen Angels.* New York: Scholastic.

National Institute of Child Health and Human Development. (2000a). *Put reading first: The research building blocks for teaching students to read.* Washington, DC: U.S. Department of Education.

National Institute of Child Health and Human Development. (2000b). *Report of the National Reading Panel. Teaching students to read: An evidence based assessment of the scientific research literature on reading and its implications for reading instruction* (NIH Publication No. 00-4769). Washington, DC: Government Printing Office.

National Research Council. (2002). *Minority students in special and gifted education.* Washington, DC: National Academy Press.

Nieto, S. (1996). *Affirming diversity: The sociopolitical context of multicultural education* (2nd ed.). White Plains, NY: Longman.

Obiakor, F. E., & Utley, C. A. (2004). Educating culturally diverse learners with exceptionalities: A critical analysis of the Brown case. *Peabody Journal of Education, 79,* 141–156.

O'Shea, L. J., & O'Shea, D. K. (1994). A component analysis of metacognition in reading comprehension: The contributions of awareness and self-regulation. *International Journal of Disability, Development and Education, 41*(1), 15–32.

O'Shea, L. J., Sindelar, P. T., & O'Shea, D. J. (1985). The effects of repeated reading and attentional cues on the reading fluency and comprehension of learning disabled readers. *Learning Disabilities Research, 2,* 103–109.

Rasinski, T. V. (2000). Speed does matter in reading. *Reading Educator, 54,* 146–151.

Rasinski, T. V., & Padak, N. (2004). *Effective reading strategies: Teaching children who find reading difficult.* Upper Saddle River, NJ: Pearson Merrill, Prentice Hall.

Rasinski, T. V., Padak, N. D., McKeon, C., Wilfong, L., Friedauer , J., & Heim, P. (2005). Is reading fluency a key for successful high school reading? *Journal of Adolescent & Adult Literacy, 49*(1), 22–27.

Richards, M. (2000). Be a good detective: Solve the case of oral reading fluency. *Reading Educator, 53,* 534–539.

Rinehart, S., & Platt, J. (2004). Metacognitive awareness and monitoring in adult and college readers. *Forum for Reading, 15*(2), 54–62.

Rist, C. (1971). Student social class and teacher expectations: The self-fulfilling prophecy in ghetto education. *Challenging the myth: The schools, the Blacks, and the poor* (Reprint Series No. 5). Cambridge, MA: Harvard Educational Review.

Salinger, T. (2003). Helping older, struggling readers. *Preventing School Failure, 47*(2), 79.

Samuels, J. (1997). The method of repeated readings. *Reading Teacher, 50*(5), 376–381.

Santa, C. M. (2006). A vision for literacy: Ours or theirs? *Journal of Adolescent & Adult Literacy, 49*(6), 466–476.

Sheets, R. (1999). Relating competence in an urban classroom to ethnic identity development. In R. Sheets (Ed.), *Racial and ethnic identity in school practices: Aspects of human development.* Mahwah, NJ: Lawrence Erlbaum Associates.

Shippen, M., Simpson, R., & Crites, S. (2003). A practical guide to functional behavioral assessment. *Teaching Exceptional Children, 35*(5), 36.

Snow, C. E., Burns, M. S., & Griffin, P. (1998). *Preventing reading difficulties in young children.* Washington, DC: National Research Council, Committee on the Prevention of Reading Difficulties in Young Children.

Soto, G. (2003). *Taking Sides.* New York: Harcourt Books. (Original work published 1991)

Speece, D. L., Mills, C., Ritchey, K. D., & Hillman, E. (2003). Initial evidence that letter fluency tasks are valid indicators of early reading skill. *Journal of Special Education, 36*, 223–233.

Stahl, S. A., & Kuhn, M. R. (2002). Center for the improvement of early reading achievement. *Reading Educator, 55*, 582–584.

Stanovich, K. E., & Stanovich, P. J. (1995). How research might inform the debate about early reading acquisition. *Journal of Research in Reading, 18*(2), 87–105.

Steptoe, J. (1987). *Mufaro's beautiful daughters.* NY: HarperCollins.

U.S. Department of Education. (2005). *The nation's report card: Reading 2005* (NCES Report No. 2006–451). Washington, DC: Institute for Education Sciences.

U.S. Department of Health, Education, and Welfare. (2003). *Education Press Release.* Washington, DC: U.S. Government Printing Office.

Vaughn, S., Bos, C. S., & Schumm, J. S. (2005). *Teaching exceptional, diverse, and at-risk students in the general education classroom* (update ed.). Upper Saddle River, NJ: Pearson Education.

Villegas, A. M. (1991). *Culturally responsive pedagogy for the 1990s and beyond.* Washington, DC: ERIC Clearinghouse on Teacher Education.

Wolf, M., & Katzir-Cohen, T. (2001). Reading fluency and its intervention. *Scientific Studies of Reading, 5*, 211–239.

Wood, J. (2006). *Living voices: Multicultural poetry in the middle school classroom.* Retrieved April 25, 2007, from http://www.ncte.org

Yep, L. (Ed.). (1993). *American dragons: Twenty-five Asian-American voices.* New York: HarperCollins.

CHAPTER 5

Al-Hassan, S. (2003). *Reciprocal peer tutoring effect on high frequency sight word learning, retention, and generalization of first- and second-grade urban elementary school students.* Unpublished doctoral dissertation, The Ohio State University, Columbus.

Anderson, R. C., & Nagy, W. E. (1991). Word meanings. In R. Barr, M. L. Kamil, P. B. Mosenthal, & P. D. Pearson (Eds.), *Handbook of reading research: Vol. 2* (pp. 690–724). White Plains, NY: Longman.

Baker, S. K., Simmons, D. C., & Kame'enui, E. J. (1998). Vocabulary acquisition: Research bases. In D. C. Simmons & E. J. Kame'enui (Eds.), *What reading research tells us about children with diverse learning needs* (pp. 183–218). Mahwah, NJ: Lawrence Erlbaum.

Baumann, J. F., Edwards, E. C., Boland, E. M., Olejnik, S., & Kame'enui, E. J. (2003). Vocabulary tricks: Effects of instruction in morphology and context on fifth-grade students' ability to derive and infer word meanings. *American Educational Research Journal, 40*(2), 447–494.

Baumann, J. F., & Kame'enui, E. J. (1991). Research on vocabulary instruction: Ode to Voltaire. In J. Flood, D. Lapp, & J. R. Squire (Eds.), *Handbook of research on teaching the English language arts* (pp. 604–632). New York: Macmillan.

Biemiller, A., & Slonim, N. (2001). Estimating root word vocabulary growth in normative populations: Evidence for a common sequence of vocabulary. *Journal of Educational Psychology, 93*(3), 498–520.

Blachowicz, C. L. Z., Fisher, P. J. L., Ogle, D., & Watts-Taffe, S. (2006). Vocabulary: Questions from the classroom. *Reading Research Quarterly, 41*(4), 524–539.

Burns, M. K., Dean, V. J., & Foley, S. (2004). Preteaching unknown key words with incremental rehearsal to improve reading fluency and comprehension with children identified as reading disabled. *Journal of School Psychology, 42*, 303–314.

Cartledge, G., & Lo, Y. (2006). *Teaching urban learners: Culturally responsive strategies for developing academic and behavioral competence.* Champaign, IL: Research Press.

Cohen, L., & Byrnes, K. (2007). Engaging children with useful words: Vocabulary instruction in a third-grade classroom. *Reading Horizons Journal, 47*(4), 271–293.

Coyne, M. D., Simmons, D. C., Kame'enui, E. J., & Stoolmiller, M. (2004). Teaching vocabulary during shared storybook readings: An examination of differential effects. *Exceptionality, 12*(3), 145–162.

Curtis, M. E., & Longo, A. M. (2001). Teaching vocabulary to adolescents to improve comprehension. *Reading Online, 5.* Available August 5, 2008, at http://www.readingonline.org/articles/art_index.asp?HREF=curtis/index.html

Davidson, J., Elcock, J., & Noyes, P. (1996). A preliminary study of the effect of computer-assisted practice on reading attainment. *Journal of Research in Reading, 19*, 102–110.

Dickinson, D. K., & Smith, M. W. (1994). Long-term effects of preschool teachers' book readings on low-income children's vocabulary and story comprehension. *Reading Research Quarterly, 29,* 104–122.

Draper, S. (2006). *Copper sun.* New York: Atheneum.

Espin, C. A., & Deno, S. L. (1993). Content-specific and general reading disabilities of secondary-level students: Identification and educational relevance. *The Journal of Special Education, 27,* 321–337.

Espin, C. A., & Deno, S. L. (1994–1995). Curriculum-based measures for secondary students: Utility and task specificity of text-based reading and vocabulary measures for predicting performance on content-area tasks. *Diagnostique, 20,* 121–142.

Espin, C. A., & Foegen, A. (1996). Validity of three general outcome measures of predicting secondary students' performance on content-area tasks. *Exceptional Children, 62,* 497–514.

Espin, C. A., Shin, J., & Busch, T. W. (2005). Curriculum-based measurement in the content areas: Vocabulary matching as an indicator of progress in social studies learning. *Journal of Learning Disabilities, 38,* 353–363.

Graves, M. F. (1986). Vocabulary learning and instruction. *Review of Research in Education, 13,* 49–89.

Graves, M. F. (2000). A vocabulary program to complement and bolster a middle-grade comprehension program. In B. M. Taylor, M. F. Graves, & P. van den Broek (Eds.), *Reading for meaning: Fostering comprehension in the middle grades* (pp. 116–135). New York and Newark, DE: Teachers College Press and International Reading Association.

Hart, B., & Risley, T. R. (1995). *Meaningful differences in the everyday experience of young American children.* Baltimore: Paul H. Brookes.

Hedrick, W. B., Harmon, J. M., & Linerode, P. M. (2004). Teachers' beliefs and practices of vocabulary instruction with social studies textbooks in Grades 4–8. *Reading Horizons, 45*(2), 103–125.

Heller, J. H., Sturner, R. A., Funk, S. G., & Feezor, M. D. (1993). The effects of input mode on vocabulary identification performance at low intensity. *Journal of Educational Computing Research, 9,* 509–518.

Hooley, D. (2007). The importance of high school debate. *English Journal, 96*(5), 18–19.

Jitendra, A. K., Edwards, L. L., Sacks, G., & Jacobson, L. A. (2004). What research says about vocabulary instruction for students with learning disabilities. *Exceptional Children, 70*(3), 299–322.

Joshi, R. M. (2005). Vocabulary: A critical component of comprehension. *Reading & Writing Quarterly, 21,* 209–219.

Kame'enui, E., Carnine, D., & Freschi, R. (1982). Effects of text construction and instructional procedures for teaching word meanings on comprehension and recall. *Reading Research Quarterly, 17,* 367–388.

Kourea, L., Cartledge, G., & Musti-Rao, S. (2007). Effects of total class peer tutoring on the sight-word acquisition, maintenance, reading fluency and reading comprehension of urban learners. *Remedial and Special Education, 28*(2), 95–107.

Musti-Rao, S., & Cartledge, G. (in press). Early reading intervention for urban learners: Implications for practice. *Multiple Voices.*

National Reading Panel. (2000). *Teaching children to read: An evidence-based assessment of the scientific research literature on reading and its implications for reading instruction; Reports of the subgroups.* Bethesda, MD: National Institute of Child Health and Human Development. Available August 5, 2008, at http://www.national readingpanel.org/Publications/publications.htm

Nelson, J. R., & Stage, S. A. (2007). Fostering the development of vocabulary knowledge and reading comprehension through contextually based multiple meaning vocabulary instruction. *Education and Treatment of Children, 30*(1), 1–22.

O'Donnell, P., Weber, K. P., & McLaughlin, T. F. (2003). Improving correct and error rate and reading comprehension using key words and previewing: A case report with a language minority student. *Education and Treatment of Children, 26,* 237–254.

Pearson, P. D., Hiebert, E. H., & Kamil, M. L. (2007). Vocabulary assessment: What we know and what we need to learn. *Reading Research Quarterly, 42*(2), 282–296.

Roberts, T. A. (1988). Development of pre-instruction versus previous experience: Effects on factual and inferential comprehension preview. *Reading Psychology, 9,* 141–157.

Ryder, R. J., & Graves, M. F. (1994). Vocabulary instruction presented prior to reading in two basal readers. *Elementary School Journal, 95,* 139–153.

Schwartz, R. M., & Raphael, T. E. (1985). Instruction in the concept of definition as a basis for vocabulary acquisition. In J. A. Niles & R. V. Lalik (Eds.), *Issues in literacy: A research perspective: Thirty-fourth yearbook of the national reading conference* (pp. 116–124). Rochester, NY: The National Reading Conference.

Stahl, S. A. (1986). Three principles of vocabulary instruction. *Journal of Reading, 29*(1), 662–668.

Stahl, S. A., & Fairbanks, M. M. (1986). The effects of vocabulary instruction: A model-based meta-analysis. *Review of Educational Research, 56,* 72–110.

Stahl, S. A., & Shiel, T. G. (1999). *Teaching meaning vocabulary: Productive approaches for poor readers.* In *Read all about it! Readings to inform the profession* (pp. 291-321). Sacramento: California State Board of Education.

Talbert-Johnson, C. (2004). Structural inequities and the achievement gap in urban schools. *Education and Urban Society, 37,* 23–36.

Tam, K. Y., Heward, W. L., & Heng, M. A. (2006). A reading instruction intervention program for English-language learners who are struggling readers. *The Journal of Special Education, 40*(2), 79–93.

Terrill, M. C., Scruggs, T. E., & Mastropieri, M. A. (2004). SAT vocabulary instruction for high school students with learning disabilities. *Intervention in School and Clinic, 39,* 288–294.

White, T. G., Graves, M. F., & Slater, W. H. (1989). Growth of reading vocabulary in diverse elementary schools. *Journal of Educational Psychology, 42,* 343–354.

Whitehurst, G. J., Arnold, D. H., Epstein, J. N., Angell, A. L. Smith, M., & Fischel, J. E. (1994). A picture book reading intervention in day care and home for children from low-income families. *Developmental Psychology, 30*(5), 679–689.

CHAPTER 6

Alliance for Excellent Education. (2005). *Six key strategies for teachers of English-language learners.* Retrieved August 5, 2008, from www.all4ed.org

Association for the Advancement of Health Education. (1994). *Cultural awareness and sensitivity: Guidelines for health educators.* Reston, VA: Author.

Bermudez, A. B., & Palumbo, D. (1994). Bridging the gap between literacy and technology: Hypermedia as a learning tool for limited English proficient students. *The Journal of Educational Issues of Language Minority Students, 14,* 165–184.

Bieger, E. M. (1996). Promoting multicultural education through a literature-based approach. *The Reading Teacher, 49,* 308–312.

Bruning, R., Schraw, G., & Ronning, R. (1999). *Cognitive psychology and instruction* (3rd ed.). Upper Saddle River, NJ: Prentice Hall.

Cameron, C., & Lee, K. (1997). Bridging the gap between home and school with voice-mail technology. *Journal of Educational Research, 90,* 182–190.

Cawelti, G. (Ed.). (1995). *Handbook of research on improving students achievement.* Arlington, VA: Educational Research Service.

Chion-Kenney, L. (1994). Weaving real-life images and experiences into Native education: Comment. *R&D Preview, 9*(1), 4–5.

Cohen, B. (with Jones, J. N., ill.). (1994). *Make a wish, Molly.* New York: Bantam Doubleday Dell.

Dale, E. (2005). *Learning pyramid.* Bethel, ME: National Training Laboratories.

Edwards, P. A. (2004). *Children's literacy development: Making it happen through school, family, and community involvement.* Boston: Allyn & Bacon.

Edwards, P. A., Danridge, J., McMillon, G. T., & Pleasants, H. M. (2001). Taking ownership of literacy: Who has the power? In P. R. Schmidt & P. B. Mosenthal (Eds.), *Reconceptualizing literacy in the new age of multiculturalism and pluralism* (pp. 111–134). Greenwich, CT: Information Age.

Eggen, P., & Kauchak, D. (2001). *Educational psychology: Windows on classrooms* (5th ed). Upper Saddle River, NJ: Prentice Hall.

Epstein, J. L., & Mac Iver, D. J. (1992). *Opportunities to learn: Effects on eighth graders of curriculum offerings and instructional approaches.* Baltimore, MD: Johns Hopkins University Center for Research on Effective Schooling of Disadvantaged Students.

García, S. B., & Ortiz, A. A. (2004). *Preventing disproportionate representation: Culturally and linguistically responsive prereferral interventions.* Tempe: National Center for Culturally Responsive Educational Systems (NCCRESt), Arizona State University. Available online August 5, 2008, at http://www.nccrest.org/briefs/Pre-referral_Brief.pdf

Gay, G. (2000). *Culturally responsive teaching: Theory, research, and practice.* New York: Teachers College Press.

Gay, G. (2002). Preparing for culturally responsive teaching. *Journal of Teacher Education, 53*(2), 106–116.

Hemmings, A. (1994, April). *Culturally responsive teaching: When and how high school teachers should cross cultural boundaries to reach students.* Paper presented at the annual meeting of the American Educational Research Association, New Orleans, LA.

Irwin, P., & Mitchell, J. (1991). *Retelling methodologies.* Unpublished manuscript.

Kalyanpur, M., & Harry, B. (1999). *Culture in special education: Building reciprocal family-professional relationships.* Baltimore: Brookes.

Lopez, G., & Schribner, J. (1999, April). *Discourses of involvement: A critical review of parent involvement research.* Paper presented at the annual meeting of the American Educational Research Association, Montreal, QC, Canada.

McCauley, J. K., & McCauley, D. S. (1992). Using choral reading to promote language learning for ESL students. *The Reading Teacher, 45,* 526–535.

Means, B., & Olson, K. (1994). The link between technology and authentic learning. *Educational Leadership, 51*(7), 15–18.

Morrow, L. O. M. (1992). The impact of literature-based program on literacy achievement, use of literature, and attitudes of children from minority backgrounds. *Reading Research Quarterly, 27,* 250–275.

Needels, M., & Knapp, M. (1994). Teaching writing to children who are under-served. *Journal of Educational Psychology, 86*(3), 339–349.

Nichols, W. D., Rupley, W. H., Webb-Johnson, G., & Tlusty, G. (2000). Teachers role in providing culturally responsive literacy instruction. *Reading Horizons, 41*(1), 1–18.

Norton, D. (1995). *Through the eyes of a child: An introduction to children's literature* (4th ed.). New York: Merrill/Macmillan.

Padrón, Y. N., & Waxman, H. C. (1999). Effective instructional practices for English language learners. In H. C. Waxman & H. J. Walberg (Eds.), *New directions for teaching practice and research* (pp. 171–203). Berkeley, CA: McCutchan.

Padrón, Y. N., Waxman, H. C., & Rivera, H. H. (2002). *Educating Hispanic students: Effective instructional practices.* Retrieved May 22, 2007 from www.cal.org/crede/pubs/PracBrief5.htm

Russell, J. F. (1997). Relationships between the implementation for middle-level program concepts and student achievement. *Journal of Curriculum and Supervision, 12,* 152–168.

Schmidt, P. R. (2000). Emphasizing differences to build cultural understandings. In V. J. Risko & K. Bromley (Eds.), *Collaboration for diverse learners: Viewpoints and practices.* Newark, DE: International Reading Association.

Schmidt, P. R. (2005). *Culturally responsive instruction: Promoting literacy in secondary content areas.* Naperville, IL: Learning Point Associates.

Shumow, L., & Harris, W. (1998, April). *Teachers' thinking about home-school relations in low-income urban communities.* Paper presented at the annual meeting of the American Educational Research Association, San Diego, CA.

Special Connections. (n.d.). *Teaching during reading self-questioning strategies.* Retrieved August 5, 2008, from http://www.specialconnections.ku.edu/cgi-bin/cgiwrap/specconn/main.php?cat=instruction&section=main&subsection=rc/during

Steinitz, V. A., & Solomon, E. R. (1986). *Starting out: Class and community in the lives of working-class youth.* Philadelphia: Temple University Press.

Stevens, R. J., & Durkin, S. (1992). *Using student team reading and student team writing in middle school.* Baltimore, MD: Johns Hopkins University, Center for Research on Effective Schooling for Disadvantaged Students.

Tharp, R. G., & Gallimore, R. (1988). *Rousing minds to life: Teaching, learning, and schooling in social context.* Cambridge, England: Cambridge University Press.

Therrien, W. J. (2004). Fluency and comprehension gains as a result of repeated readings. *Remedial and Special Education, 25,* 252–261.

Time for Learning. (n.d.). *Learning reading comprehension skill.* Retrieved August 5, 2008, from http://www.time4learning.com/readingpyramid/Comprehension.htm

Tomlinson, C. A. (1999). *The differentiated classroom: Responding to the needs of all learners.* Alexandria, VA: Association for Supervision and Curriculum Development.

Vacca R. T., & Vacca, J. L. (2005). *Content area reading* (8th ed.). Boston: Allyn & Bacon.

Villegas, A. (1991). *Culturally responsive pedagogy for the 1990s and beyond.* Princeton, NJ: Educational Testing Service.

Waxman, H. C., Padrón, Y. N., & Knight, S. L. (1991). Risks associated with students: Limited cognitive mastery. In M. C. Wang, M. C. Reynolds, & H. J. Walberg (Eds.), *Handbook of special education: Vol. 4. Emerging programs* (pp. 235–254). Oxford, England: Pergamon.

Wiggins, G., & McTighe, J. (1998). *Understanding by design.* Alexandria, VA: Association for Supervision and Curriculum Development.

CHAPTER 7

Afferbach, P. (1990). The influence of prior knowledge on expert readers' main idea construction strategies. *Reading Research Quarterly, 25,* 31–36.

Allen, V. G. (1991). Teaching bilingual and ESL children. In J. Flood, J. M. Jensen, D. Lapp, & J. R. Squire (Eds.), *Handbook of research on teaching the English language arts* (pp. 356–364). New York: Macmillan.

Allen, V. G. (1994). Selecting materials for the reading instruction of ESL children. In K. Spangerberg-Urbschat & R. Pritchard (Eds.), *Kids come in all languages: Reading instruction for all ESL students* (pp. 108–131). Newark, DE: International Reading Association.

Bazron, B., Osher, D., & Fleischman, S. (2005). Culturally responsive schools. *Educational Leadership, 63*(1), 83–84.

Cummins, J. (1994). Assessment and intervention with culturally and linguistically diverse learners. In S. R. Hollins & J. V. Tinajero (Eds.), *Literacy assessment of second language learners* (pp.115–129). Boston: Allyn and Bacon.

Cummins, J., Bismilla, V., Chow, P., Cohen, S., Giampapa, F., Leoni, et al. (2005). Affirming identity in multilingual classrooms. *Educational Leadership, 63*(1), 38–43.

DeBruyn, R. L. (1984). Upholding the tenets of education. *The Master Teacher, 15*(32), 1.

Delpit, L. (1995). *Other people's children: Cultural conflict in the classroom.* New York: The New Press.

Delpit, L., & Dowdy, J. (Eds.). (2002). *The skin that we speak: Thoughts on language and culture in the classroom.* New York: The New Press.

Edwards, L. (2001). We teach ourselves. In C. F. Stice & J. E. Bertrand (Eds.), *Teaching at-risk students in the K–4 classrooms: Language, literacy, and learning* (pp.1–18). Norwood, MA: Christopher-Gordon.

Flint, A. S. (2008). *Literate lives: Teaching reading and writing in elementary classrooms.* Hoboken, NJ: John Wiley & Sons.

Flood, J., & Anders, P. L. (2005). *Literacy development of students in urban schools: Research and policy.* Newark, DE: International Reading Association.

Freire, P. (1970). *The pedagogy of the oppressed.* New York: Herder and Herder.

Gay, G. (2000). *Cultural responsive teaching: Theory, research, and practice.* New York: Teachers College Press.

Gutiérrez, K. D. (2005). The persistence of inequality: English-language learners and educational reform. In J. Flood & P. L. Anders (Eds.), *Literacy development of students in urban schools: Research and policy* (pp. 288–304). Newark, DE: International Reading Association.

Hilliard, A. G. (1992). The pitfalls and promises of special education practice. *Exceptional Children, 59*(2), 168–172.

Hirsh, E. D. (1987). *Cultural literacy: What every American needs to know.* Boston: Houghton Mifflin.

Jenkins, W. (2006). *What's missing in the education of African-American children: The real reasons behind the gap.* St. Louis, MO: William Jenkins Enterprises.

Kozol, J. (2005). *The shame of the nation: The restoration of apartheid schooling in America.* New York: Crown Publishers.

Lau v. Nichols. 414 U.S. 563 (1974); Lau v. Hopp (N.D. Cal., No. C 70-627 LHB).

Lessen, P. P. M., & Dejong, P. F. (2001). Home literacy: Opportunities, instruction, cooperation, and social-emotional quality predicting early reading achievement. *Reading Research Quarterly, 33*, 294–318.

Manzo, A. V., Manzo, U. C., & Thomas, M. M. (2005). *Content area literacy: Strategic teaching for strategic learning* (4th ed.). Hoboken, NJ: John Wiley & Sons.

No Child Left Behind Act of 2001, Pub. L. 107-110, § 1001. Available August 5, 2008, at http:/ed.gov/legislation/ESEA02/

Obiakor, F. E. (2001). *It even happens in "good" schools: Responding to cultural diversity in today's classrooms.* Thousand Oaks, CA: Corwin Press.

Obiakor, F. E. (2004). Impact of changing demographics on public education for culturally diverse learners with behavior problems: Implications for teacher preparation. In L. M. Bullock & R. A. Gable (Eds.), *Quality personnel preparation in emotional/behavioral disorders: Current perspectives and future directions* (pp. 51–63). Denton: University of North Texas, Institute for Behavioral and Learning Differences.

Obiakor, F. E. (2007). *Multicultural special education: Culturally responsive teaching.* Upper Saddle River, NJ: Pearson Merrill/Prentice Hall.

O'Brien, C. A. (1973). *Teaching the language-different child to read.* Columbus, OH: Merrill/Prentice Hall.

Rueda, R. (2005). Culture, context, and diversity: A perspective on urban school reform: A response to Kris Gutiérrez. In J. Flood and P. L. Anders (Eds.), *Literacy development of students in urban schools: Research and policy* (pp. 305–313). Newark, DE: International Reading Association.

Ryan, K., & Cooper, J. (1998). *Those who can, teach.* New York: Houghton Mifflin.

Smith, D. (1999). *Stepping inside the classroom through personal narratives.* Lanham, MD: University Press of America.

Smitherman, G. (2001). *Talkin that talk: Language, culture, and education in African America.* New York: Routledge.

Utley, C. A., Obiakor, F. E., & Kozleski, E. B. (2005). Overrepresentation of culturally and linguistically diverse students in special education in urban schools: A research synthesis. In J. Flood & P. L. Anders (Eds.), *Literacy development of students in urban schools: Research and policy* (pp. 315–344). Newark, DE: International Reading Association.

Williams, R. (1975). *Ebonics: The true language of Black folks.* St. Louis, MO: R. W. Associates.

Winzer, M. A., & Mazurek, K. (1998). *Special education in multicultural contexts.* Upper Saddle River, NJ: Merrill/Prentice Hall.

Zimmerman, J. (2002). *Whose America? Cultural wars in the public schools.* Cambridge, MA: Harvard University Press.

Index

CORWIN PRESS

The Corwin Press logo—a raven striding across an open book—represents the union of courage and learning. Corwin Press is committed to improving education for all learners by publishing books and other professional development resources for those serving the field of PreK–12 education. By providing practical, hands-on materials, Corwin Press continues to carry out the promise of its motto: **"Helping Educators Do Their Work Better."**